Industrial Cowboys

Industrial Cowboys

Miller & Lux and the Transformation of the Far West, 1850–1920

David Igler

UNIVERSITY OF CALIFORNIA PRESS
Berkeley · Los Angeles · London

University of California Press
Berkeley and Los Angeles California

University of California Press, Ltd.
London, England

First paperback printing 2005

Library of Congress Cataloging-in-Publication Data

Igler, David, 1964–.
    Industrial Cowboys : Miller & Lux and the
transformation of the Far West, 1850–1920 /
David Igler.
        p.   cm.
    Includes bibliographical references and index.
    ISBN 0-520-24534-2 (pbk : alk. paper)
    1. Miller & Lux—History.   2. Cattle trade—
West (U.S.)—History.   3. Animal industry—
West (U.S.)—History.   4. Packinghouses—West
(U.S.)—History.   5. Land use—West (U.S.)—
History.   6. Water rights—West (U.S.)—His-
tory.   7. Big business—West (U.S.)—History.
8. Industrialization—West (U.S.)—History.
    I. Title.
HD9433.U52 M554   2001
333.76'0978—dc21   00-055171

13   12   11   10   09   08   07   06   05
10   9   8   7   6   5   4   3   2   1

For my parents, Ralph and Lynne Igler

Contents

Illustrations

FIGURES

MAPS

Acknowledgments

Research projects rarely follow the best-laid plans. Instead, they evolve in all sorts of unanticipated directions while consuming years of one's life. Such was the mystery and pleasure of writing this book. What began as a dissertation prospectus that offered some tentative claims about Miller & Lux and the politics of land monopoly in California developed into a manuscript about the transformation of the Far West between 1850 and 1920. Miller & Lux still remained at the center of the narrative, but issues of environmental change, political economy, social conflict, business modernization, and industrialism also rose to the forefront. This project, thankfully, forced me out of the archives and into the Far West's rural and urban landscapes. From San Francisco to eastern Oregon to countless journeys through the San Joaquin Valley, some of my most productive and enjoyable moments were those spent on the lands discussed in the following pages. Along the way, I received support from numerous institutions and guidance from friends and colleagues too many to list. But let me try.

The history department at the University of California at Berkeley provided extensive financial support, great friends, and a number of excellent mentors. I thank Waldo Martin and Robert Middlekauff for their assistance and advice throughout my time at Berkeley. Robin Einhorn generously read the entire manuscript at a crucial stage and returned it with pages of invaluable comments. Paul Sabin has labored through more chapter drafts than he (or I) care to remember. His good cheer and probing criticisms kept me going through the toughest parts. I owe a great debt to my marvelous dissertation committee. Carolyn Merchant introduced me to environmental history and convinced me of all the ways that the environment was central to this study. Dick Walker has influenced my work more than he knows; his vast knowledge and critical understanding of California and the Far West filled the gaping holes in my own knowledge of this subject. Jim Gregory has mentored me during many important junctures in my professional life and always offered sound and comforting advice. Jim encouraged me to break apart the manuscript's constricting seams, look at issues from new directions, and ultimately, reconsider this study's larger framework. Finally, Jon Gjerde was a superb chair and critic. He skillfully guided me through the writing process and, perhaps unknowingly, encouraged me with his dry Norwegian humor. I am grateful for all his insights.

Revising this manuscript required time, patience, and the help of numerous colleagues and friends. I have borrowed ideas freely and usually with attribution. I would especially like to thank Hal Rothman, Kevin Gilmartin, Donald Pisani, Doug Sackman, David Vaught, Jessica Teisch, Gabi Arredondo, Gray Brechin, and David Johnson. Gratitude is due to Clarence Walker for his continuing comraderie as well as his general skepticism of western and environmental history. Charles Wollenberg read the entire manuscript and provided many important suggestions. Steve Aron has profoundly influenced my research and given me a tremendous amount of professional guidance. Many thanks for his time, expertise, and encouragement.

A number of Henry Miller's descendants offered their assistance with family history, including George Nickel Jr., Henry Bowles, Jack Nickel, and Thomas Tucker Mein. While this book may not present Henry Miller in an entirely flattering way, I hope they will nonetheless see the importance of their ancestor from a new perspective. I also wish to extend my gratitude to Jamy Faulhaber of the Bancroft Library Oral History Project, Mary Morganty and David Kessler of the Bancroft Library at U.C. Berkeley, and J. Walter Schmitz III for information on his grandfather.

A postdoctoral fellowship sponsored by the California Institute of Technology and the Huntington Library allowed me the time to rethink and expand this project. These two years in Pasadena also offered me the chance to mature as a scholar, initiate new research, and reconsider my northern Californian disdain for southern California. During this time I received generous support from the W. M. Keck Foundation, the Barbara Thom Foundation, the Mellon Foundation, and Caltech's Division of Humanities and Social Sciences.

For many other scholars and myself the Huntington Library is the finest home away from home. Robert C. Ritchie, Director of Research, made my tenure as a Huntington fellow immensely educational and pleasurable. I truly appreciate his sound advice on professional and personal issues. Bill Frank and Alan Jutzi helped me with all matters curatorial, while Kate McGinn and Jenny Watts shared their vast knowledge of photography, the American West, and much else. The Huntington Library's fabulous collection of scholars provided a model intellectual community; I especially thank Martin Ridge, Hal Barron, Cheryl Koos, David Wrobel, Nancy Quam-Wickham, and Erika Bsumek. For affairs academic and otherwise, I thank Janet Fireman.

Huntington Library regulars Clark Davis, Doug Smith, and Philip Goff offered the intellectual and personal companionship that made work and play almost indistinguishable. Clark read an early version of this entire manuscript and provided vital suggestions on style, content, and the field of business history. Doug took over where Clark left off and encouraged me to think about region and regionalism in new ways. They were both candid and charitable critics. Philip Goff endured my discussion of cattle, rivers, and meatpacking during our long walks in the Pasadena arroyo. I thank him for keeping me on course. Bill Deverell has influenced my work more than anyone else during the past few years. With great patience he has read most of what I've produced and has always offered valuable feedback. Most of all I appreciate his friendship.

I completed this manuscript with tremendous support from the University of Utah. My new colleagues, including Megan Armstrong, Beth Clement, Bruce Dain, Bob Goldberg, Ray Gunn, Eric Hinderaker, Dean May, Isabel Moreira, Bradley Parker, Susie Porter, Raul Ramos, Wes Sasaki-Uemura, and Janet Theiss, always provided good cheer and sound advice.

Finally, I would like to acknowledge a few longtime friends and family members. John Minkus brought Miller & Lux to my attention over a decade ago—he won't remember the conversation, but I do. Another childhood friend and fellow historian, Michael Willrich, keeps me company in a profession that often requires more than one head to unravel its twists of fate. My editor at the University of California Press, Monica McCormick, receives my admiration and gratitude for guiding me through what could have been a tortuous process. For support throughout, I would like to thank Marc Igler, Jennifer Cray, Louise Aplington, Jackie Foret, Mabel and Laurel Edlund, and Kimberly and Cheryl Willard. For their love and patience, this book is dedicated to my parents, Ralph and Lynne Igler. Cynthia Willard knows the many debts I owe her. I look forward to repaying them.

Industrial Cowboys
in the Far West

Haying at Buena Vista Farm, 1881. The photographer carefully arranged this scene so that the wagons, machinery, and workers would lend perspective to the towering haystack. (See figure 1.) An abrupt horizon bisects the giant mound, and three horsemen pose in the foreground. Loaded wagons wait in line, pointing to the haystack. A man wearing a white shirt stands silhouetted against its dark shadow. He halts a three-pronged "Jackson Fork" derrick in position; its payload hovers above the stack, which rises sixty feet from the ground. Six men wait atop the haystack. They wear broad-brimmed straw hats to shield their faces from the San Joaquin Valley's blistering midday sun. The unseen photographer directs the activity from the roof of a horse-drawn carriage. He has stopped the action and carefully composed the image. But the stillness of the photograph belies the laborers' continuous, systematic movements. The hayers, mowers, and teamsters will wait only long enough for the photographer to capture the scene before proceeding with their assigned tasks. The ranch superintendent and his *vaquero* foreman, facing the camera, will make certain of that. The photograph's subject is not the haystack or its impressive scale, but rather the labor involved in creating it: *haying* at Buena Vista Farm.   ⌐a labor photo

The San Francisco photographer Carleton Watkins took two trips to Kern County, California, at the behest of the multimillionaire land developer James Ben Ali Haggin.[1] During his second visit, in 1888, Watkins photographed many scenes: the county seat of Bakersfield, prominent

Figure 1. In Carleton Watkins's *Haying at Buena Vista Farm* (1881), the two men facing the camera are Miller & Lux's Kern County divisional superintendent, S. W. Wible, and the vaquero boss Rafael Cuen. (Reproduced by permission of The Huntington Library, San Marino, California.)

citizens with their families, and the extensive ranch operations that composed Haggin's Kern County Land Company. Haggin desired publicity for his land development projects, and the financially strapped Watkins was always pleased to assist his friend and wealthy benefactor. But Watkins's earlier trip to Kern County, in 1881, had served a different purpose. In 1881 Haggin found himself embroiled in what soon became the American West's most notorious water rights battle, *Lux v. Haggin.* To document his company's water rights on the Kern River, Haggin hired Watkins to photograph the landscape as well as his irrigation and ranching enterprises.[2] Watkins fulfilled Haggin's wishes, using an enormous camera equipped with fourteen-by-twenty-one-inch glass negatives. During this engagement, however, Watkins also worked for the Kern County operations of Haggin's courtroom opponent—the land, cattle, water, and meatpacking firm of Miller & Lux. *Haying at Buena Vista Farm* derived from this series of images.

Watkins left few written records of his work for Miller & Lux, James Haggin, or any of the large-scale firms in the Far West that employed his photographic talents. Although thousands of Watkins's photographs and documents were destroyed in the 1906 earthquake and fire, the remaining work is virtually unparalleled for its stark juxtaposition of the western landscape, industrial enterprise, and the region's laboring populations. In one image a giant steel harvester with wooden-spoke wheels dwarfs the workers who rest in its shadow. Another photograph shows miles of Southern Pacific Railroad track snaking precipitously up the central California foothills en route to a distant mountain pass. A third print reveals the skeletal frame of a massive dam, under construction by the Golden Gate and Golden Feather Mining Company, standing half-finished beside the Feather River. Watkins also photographed the sculpted gardens of rural estates and the perfect symmetry of peach-filled shipping crates—elegant scenes that evoked the California myths of sunshine and leisure. Yet even these bucolic images suggest the intersection of landscape, work, and industry.[3] Watkins's keen eye for nineteenth-century industrialism could not have found a more fitting subject than Miller & Lux's Buena Vista Farm.

Haying at Buena Vista Farm captures many elements of Miller & Lux's production system. Though unidentified by Watkins, the superintendent in the foreground is S. W. Wible, a self-trained irrigation engineer who entered Miller & Lux's employ after twenty years of scraping a hard living from the surrounding plains. Wible supervised the activities of numerous ranch managers and irrigation canal foremen, who in turn directed the work of countless wage laborers. The man to Wible's left is most likely Rafael Cuen, a skilled vaquero boss whom Miller & Lux hired away from James Haggin's Kern County Land Company. Cuen, like some of the firm's other Mexican or Mexican American vaqueros (or cowboys), worked on company land once owned by his father.[4] The haystack behind these two men represented a key fixture of corporate ranching in the Far West. Similar structures dotted Miller & Lux's contiguous properties for two hundred miles north of Buena Vista Farm, and together the haystacks symbolized one step in the firm's struggle to transform and capitalize on the natural landscape. That struggle required a labor force often exceeding twelve hundred migrant workers, a highly coordinated corporate system, and large sums of investment capital, earned in San Francisco's meatpacking industry. It also demanded extensive water rights, secured in court cases such as *Lux v. Haggin. Haying at Buena Vista Farm* illustrates a point in Miller & Lux's system where landscape, labor, capital, politics, law, and industry converge.

Like Watkins's photograph, this book situates Miller & Lux within the region's industrial transformation. The Far West that emerged after the 1849 gold rush featured an instant market economy, dynamic urban cores, and large corporate enterprises. In short, the West had a "machine in the garden" that moved across the region with shocking speed.[5] Here, resource-dependent industries drew upon nature's wealth as they organized efficient business systems. The companies that propelled western industrialism both shaped and were shaped by their physical surroundings. Among the top corporations directing the region's industrial activity was Miller & Lux.[6]

Miller & Lux entered the twentieth century as one of the nation's largest industrial enterprises. The firm dominated Pacific Coast meat markets with annual sales exceeding $5 million in 1913. The corporation's herd of one hundred thousand cattle grazed upon 1.25 million acres of company land in three western states. Water, the most prized commodity throughout the Far West, flowed across Miller & Lux properties in a labyrinthine grid—a testament to the work of thousands of immigrant laborers, water rights litigators, and political lobbyists. The firm's innovative and imperious founders, Henry Miller and Charles Lux,[7] had created a vast machine to engineer the natural landscape and regulate the geography of western meat production. At one end of the business were concentrated the lucrative meat markets that fed San Francisco's burgeoning population. The other end fanned out horizontally from San Francisco into the San Joaquin Valley, northern Nevada, and eastern Oregon. (See map 1.) In these hinterlands, Miller & Lux mobilized capital and labor to a degree far surpassing most eastern manufacturing firms. An anomaly in a nation still clinging to its family farm tradition, Miller & Lux was the only agricultural corporation ranked among the nation's top two hundred "industrial enterprises" at the century's turn.[8]

"Industrial cowboys"—this phrase characterizes the firm's founders, but it also functions as a metaphor for the enterprises dominating the Far West's late-nineteenth-century landscape. "Industrial cowboys" juxtaposes the nineteenth century's most powerful transformation with the individualistic ethos of our mythic creation, the American cowboy. Many western firms embodied this amalgam. They were large-scale and ambitious ventures that rode roughshod over the region's terrain. Investment capital financed a variety of western enterprises after 1849: railroad, timber, agriculture, mining, real estate, and irrigation companies, to name only a few. Wild speculation drove some firms into bankruptcy. Others, such as Miller & Lux, cornered markets and forged profitable links with government agencies to claim the region's public domain. The success of many of these enterprises revealed the speculative frenzy dramatized in western lore as well as the coordinated exploitation of the West's social and natural environment. Here was the "westering" of industrialization, the creation of modern capitalist relations in a new and different landscape.

Miller & Lux operated in ways similar to the nation's other emerging industrial firms—by reducing risks, segmenting labor, and creating vertically integrated production units. But the firm also represents a western variant of American business enterprise. The extractive nature of the region's industries necessitated more than the vertical integration of production and marketing: it also demanded unparalleled horizontal consolidation of natural resources. For enterprises like Miller & Lux, monopolizing land, water, and other resources provided an insurance policy against the West's drought and flood cycles and its complex natural environment.[9] Securing land and water rights was not an end in itself. Rather, such rights enabled capitalized interests to transform the landscape and reap huge profits. Miller & Lux's activities ultimately fostered enduring contradictions between the Far West's natural and social landscapes. Conflicts over the control of natural resources produced and exacerbated these contradictions, as they transpired simultaneously in the courtrooms, legislatures, and marketplace and on the land itself. In each forum the central issue remained consistent: who held the right and power to engineer the landscape for market production? — a major point

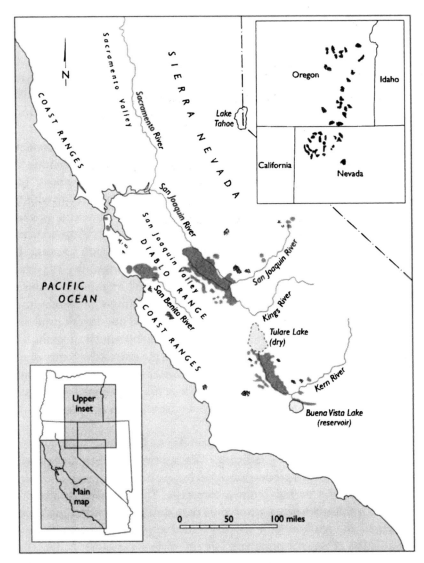

Map 1.   Miller & Lux lands (shaded areas). Miller & Lux acquired 1.25 million acres of land in California, Nevada, and Oregon—though Henry Miller claimed that his firm "control[led] ten times the amount of land we actually own."

INDUSTRIAL ENTERPRISES ON THE LAND

The large-scale firms at the center of western industrialization drew upon several power bases. Financed with private capital, western firms utilized public officials and the larger political state to secure vast holdings of land and natural resources.[10] They developed remarkably dynamic investment strategies and corporate structures; many companies, in addition to creating vertical chains of production, spun off subsidiaries in different business sectors. Far western firms, furthermore, operated out of metropolitan "cores" and incorporated "peripheral" hinterlands into urban markets and business networks.[11] San Francisco (and California as a whole) propelled this regional system. Finally, industrial enterprise in the Far West thrived by engineering natural landscapes and mobilizing large labor forces. These two tactics—manipulating nature and exploiting human labor—reinforced one another throughout the region.[12] These characteristics were certainly not exceptional to western industry. Indeed, they illustrate some common processes through which big business emerged across the nation. Yet a particular type of industrial activity quickly took root in the region—much earlier and farther to the West than acknowledged by conventional understandings of industrialization.[13]

[margin note: ~ making a connect between urban & rural]

The extractive nature of most western industries made extensive landownership a crucial asset of corporate power across the region. Private rights to millions of acres gave the California and Pacific Northwest timber industry access to vast stretches of old-growth redwood, ponderosa pine, and Douglas fir. Highly capitalized mining corporations extracted the West's deposits of gold and silver through contiguous mineral claims, reinvesting their profits in other land-based operations. The Southern Pacific and Northern Pacific Railroads, largely financed by government gifts of land in the public domain, remained the West's largest landowning corporations during the nineteenth century. By striking deals with other western industrialists, these railroads passed their bounty into the hands of the region's leading firms.[14] Land, therefore, provided the means for capitalized industries to expand across the Far West.

Capitalization was another key component of western industrial growth and power. Lacking its own investment funds in the 1850s and 1860s, Miller & Lux gained support from San Francisco's top financial institutions: Parrott & Company and the Bank of California. Such capital enabled Miller & Lux and many other land-based enterprises to gain unparalleled influence over federal land policy.[15] James Haggin and his partners in the Kern County Land Company all but drafted the 1877

- semi-slimey
- business
influence

Desert Land Act before grabbing large portions of Kern County under its provisions.[16] Miller & Lux lobbied successfully against the acreage limitations contained in the Swamp Land Act, and then proceeded to claim entire townships of questionable "swampland" in California, Nevada, and Oregon. The corporation's network of agents ranged from county surveyors to high-priced lobbyists in the nation's capital. Like other western enterprises, Miller & Lux effectively merged public land policies with its private interests and seized large rewards in the process.

While access to capital and public land agencies allowed corporations to claim western land, San Francisco provided the geographic nexus through which land consolidations and market relations flourished.[17] The Central Pacific Railroad, the Union Lumber and Pacific Lumber Companies, the Kern County Land Company, George Hearst's various mining companies, and the California Sugar Refinery Company—these San Francisco–based enterprises all used landownership in the countryside as a vehicle for corporate growth. In the process, they reinforced San Francisco's preeminent position throughout the region. Miller & Lux's expansion, perhaps more than that of any other western enterprise, demonstrates the centralizing grasp of the Pacific Coast metropolis.

ECOLOGIES OF INDUSTRY AND NATURE

Though substantially influenced by regional factors, western industry did not remain isolated from its eastern counterpart. Rather, the contemporaneous growth of big business across the nation demands a broader perspective on industrial America. The typical narrative of America's industrial transformation emphasizes eastern factories and European immigrant laborers, manufacturing and Wall Street financiers, and vertical chains of production guided by the "visible hand" of salaried managers.[18] Two developments apparently proved crucial to this transformation: the vertical integration of factory production and marketing, and the emergence of modern managerial systems. While this narrative suggests many key elements of industrial change, it is nonetheless rooted in a particular idea of business expansion that accounts well for the emergence of manufacturing and transportation but fails to register the diversity of modern enterprise and its multifold consequences. As a result, the usual story of U.S. industrialization suggests vital lessons about that well-trod beltway from Lowell, Massachusetts, to Detroit but remarkably little about Montana's copper mines, corporate land reclamation in California, and various other trajectories of industrial mod-

ernization. To the extent that the American West informs the discussion
of industrialization, it appears as a natural-resource colony plundered
by eastern capitalists and firms.[19] Some western historians have served
important correctives to this regional bias, but the broad contours of
late-nineteenth-century industrialism remain largely unexplored.[20]

As a corporation, Miller & Lux illustrates many features of business
modernization during the late nineteenth century: the central role of investment capital; vertical chains of production and marketing; a large,
ethnically segmented labor force; and a distinct managerial structure. But
the example of Miller & Lux also cautions us against creating an inflex-
ible model of industrial development. Beginning as meat wholesalers,
Henry Miller and Charles Lux quickly expanded their business to en-
compass cattle, land, irrigation, and land reclamation projects—hardly
the typical factors of industrial production. Only later did Miller & Lux
integrate forward into marketing meat by-products nationally. Like
other industrial firms, Miller & Lux faced uncertain markets, new competitors, and labor problems. But unlike risks faced by eastern manufacturing companies, Miller & Lux's most significant risks sprung from
the environment. Nature impacted the corporation as much as the corporation shaped its natural surroundings.[21] One brief example: soon after
Miller & Lux began purchasing land, a massive winter flood (1861–62)
destroyed California's crops and littered the landscape with livestock
carcasses. Two years of devastating drought (1862–64) immediately followed the flood, demonstrating the hydraulic extremes that characterized California's natural environment. These natural "disasters" might
have marked the end of the state's ranching industry.[22] Instead, these conditions set some ranching enterprises on a different path, one marked by
modern business systems and extensive land consolidations. In the midst
of flood and drought, Miller & Lux entered a period of furious land acquisition remarkably similar to other firms' resource stockpiling strategies.[23]
But the western terrain represented more than a potential resource warehouse. This rugged and vast landscape decidedly influenced the actions
and ideas of those who inhabited the region. A dialectical interaction of
humans and the natural environment, rather than a one-sided conquest
of nature, framed the processes by which western society and industry
established its foothold.[24]

A natural environment of vast complexity and unpredictable extremes
confronted all immigrants to the Far West. Here, environmental disturbance and disorder set the standard.[25] Earthquakes, repeated forest and
grassland fires, floods, and droughts constantly transformed the land-

scape. But natural change had little place in the ordered and productive "garden" envisioned by most westerners, and by agriculturalists in particular.[26] For individual farmers and the industry as a whole, irrigation and land reclamation offered the possibility of dependable production amid unpredictable natural conditions.[27] This effort to change the water-scape represented one part of a larger engineering agenda that sought to simplify nature's complexity, redesign ecosystems, and restrict environmental change. Though radically transformed—"broken with steam and with steel," one agricultural booster commented—the natural environment still remained an active agent in the Far West's development.[28] Human labor and technology could neither halt the forces of natural change nor regulate the region's many variations. The engineered landscape produced great wealth, but it also produced unexpected environmental and social consequences.[29]

Transforming the waterscape emerged as a key determinant of regional development, and Miller & Lux's consolidation of the largest irrigation companies illustrates how private interests during the late nineteenth century dominated the environmental engineering agenda. The monumental importance of water has led some historians to characterize the West as a "hydraulic society"—a "social order based on the intensive, large-scale manipulation of water and its products in an arid setting."[30] California's Central Valley, the southern half of which is the San Joaquin Valley, was especially "representative of an emerging West and its sudden transition . . . from wilderness to technological dominance." But the West was hardly unique according to this line of reasoning. Rather, it represented the modern fulfillment of hydraulic societies dating back to ancient Egypt and China. Like these powerful predecessors, the West's hydraulic engineering ultimately supported a "coercive, monolithic, and hierarchical system."[31]

Many historians have criticized this deterministic approach to western water and its grim depiction of western society. Did a monolithic and coercive state surround the West's irrigation canals, or, as other historians contend, did various factors create avenues for reform and democratic possibilities?[32] The study of Miller & Lux, one of the principal architects of the West's waterscape, illuminates a western society constructed around several intersecting systems of power. The corporation's water engineering functioned as only one part of its relationship to government, markets, smaller landowners, workers, and the natural landscape. Western society, furthermore, contained far more important connections to the industrializing eastern states than it did to ancient irrigation civilizations. Miller & Lux's rise reveals a process of western industrialization in which market relations commodified and transformed all natural resources, not just water.[33] An industrial capitalist society, rather than a singularly hydraulic one, propelled the Far West's development during the late nineteenth century.

Private property rights constituted another critical component of western incorporation. Private landownership carried distinct and personal meaning to the individual claimant, but the legal relationships between land, minerals, water, and other resources were less concrete and had to be continually negotiated through political institutions and capitalist markets. Here, the West contributed to the national transformation from a "static agrarian conception" of property to a "dynamic, instrumental, and more abstract view" that accompanied industrialization.[34] Privatizing property ultimately centered on controlling access to the land's resources; it was simultaneously an act of inclusion and exclusion.[35] In the 1860s, for instance, Miller & Lux carved out the rich bottomlands of sixteen former Mexican land grants, excluding the *rancheros* and Anglo settlers alike from the properties' most valuable resources. The following decade, Miller & Lux used its private property along the San Joaquin River to seize extensive water rights and take over the West's largest irrigation canal. During the 1880s, the firm formalized in court the connection between property in land and property in water: *Lux* v. *Haggin* (1881–86) supported Miller & Lux's riparian right to the Kern River's flow despite the adverse claims of upstream irrigators. While these examples revolve around the annexation of water, Miller & Lux also exercised its property rights to secure many other company interests.

Engineering the landscape and securing property rights were two means that Miller & Lux used to attain wealth and power in the Far West. A third was the exploitation of regional opportunities. As the firm extended its system of production across a vast region, it reinforced San Francisco's power in the hinterlands. In many ways, the city's imperial scope mirrored the expansion of contemporaneous midwestern cities. One recent study of Chicago skillfully recounts how the exchange of natural resources and produced goods linked the city with its hinterlands: meat, wheat, timber, and other products from the countryside entered Chicago's markets in exchange for various manufactured goods. This process ultimately linked "first nature" landscapes with "second nature" resources and commodities, even as the market "concealed the very linkages it was creating."[36] In this study, Chicago merchants propelled urban expansion, and the mercantile system facilitated city-hinterland relationships.

San Francisco followed a similar path of urban imperialism in that its meteoric rise resulted largely from the high value of natural resources extracted from the hinterlands. But an industrial system, not a mercantile one, played the decisive role in transforming San Francisco and the Far West. The city's leading firms took their capital, technology, labor forces, and systems of production to the countryside and appropriated its natural wealth. Miller & Lux, like other San Francisco–based firms, actually owned the hinterland soil upon which its production took place. These powerful corporations established the terms of wage labor in local communities, and when rural labor pools proved insufficient, they imported workers from the city. San Francisco firms built company towns to centralize secondary industries, often displacing previous population centers. They used political leverage in rural communities to further specific business agendas and undermine popular demands for reform. Like Chicago merchants, San Francisco merchants certainly facilitated trade patterns throughout the region.[37] But the San Francisco corporations that spread industrial relations across the landscape held a far more material presence, and their activities reduced significantly the power of local communities to make autonomous decisions about their development and livelihood.

HENRY MILLER AND CHARLES LUX:
FROM THE OLD COUNTRY TO THE FAR WEST

Though not specifically a study of Henry Miller or Charles Lux, this book inevitably confronts the decisions and ideas of these two business entrepreneurs. Why did Miller and Lux join together to form what would become one of the West's most powerful enterprises? What forces motivated their business decisions—to integrate backward, stage hostile corporate takeovers, and pursue a modern litigation strategy? What inspired the transformation from immigrant butcher to industrial cowboy? To answer these questions we must move beyond standard tropes of the heroic West (the partners were individualistic "empire builders," according to the author of a 1930 novel about the firm) and reductionist notions of ethnicity (Miller acted in a "thoroughly, virtuously Germanic" fashion, wrote Mary Austin) to examine their experience as European immigrants.[38]

Charles Lux (see figure 2) was born in 1823 in Hatten, a small Alsatian town in southwestern Germany.[39] His family belonged to the German Catholic Church, and his father worked as a wheelwright, most likely managing his own shop. Henry Miller (see figure 3) was born four years later in Brackenheim, a small town in the southwestern German province of Wurttemberg. Miller's birth name was Heinrich Alfred Kreiser. Kreiser's parents were Protestant, and his father worked as a skilled master butcher and cattle trafficker. Kreiser attended public school until the age of thirteen and served as an apprentice to his father. In Germany, Kreiser-Miller later recalled, "the butcher business comprised [all aspects of the trade]. [The butcher] had to know how to clean guts of sheep and turn them into fiddle stings; he had to know how to cure meat and to make sausage and everything connected in that trade."[40] Apparently, both Lux and Kreiser chafed under parental authority. Lux had no desire to join his father's trade, while Kreiser enjoyed the trade but had little desire to work under his father before entering the butchers' guild as a master tradesman.[41] By their midteens, Lux and Kreiser had each left southwestern Germany in search of greater opportunity abroad.

By leaving Germany in 1839 and 1842 respectively, Lux and Kreiser participated in the early stage of the country's nineteenth-century emigration process. This initial wave of German immigrants came from the southwestern provinces of Wurttemberg, Baden, and Alsace and was made up of farmers and artisans affected by the region's poor harvests, overpopulation, and economic crisis associated with early German industrialism.[42] Kreiser also had personal reasons for leaving. "The [German] people and I could never assimilate," he explained years later in an interview resonating with profound ambivalence for his German homeland. "What was pleasure for them was simply an annoyance for me and it [Germany] was not a pleasant country for me to live in. My sympathies or attachments were never for the people but for the soil I was raised on."[43] The United States attracted Kreiser, he noted, for its "freedom and greater opportunity," but the possibility of actually own- —*land!* ing "soil" also ranked high on the list.[44] He would not be disappointed.

Lux arrived in New York City in 1839 and apprenticed with a butcher for six dollars a month. He learned to speak English fluently and soon found himself in charge of the busy shop. By December 1849, Lux had saved enough money to book passage to San Francisco onboard the *Ohio*. Kreiser, meanwhile, arrived in New York City in 1847 after working in Holland for three years and England for two years.[45] He found work at a "hog shop" in the middle of New York's bustling Washing-

Figure 2.   Charles Lux managed the firm's affairs in San
Francisco. Charles Joseph Carlson painted this portrait after
Lux's death, and it hung in the library of the Lux School of
Industrial Training. (Courtesy of the California Historical
Society, FN-31909. Photograph by Gabriel Coulin.)

ton Market. Sleeping on a cot in the back room, Kreiser spent his days
dressing meats and making deliveries. His wages derived from the sale
of hogs' offal—"guts, heart, liver and lights . . . which amounted to almost a dollar a day."[46] During his three years in New York, Heinrich
Kreiser longed for greater independence: economic independence for certain, but also the independence of open space. His opportunity arrived

Figure 3.   Henry Miller, cofounder of Miller & Lux, directed
the firm's cattle, land, and water business for six decades.
(Courtesy of George Nickel Jr.)

when an acquaintance named Henry Miller offered him a ticket to California onboard the steamer *Georgia*. "When he looked at the ticket," Edward F. Treadwell wrote in his 1931 "dramatized" biography of Henry Miller, "he saw it was in the name of 'Henry Miller' and was marked 'Not Transferable.' He was anxious to go and was unfamiliar with business affairs, and feared that if he told that he had bought the ticket he could not go, so he decided to go as 'Henry Miller.' As Henry Miller he did go, and under that name he continued till the time of his death."[47] Treadwell's story remains the only account of Kreiser's transformation

perchance name —
change —
a chance
to
assimilate

to Henry Miller, for Miller himself never mentioned it. He arrived in San Francisco in September 1850 as Henry Miller and evidently felt his new Anglican name fit his new city, despite the fact that Germans ranked only a little behind the English as a percentage of the city's immigrant population.[48] The new name also served a conscious strategy of assimilation: "Henry Miller" veiled his connection to a homeland he had deliberately left behind.

Miller and Lux found work as butchers in San Francisco and quickly rose to the position of independent proprietors. By July 1851, Miller ran his own retail butcher shop on Jackson Street in the heart of San Francisco's small commercial district. Lux owned a similar establishment, and by 1853 he had saved enough capital to enter the wholesale cattle trade with an Englishman named Alfred Edmondson. Lux and Edmondson strengthened their partnership in December 1853 with the purchase of 1,700 acres of Rancho Buri Buri from the indebted heirs of José Antonio Sánchez. Lux purchased his partner's share of Buri Buri three years later.[49] The following year, Miller and Lux invested together in a rare herd of 1,600 Texas cattle (most cattle in California during the 1850s were Mexican bred). They purchased the herd, slaughtered and sold off the meat wholesale, and went their separate ways. In 1858 Miller and Lux formed a permanent partnership, which would last until Lux's death in 1887.

A natural partnership by all appearances, Miller & Lux exhibited all the characteristics of a successful nineteenth-century "ethnic" enterprise. The two partners came from southwestern German towns less than a hundred miles apart and followed remarkably similar migration routes to New York and, later, San Francisco. While Lux probably possessed more capital than Miller, they both belonged to the same class of rising entrepreneurs who often sought security through ethnically based partnership.[50] Whether the partnership spirit in San Francisco was born out of choice (as in the case of Germans, Irish, or English) or more out of necessity (such as in the case of the Chinese, who faced individual and institutional discrimination), it remained a positive business strategy that revealed the significance of common sensibilities, language, and place of birth.

Though partners in business, Miller and Lux lived in two different social worlds. Charles Lux, through financial success and his marriage into a prominent family, gained entrance to San Francisco's rather permeable elite society. In 1857, he married the recently widowed Miranda Wilmarth Sheldon and built a family home in the fashionable South Park neighborhood for his new bride and stepson.[51] When "the days of [South

Park's] aristocratic locality had passed," as his realtor explained in 1875, Lux moved his family to the new upper-class environs of Nob Hill.[52] On weekends, they retreated to their mansion on Rancho Buri Buri just south of the city. Though business often took Lux away from San Francisco, he mostly tended to the city end of the business at Miller & Lux's downtown headquarters. Lux dined at his social club with bankers, lawyers, politicians, and railroad tycoons, managing the relationships that ensured Miller & Lux's success. *— Lux handled city business*

Henry Miller could hardly have been more different. He possessed little tolerance for lawyers, politicians, and city society in general. He preferred the open space of the San Joaquin Valley and the company of a large herd of cattle. In 1858, shortly after Miller and Lux joined forces, Miller cemented the partnership by marrying Lux's sister-in-law, Nancy Wilmarth Sheldon. She died in childbirth the following year, but by 1860 Miller had married her twenty-year-old niece, Sarah Elizabeth Wilmarth Sheldon. They soon moved to Miller's 1,700-acre Bloomfield Farm near Gilroy, where Miller could direct the rapidly expanding land and cattle end of the business. Only one of their four children would outlive Miller, who died in 1916 at the age of eighty-nine. His thirty-year partnership with Lux was cordial yet distant; Miller stated bluntly that "there is no similarity between Lux and myself—not in sympathy nor in views nor nothing." After Lux's death, Miller had the impudence to claim he had "made [a fortune] for my partner." For two German immigrants, they shared few sensibilities beyond the profit margin, and Miller all but dismissed their common ethnicity: "He [Lux] was a native of Germany, and his stock is more German than mine."[53]

But the differences between Miller and Lux worked to their advantage. At home in San Francisco, Lux could cultivate the necessary business and political connections for a successful corporate enterprise, leaving Miller free to build the landed empire from the ground up. Miller's stern business manner, which was too coarse for urban society, nevertheless worked well among cattle and land dealers. Miller and Lux brought their skills to gold rush California and had the foresight to recognize that the state's true business frontier existed in San Francisco, not in the Sierra foothills. Ambitious and independent—neither one had remained satisfied for long as a hired hand—both were willing to assume more entrepreneurial risk than typical immigrant businessmen. They shared a mutual drive for business expansion and consolidation. In the Far West, the two German butchers discovered a landscape that promised escape from European confinement and fulfilled their ideas of American opportunity. To become industrial capitalists, they married into the same elite San Francisco family, developed ties to the city's business leaders, and began exploiting the systems of private property and government agencies. They utilized institutional and natural resources to construct a ranching empire, and by rationalizing labor and nature, they flourished as industrial cowboys. To understand Miller & Lux's development into one of the nation's most important nineteenth-century enterprises, we must examine the broader context of the American Far West. The California landscape, where Miller and Lux built their business, is the point of departure.

CHAPTER I

The San Joaquin Valley

Landscape, History, and Memory

In 1854, four years after arriving in San Francisco with a few dollars to his name, Henry Miller paid $33,000 in cash for a herd of American cattle. Thirty years later he recounted the precise details of this incident. Miller remembered his small shop, a storefront-turned-slaughterhouse on the corner of Fifth and Howard Streets. He recalled his partner at the time, a man named Zimmerman, who had no capital but good butchering skills. "I went over to the San Joaquin," he remembered, "and bought [this] band of American cattle from Livingston and Kincaid[;] and I paid for that band of cattle $33,000[,] and paid cash down for them."[1] The cattle dealers Livingston and Kincaid had driven the herd from Salt Lake City, and it was the first sizeable band of American stock to reach San Francisco. The price far exceeded the current rate for Mexican cattle, Miller emphasized, but he believed the higher-quality American beef would sell fast. He made a great profit. The herd contained 300 cattle and he paid $110 a head. Miller marketed the beef at 18 to 20 cents a pound wholesale. The average carcass weighed over 800 pounds. Such facts Miller remembered effortlessly.

Henry Miller possessed a sound mind for details. In the thirty years since this purchase, Miller had closed thousands of similar deals and could likely recollect the size of each herd if not the weight of each steer. He remembered the purchase price and seller's name, the ranch on which he stocked the cattle, and, as he often remarked about the slaughtering process, how "good they killed." Miller knew his firm's property in a similar way: the boundary lines, the twists and turns of a particular slough, and the alfalfa yield on any given field. Important details like the price of his 1854 purchase stuck in Miller's mind, while related events received only an obligatory word. For instance, he failed to mention that this transaction had allowed him a first glimpse of the San Joaquin Valley's Westside, a landscape Miller & Lux would control for the next fifty years. Instead, he referred in passing to one aspect of the valley's wildlife. "Over in the San Joaquin Valley," Miller remembered, "there were wild horses and elk and you could see them running in every direction."[2]

Memory is a tricky tool for reconstructing the past.[3] It speaks with the authority of individual experience unchallenged by contrary data or dissent. Henry Miller *saw* wild horses and elk running across the valley floor, and given his knowledge of large ungulates, we might accept this statement as an accurate account of the landscape's wildlife prior to widespread American settlement. Memories from other San Joaquin visitors and residents could help us reconstruct many aspects of this natural environment. Edward Bosqui, who explored the valley in the 1840s, remembered "bands of elk, deer and antelope in such numbers that they actually darkened the plains for miles and looked in the distance like great herds of cattle." Jessie Benton Fremont recalled a "broad belt of trees" lining the San Joaquin River as late as 1860. The San Joaquin Yokut Indians began their creation stories with water covering the entire valley—a common event throughout the millennia and into the nineteenth century.[4] Each recollection contributes to a reconstruction of the San Joaquin's past: a landscape of wild game, dense riparian forests, and often an inland sea. But memory is not a precise tool. In separating past landscapes from the present, memory accentuates the distance between a supposedly "pristine" nature and the succeeding engineered environment. Memory triangulates the shift from one landscape to another, and in so doing, it often represents the two as distinct places that share little common history.

Henry Miller *may* have left the valley in 1854 with his 300 cattle and a first sighting of elk. More than likely, however, he saw no elk that day because market hunters had substantially reduced their population, and the surviving elk had retreated from sight into the tule marshes.[5] But Miller probably did leave the San Joaquin with a vision fixed in his mind of its boundless grasslands. Like many western empire builders, Miller recognized the potential for vast wealth when he gazed at the natural landscape. He saw a land rich in resources and possibilities, an open invitation to leave his mark on a seemingly untouched place. Recalling this first visit to the valley, Miller quite likely remembered seeing elk "run-

ning in every direction" because the disappearance of wild game symbolized his firm's very success at containing and engineering a vast portion of the region's environment.

The Far West's natural landscapes, however, constituted more than a
symbolic backdrop for the development of large-scale enterprises like
Miller & Lux. The landscape provided a source of power for those who
could engineer its resources; it became a staging area where new ideas
and technologies took root in the late nineteenth century. From the gold-
laden Sierra to Nevada's Comstock Lode to the old-growth forests of
Oregon and Washington, the landscape and its potential sat at the center of the region's dynamic growth.[6] The San Joaquin Valley represented
such a landscape for Miller & Lux, and an understanding of the firm's
place within a broader history must begin with this environment.

A long history of natural change linked the seemingly wild landscape
Miller remembered and the highly managed landscape of later decades.
Beginning with the first Native Americans, successive human populations
altered every component of the San Joaquin landscape. This process, centuries old already, gained momentum in the early nineteenth century and
rapidly accelerated at midcentury. Plants and animals, free-running
rivers and marshy bottomlands, riparian forests and the valley's very soils
were all transformed by introduced species and increased human engineering of natural systems. But placing human actors at the center of ecological change can divert attention from the many ways landscapes evolve
on their own. The supposedly "pristine" valley seen by Miller (and every
generation before him) resulted from natural disturbances and chaotic
events throughout the millennia, and these natural processes did not cease
with American conquest and its landscape engineers. Instead, forces of
natural change persisted and repeatedly frustrated the plans of those who
sought to alter the landscape for their own agendas.[7] _ nature had influence

Natural extremes also connected the remembered landscape to the
engineered one. If, as the historian Walter Prescott Webb wrote, the arid
West is "a semidesert with a desert heart," then the San Joaquin Valley
is close to that heart.[8] The valley presented homestead farmers and land
barons alike with some of the most arid conditions west of the Mississippi River. Yet the opposite extreme materialized with surprising fre-
quency. During years of heavy rain the inundated rivers could suddenly
transpose the San Joaquin floor into a vast inland sea stretching a hundred miles from north to south. These hydrological counterparts—
flooding and aridity—constituted only the most conspicuous natural
extremes of this Mediterranean landscape.[9] The land and its biotic com-

- San Joaquin Valley was prone to floods

munities varied enormously across the valley floor: different soil types, flora and fauna communities, alkaline flats, and extensive wetlands produced a patchwork of natural systems that tested human endurance and ingenuity.[10] In short, the boundless and seemingly static landscape Americans entered in the 1850s was in fact a remarkably complex and evolving region. They would soon discover this fact.

AN INLAND SEA, AN INLAND DESERT

All migrants to the American West altered their natural surroundings for various reasons—whether because they sought food or extracted resources, or as a result of pioneering hubris and the need to find comfort in an alien place. Such explanations framed the Central Valley's settlement, but with American conquest attention quickly turned to the valley's hydrological extremes. Anyone doubting this fact need only consult the events of the early 1860s, recorded by the California Geologic Survey leader, William H. Brewer. On October 10, 1861, Brewer and his party entered the north end of the San Joaquin Valley and began traveling south along the base of the Mount Diablo range. "We strike out on the plain—oh! what a tedious plain—league after league stretches away, it seems as boundless as the sea," wrote Brewer, whose 1860–64 journal of the expedition represents one of the most vivid accounts of California's landscape in the nineteenth century. "The [valley] soil is fertile enough," he admitted, "but destitute of water, save the marshes near the river and near Tulare Lake."[11]

Three months later, however, Brewer described a very different landscape: "The great central valley of the state is under water—the Sacramento and San Joaquin valleys—a region 250 to 300 miles long and an average of at least twenty miles wide." He detailed the devastation of the capital city, Sacramento, which sat under six feet of water. He saw steamboats traversing the typically dry plains. "There [is] such a body of water," Brewer wrote, "that the winds made high waves which beat the farm homes in pieces." The floodwaters submerged thousands of farms, he reported, and cattle were both "starving *and* drowning," a fact that Henry Miller understood well, since he had thousands of cattle on rented land that bordered the San Joaquin River. Attempting to summarize the devastation caused by this El Niño season, Brewer claimed that "America has never before seen such desolation by flood as this has been, and seldom has the Old World seen the like."[12]

The sight truly unsettled Brewer. Raised on a small farm in Enfield, New York, he sympathized with those farmers forced to witness the destruction of their hard work. But another factor also disturbed the thirty-four-year-old Yale-trained scientist. He had described the valley months before as "boundless as the sea" but "destitute of water." Nature had now inverted this landscape: an inland sea covered all the land. The juxtaposition of these different landscapes challenged both his memory and training. Brewer was not alone in his bewilderment. Between 1861 and 1864, Californians watched helplessly while their natural surroundings shifted from one extreme to the other. One "disaster" followed another; but these events were entirely commonplace in the valley's natural history.[13]

The 1861–62 flood illustrated both nature's power for destruction and the valley's need for radical "improvements." The city of Sacramento received the brunt of the force. Heavy rains fell throughout November 1861, and by December Sacramento's residents nervously waited as the water climbed the levees surrounding their city. Sacramento had experienced severe flooding nine years earlier, prompting city leaders to raise the streets of its business district by a height of one to five feet and strengthen the main levee. By 1861, this levee stood twenty-two and a half feet above the low-river mark.[14] Sacramento residents believed they had sufficiently fortified their city against every contingency, but on December 9, 1861, the American River's raging waters ripped through the levee northeast of Sacramento and quickly filled the walled city. Small frame houses floated freely down the main thoroughfares while boats plied the city streets, rescuing residents from second-story windows and rooftops. When the city engineers cut an opening for drainage, the *California Farmer* reported, "the rush of water out was so great as to take along twenty or thirty buildings and even two-story houses, which were dashed to pieces below, while every description of furniture, including pianos, bureaus, etc. was distributed over the county all the way to Sutterville."[15] Unfortunately, the worst was yet to come.

In Sacramento's immediate vicinity twenty-five inches of rain fell during the following two months, almost four times the average rainfall. The Sacramento River surged at three times its normal seasonal flow of 285,000 cubic feet per second, inundating the Sacramento–San Joaquin Delta region and putting thousands of farms under water.[16] Landowners on the banks of the Sacramento River watched helplessly as their protective levees vanished under the torrent of muddy water and debris. The perennially optimistic *California Farmer* urged its readers to " 'look on the bright side,' and murmur not at the Storm: for it was beyond your control." But residents of Marysville found little comfort in such philosophizing; there, the death toll reached sixty-two persons, a figure the

California Farmer admitted "makes no account [for] the hundreds of Chinamen known to have perished."[17] In Marysville as elsewhere in the Golden State, deaths of Chinese people were rarely remembered in the public record.

The San Joaquin Valley experienced similar devastation. While the San Joaquin River usually carried far less water than the Sacramento River, in December and January the San Joaquin rose from 24,000 to approximately 133,000 cubic feet per second, a fivefold increase.[18] Floating farmhouses broke the telegraph wires on the outskirts of Stockton, and all the bridges on the Stanislaus River save one disappeared. The *Stockton Independent* estimated in January that 100,000 cattle perished in the valley. This loss of cattle, opined the *California Farmer,* would ultimately assist the stock raisers by driving up prices and killing off the inferior "Mexican" stock.[19] Ranchers like Henry Miller felt little enthusiasm at this prospect, as they struggled to drive their cattle to higher ground and watched the stragglers float downstream. In the southern end of the San Joaquin Valley, Tulare Lake stretched across some 486,400 acres, four times its average size.[20]

Many residents remembered the 1861–62 flood for the rest of their lives. "I can remember it very well," William Browning claimed sixty years later.[21] He recalled the body of water a dozen miles wide and a hundred miles long. He recounted how a steamboat ran through the back wall of the Russ Hotel in the crossroad town of Hill's Ferry. Browning felt no need to exaggerate the enormity of the flood, because the events held their own power of persuasion. While Browning and other residents remembered the event as a unique benchmark against which they measured all future natural catastrophes, the 1861–62 flood hardly qualified as an extraordinary ecological event. Though floods were unpredictable, the fact that another would soon occur was certain.

The flood nonetheless marked a crucial turning point in the San Joaquin Valley's social and environmental history. It made property owners painfully aware of the problems associated with living in a natural floodplain. Plans for flood control and swampland reclamation soon gained momentum—projects that held far-reaching consequences for the valley's natural communities.[22] Some small landowners reconsidered the practicality of farming in a region visited by such devastating floods; many simply moved on. Aspiring agrarian capitalists like Miller and Lux, William Chapman, and Isaac Friedlander seized the opportunity to expand their land-based operations during the downswing in real estate prices. Large-scale land consolidation, they believed, could protect their

- many leave the valley; M & L see opportunity - then drought

enterprises against nature's inconsistencies. This theory partially explained the Miller & Lux partnership's unabated land acquisitions over
the next forty years. But if the 1861–62 flood held significant implications for the Central Valley's landscape and landholding patterns, the
drought that followed the flood only reinforced those patterns.

For the next two years Sacramento received less than half its normal
rainfall, and the San Joaquin Valley fared even worse. "We have had no
rain of consequence for 11 months," the *Stockton Independent* reported
on February 27, 1864. "It excites a fear that we may not have any for
eight or ten months more."[23] Wheat and barley fields around Stockton
turned a "sickly" yellow color, and in the next month those crops dried
out completely. In a last-ditch effort to rescue cattle from starvation, stock
raisers drove their best cattle to the wetlands that bordered the San
Joaquin River.[24] In the first year of this drought, William Brewer described
the San Joaquin as "a plain of absolute desolation." Fifteen months later
he traversed the same ground and grimly noted, "Perfectly dry and barren, no grass."[25] The fading memory of an inland sea doubtlessly rose
in Brewer's mind as he surveyed the cracked plains.

After more than a year of severe drought, newspapers began printing
articles on the history of California droughts under headlines reading
"WILL IT RAIN?" and "THE RAINLESS YEARS OF CALIFORNIA—PASTURES,
CATTLE, SHEEP, ETC[.]," as if to assure their readers that the drought was
not a unique phenomenon.[26] Other newspapers attempted to draw lessons from the drought's effect. "Farmers will be more frugal and have a
keener and higher appreciation of the actual blessings of our climate and
country," the *San Jose Mercury* informed its readers.[27] The *California
Farmer* saw the lesson of the drought as one directed toward the state's
"stockmen" and "large [land]owners": "It is a singular fact, that with
[the] great loss of stock, no *American stock were lost.* We should esteem
it the best thing for the country to get rid of the wild and worthless [Mex-
ican] stock and breed and keep only the better kind. . . . The late drought
will, we think, compel many large owners to sell their land. This will be
a benefit to our State, and we shall see that good will come out of evil, or
rather what was esteemed a calamity, proves but 'a blessing in disguise.'"[28]
Indeed, cattle perished throughout the Central Valley, but the *California
Farmer*'s prediction that many "large owners" (primarily Anglo ranchers
and speculators) would sell their land never came true.

The drought certainly ruined some ranchers. The venerable California stockman Abel Stearns, who amassed well over 200,000 acres in
southern California during the 1840s and 1850s, faced an economic dis-

aster. Away from his ranchos during the winter of 1863–64, Stearns received weekly reports on the worsening condition of his land and cattle from his ranch superintendent, Charles Johnson:

> [November 17] Cattle are in pretty fair order for the season; your Rancho men report very few as having died.
> [December 18] Would you please sell steers to the butchers, [prices] here less than fifteen dollars!
> [January 11] The grass is very backward, though your Mayordomos say very few cattle dies [sic] as yet.
> [March 14] There is absolutely no grass, and it is the opinion of the Rancho men, the cattle will commence dying within a month. . . . All they can do on the Ranchos is to skin the cattle.[29]

Johnson's assessment of the drought's effect proved correct. In 1863, Stearns began selling his cattle to Miller & Lux for eight dollars a head.[30] The remaining steers were skinned for their hides. By 1864, the *Los Angeles Southern News* reported, "Thousands of carcasses strew the plains in all directions . . . and the sight is harrowing in the extreme."[31]

The drought finally ended in November 1864, and three "normal" rain years followed. In the winter of 1867–68 the high waters again returned, and "the whole San Joaquin Valley looked like an ocean."[32] But this flood lasted only weeks rather than months, and the following year was again dry. In all, the extreme natural conditions of the 1860s ruined many San Joaquin farmers, ranchers, and town promoters. During the coming decades the survivors would remember these events as something more than a series of natural disasters. They recalled the 1860s when they discussed the problems associated with the early landscape—prior to large-scale swampland reclamation, prior to the irrigation crusade, and prior to dams and river channelization. They remembered the devastation caused by drought and flooding as characteristic of a past landscape—usually not as a set of environmental dynamics and constraints associated with their present surroundings. Memory placed these events in the safety of the past, while those landowners who sought to control and engineer the valley's acreage planned for future catastrophes with the past firmly in mind.

AN EVOLVING LANDSCAPE:
RIPARIAN FORESTS, GRASSLANDS, AND WILDLIFE

Central Valley residents certainly remembered the drought and flooding of the 1860s for the extraordinary cost to private property. Some residents attempted to quantify the events in comparison to other hydrologic extremes during the nineteenth century.[33] A few careful observers recalled how the flooding actually reshaped parts of the valley floor, such as the course of the San Joaquin and Kern Rivers. In physically changing the valley, the flooding showed how extreme events (rather than the frequent, low-intensity events of temperate climates) dramatically conditioned this Mediterranean landscape.[34] A long history of natural change occurring long before human memory provides the context for those environmental transformations initiated by American settlement after 1850.

The geological formation of the Central Valley began roughly 220 million years ago, when the Pacific plate collided with the North American plate and forced the floor of the Pacific Ocean under the North American continent.[35] Islands, then mountains, and finally the present Pacific Coast emerged from the ocean. The Central Valley appeared between the uplift of the Coast Ranges and the Sierra Nevada, and water covered the valley until 100 million years ago. Alluvial deposits from the Sierra Nevada slowly filled the valley floor, which forced the inland waters to drain through the Suisun and San Francisco Bays. Freshwater lakes, similar to those seen in 1861–62, blanketed the area as three distinct valleys took shape (the Sacramento Valley, the San Joaquin Valley, and the Tulare Basin).[36] Plate tectonics, watercourse shifts, and soil deposits continued to refashion the valley floor, and these changes did not cease with human occupation.

The impacts made by valley residents during the mid–nineteenth century, however, began to supercede both evolutionary and catastrophic shifts in the landscape. During the years surrounding American conquest, the landscape's natural communities were altered with a rapidity to match the rate of change at any place on the continent. In particular, the valley's riparian forests, grasslands, and wildlife experienced replacements and decimation as a result of resource extraction, introduced species, and population growth.[37] The transformation of these three natural communities paved the way for the intensive landscape engineering of the coming decades.

The composition of the San Joaquin Valley's protohistoric forest—estimated to have covered well over a hundred thousand acres—varied widely from the surrounding foothills to the riparian regions alongside its rivers.[38] John C. Fremont noted this variability during his explorations of the Central Valley in the 1840s. "The uplands bordering the valleys of the large streams are usually wooded with evergreen oaks," Fremont wrote, "and the intervening plains are timbered with groves or belts of evergreen and white oaks among prairie and open land." Near the rivers on the valley floor, he reported, the "broad alluvial bottoms of very fertile soil" were often "rankly overgrown with bullrushes."[39] Indeed, the forests near the rivers exhibited the most floristic diversity. Cottonwood, California sycamore, willow, and valley oak comprised the upper story of trees. Beneath them lay an intermediate layer of box elder, Oregon ash, and smaller willow trees. On the forest floor grew vines with wild grapes and poison oak, clematis, mugwort, wild rose, and other undergrowth plant species.[40] Juan José Warner, who penetrated this thicket in the 1830s to reach the San Joaquin River, characterized it as a "labrynthian [sic] morass" of undergrowth.[41]

The catastrophic decline of the valley's Indian population during the early nineteenth century explains Warner's description, because valley Indians had intensely groomed the forests for thousands of years.[42] The forests served as an important food source for the Yokuts, who numbered as many as forty thousand prior to European contact. Acorns, gathered from the plentiful oaks bordering the valley's rivers and the adjacent foothills, were an important dietary staple. The Yokuts annually set fire to the grasslands in order to increase the acorn yield and to assist in hunting practices.[43] During dry years the fires moved through the riparian forests, clearing the understory brush and making the rivers more accessible. Fire disturbance of grasslands and forests, whether set by Indians or naturally by lightning strikes, provided natural regeneration for vegetation and soils and lowered the possibility of major conflagrations. The "labrynthian morass" described by Warner therefore represented something new, reflecting the steep decline of the Yokut population.[44]

The first two decades of American settlement brought an entirely different order of ecological change to the forests. The richness of riparian soils, demand for the wood supply, and proximity to a consistent water source led to rapid deforestation during the 1850s and 1860s.[45] Settlers thinned these forests substantially for fuel and fencing material, and steamships plying the San Joaquin and Sacramento Rivers used much of the remaining wood supply, particularly in the late 1850s, when steamboat travel markedly increased.[46] Some riparian forests remained. John Muir, for instance, happened upon what he described as "a fine jungle of tropical luxuriance" when he crossed the southern part of the valley in the early 1870s.[47] But Muir, who later championed the preservation of Sierra redwoods, viewed the valley's natural vegetation as a testament to its agricultural potential. The "fine jungle" seen by Muir grew thinner in the following decades. The lasting impact of the riparian forest depletion was not simply the disappearance of trees but rather the breakdown of vital "edge" communities that joined rivers and wetlands with the surrounding grasslands.[48] The forests' decline therefore marked a loss for the total environment. - *Euro-/Americans quickly degrade the enviro*

The valley's grasslands experienced a similar fate during the mid–nineteenth century, but their transformation had been initiated in the late 1700s and owed as much to natural processes as to human design. Dozens of different perennial and annual grass species covered the San Joaquin Valley prior to Spanish settlement, and the grasslands' composition varied widely according to soil types, degree of disturbance (such as fire), and wildlife grazing pressure.[49] Exogenous species invasion, however, set off a new chain of events. Spanish livestock driven to Alta California in 1769 carried with them exotic annual grasses, and some evidence suggests that European grass seeds arrived on the California coast even prior to Spanish settlement.[50] These Mediterranean-type grasses were well adapted to California's climate and to heavy grazing by cattle and sheep. Perhaps most significant, the introduced annuals spread rapidly in periods of drought. This combination of factors—the introduction of adapted annual grass species, a growing population of Spanish cattle, and California's dry Mediterranean climate—completely altered the grasslands' composition in the century following initial Spanish settlement.[51] *grasslands changed*

Convinced of the relationship between splendid grasslands and agricultural potential, American explorers, hunting parties, and early residents paid particular attention to California's prairie. Edwin Bryant, for instance, noted some of the grasslands' features as he traversed the northern end of the San Joaquin Valley in 1846. "The soil of the bottom[land] appears to be very rich, and produces the finest qualities of grasses," he wrote. "The grass on the upland is also abundant, but at this time it is brown and dead. We passed through large tracts of wild oats during the day; the stalks are generally from three to five feet in length." The next day he continued south across a "flat plain, generally covered with luxuriant grass, wild oats, and a variety of sparkling flowers." A member of John Charles Fremont's conquering California Battalion, Bryant envisioned California as "the future abode to millions upon millions of the sons of liberty." The grasslands' fertility symbolized this imagined future.[52]

Fremont was also fascinated by the San Joaquin's range—"good and green bunch grass," bur clover, and filaree, "a valuable plant for stock,

grass! → introduced by Euros
earlier

considered very nutritious."[53] Fremont could only begin to list the
grasses that covered the California prairie, and he was unaware that many
of these grasses, like him, were newcomers to the region.[54] Some early
settlers in the San Joaquin did recognize important changes in the grasslands. James Perkins, a sheep raiser in the 1850s, wrote, "Less than ten
years ago the traveler would ride for days through wild oats tall enough
to tie across his saddle; [they are] now dwindled down [by drought] to
a stunted growth of six or ten inches, with wide reaches of utterly barren land."[55] The "wild oats" he described were most likely *Avena fatua*
and *Brassica nigra,* both annual species introduced prior to extensive livestock grazing.[56] Unknowingly, Fremont also gave evidence of species invasion. His mention of the San Joaquin foothills being "interspersed"
with filaree *(Erodium cicutarium)* and bunchgrass (the most common of
which was *Nassella pulchra,* or purple needlegrass) suggests a transitional
phase of replacement—filaree was an introduced annual grass, while the
bunchgrasses were native perennials.[57]

Mediterranean annual grasses like wild oat, filaree, and chess grass
(Bromus rubens and *B. mollis)* had almost entirely replaced California's
native species by the end of the 1862–64 drought, and these species responded exceptionally well to ranchers' primitive range management.[58]
By the early 1870s, Miller & Lux would use flood irrigation and controlled burning to maximize the range's grazing potential. The introduced
grass species could also tolerate the heavy grazing of cattle and sheep
herds. The outcome of this transformation went beyond the replacement
of native species by imported ones. An open prairie landscape shaped by
flora diversity, indigenous grazers, wildfires, and periodic flooding gave
way to one characterized by Miller & Lux's property management system, which organized the land into discrete production sites. Meanwhile,
native grasses retreated to the isolated margins of California's valleys, a
retreat mirrored by the region's wild game.

Leaving the Central Valley en route to San Francisco on September 12,
1861, William Brewer paused to consider the inland region's declining
wildlife. "Game was once very abundant," he wrote in his diary; "bear
in the hills, and deer, antelope, and elk like cattle, in herds. [Thomas]
Russell said he had known a party of thirty or forty to *lasso* twenty-
eight elk on one Sunday. All are now exterminated, but we find their horns
by the hundreds."[59] Large game had certainly proliferated in the Central Valley during the early 1800s. Pronghorn antelope, deer, and elk
roamed in herds of more than a thousand animals, according to Span-

ish and American explorers. Recall Edward Bosqui's memory of the valley wildlife that still existed in the 1840s: "Elk, deer and antelope in such numbers that they actually darkened the plains for miles, and looked in the distance like great herds of cattle."[60] ~ *native herds killed/driven off — memories*

These memories imagined a past landscape that teemed with large game. A romanticized past is unmistakable in such passages: this was how it *used to be,* a splendid wildness removed from civilization and historical change. But such memories rendered the valley static in time— *a different story* wild game had *always* thrived here, herds of elk and deer had always roamed in "great herds" because of the valley's bountiful nature. If wild game often "darkened the plains for miles," natural forces could also litter the plains with sun-bleached horns and bones, particularly when drought coincided with wildlife overpopulation. Indian hunting prior to Spanish colonization, furthermore, kept wildlife populations at a far lower level than in the accounts of endless game presented by explorers. Only *after* the rapid decline of Indian populations did wildlife proliferate during the early- to mid-1800s.[61] Thus, the historical and protohistorical record reveals a remarkably dynamic scene of wildlife fluctuations on this landscape, one quite different from the static image conjured up by explorers' memories. Nonetheless, the mid–nineteenth century brought a different sort of change to the valley's wildlife.

Nineteenth-century hunting parties entered the valley at a moment that was opportune as a result of native population declines. In 1827 Jedediah Smith's hunting party trapped their way up the San Joaquin River and departed the following year with fifteen hundred pounds of beaver and otter pelts.[62] Six years later a hunting party from the Hudson Bay Company spent a month in the valley and amassed a body count of 395 elk, 148 deer, 17 bears, and 8 antelopes. This plunder was "certainly a great many more than was required," wrote expedition leader John Work, "but when the [hunters] have ammunition and see animals they must needs fire upon them be wanted or not."[63] An ideology of accumulation spurred on by the fur trade clearly distinguished these Anglo hunters from their native predecessors, and this ideology gained many followers by midcentury.

Spanish introductions of wild horses and cattle added another source of pressure on the valley's wildlife.[64] By the late 1820s, Mexican military expeditions in the valley could easily live off these introduced livestock. When José Sánchez, Joaquin Pina, and Mariano Vallejo led their troops into the valley pursuing the Indian rebel Estanislao in 1829, they had no trouble lassoing wild cattle to feed their troops. Pina reported the capture of fifty-seven steers in just one afternoon "for the use of the whole company," surely enough to feed his 154 men.[65] Pina's report (and many like it) confirms that herds of wild horses and cattle increased rapidly in size during the Mexican period. But these herds also challenged the native ungulates for forage, particularly in drought years, when the grasslands' carrying capacity declined and introduced diseases weakened native wildlife.[66] A combination of factors, therefore—including hunting parties, introduced livestock, and drought—led to the decline of native wildlife by the early 1850s.

It is within this context of decimated wildlife that Henry Miller's 1854 memory of elk "running in every direction" comes into question. "Tule" elk (Cervus elaphus nannodes) remained the valley's most numerous grazers until the mid-1840s.[67] On the San Joaquin's Westside in 1845, James Clyman witnessed "one herd of Elk . . . containing more than 2,000 head and covering the plain for more than a mile in length."[68] The following year Edwin Bryant also counted herds of "at least two thousand" animals, which he described as "very tame" but "not much prized" by hunters, given the ready supply of Mexican cattle.[69] The discovery of gold in 1848 and the immediate flood of hungry gold seekers dramatically changed this situation.

As early as 1849 elk and other wild game could be found on restaurant menus in San Francisco and Sacramento, and the market value of an elk hindquarter rose to forty dollars.[70] By 1854, according to the market hunter H. C. Banta, nearly all the elk in the San Joaquin Valley had been killed or "driven to the tules." Banta and other hunters then used small boats to follow these few survivors into the wetlands. "In one instance in Whiskey Slough," he recalled, "I cleaned up a band of eight single-handed, keeping out of sight. . . . Five were taken with the rifle and I returned to the boat, loaded my shotgun with heavy charge of buckshot and on returning, found the three remaining yearlings still in the vicinity near the carcasses. Following them, I got all three single file, and, as they turned their heads, I got all three at one shot, at an angle, being kicked over by the charge in the bargain."[71]

Banta's memory of this event contains no small measure of hunter's bragging rights, yet it also isolates a rare and particularly brutal moment of environmental change. The San Joaquin had experienced a century of ecological invasions and replacements that profoundly altered the region's flora and fauna. This process had many causes and explanations. Both natural forces and human actions contributed to the San Joaquin's transformation, and each set the stage for the intensive land management regime of the coming decades. Banta's story of "clean[ing] up" a final elk band freezes this historical process in time. Between the abundant game of the past and the engineered landscape of the future, only a few elk survived in the balance.

TULE ELK AND ENVIRONMENTAL CHANGE

Henry Miller's memory of wild elk also intersects with this process of environmental change. Miller had a personal attachment to tule elk at the time he recounted the event in the mid-1880s. Though for years tule elk had been considered extinct in California, a pair suddenly appeared in a swath of San Joaquin swampland that Miller & Lux was reclaiming in the late 1870s. Miller instructed his laborers to protect the elk while the reclamation work proceeded, a project that incrementally consumed their final habitat. From Miller's protected elk came the species' surviving representatives, soon penned on game reserves throughout California. Chapter 4 will explore these circumstances in greater detail, but here we should note the coincidence between a remembered event and the circumstances when that memory took place.

Miller knew that elk had once roamed throughout the San Joaquin plain, and he knew they *should* have been "running in every direction" when he first visited the valley in 1854. His recollection—like those of countless other observers—attempted to revisit the landscape in its primitive state. It used to be filled with game, crossed by riparian forests, and frequented by periodic floods. It used to be wild and unpredictable. Memory served Miller's purpose in this regard because it clearly separated the past from the present: the "wild" landscape, in which elk herds freely roamed, was distinct from a seemingly domesticated landscape in which only a few survived in pens. Miller did not long for this past landscape, but he used the memory of it to gain perspective on his present engineered surroundings.

Memory could celebrate past landscapes, such as Bosqui's vision of game that "darkened the plains for miles." Memory could also unsettle a spectator by the sharp juxtaposition of past and present—Brewer experienced this sensation as he watched the arid valley turn into an inland sea and then back to desert. For the San Joaquin Yokuts, memory (in the form of creation stories) provided an ancestral link to the landscape and a means of ordering their place in the natural world. Memory, in short, had different functions for different people as they pondered their relationship to the natural surroundings. More often than not, however, memory provided a poor rendition of how environmental change took place and the roles played by both humans and natural forces. Miller remembered that elk had been everywhere and that currently his property held the last survivors, but his memory ignored the complicated transition— and his own role in it—between these time periods.

The decline of wildlife was only the most noticeable sign of the valley's transformation. Throughout the nineteenth century, and particularly during the first few decades of American settlement, the entire landscape underwent a process of change that replaced complex ecological communities with domesticated animals, constructed waterways, and irrigated fields. The natural change and disturbance that had previously shaped the valley was superceded by human alterations of the physical environment. But the San Joaquin's natural extremes continued to play a formative role in the region's development, and despite the radical changes brought to the land, the essential conditions of the San Joaquin were not so easily altered.

Miller & Lux's horizontal expansion, originating in the late 1850s with the firm's first land acquisitions, developed in part from an understanding of California's complex landscape and natural extremes. The partners recognized the inevitability of recurrent droughts and floods, knew that range resources varied widely across the inland valleys, and understood that having a consistent water supply in the San Joaquin required controlling extensive riparian lands. By extending its property throughout the San Joaquin Valley and elsewhere, Miller & Lux sought protection from nature's unpredictability. This expansion originated in the markets of San Francisco and then moved outward from the city limits to a hinterland still claimed, in many cases, by Mexican rancheros.

CHAPTER 2

Laying the Foundation

San Francisco Networks and Hinterland Property

In 1853 Charles Lux initiated two ordinary transactions that paved the way for his future success. Lux had lived in San Francisco since 1850, and he operated a highly profitable butcher shop on the corner of Sacramento and Kearny Streets. The city's social and business elite apparently welcomed this German immigrant: within a few years Lux would marry into a wealthy family that traced its lineage back to Rhode Island's founders, and soon thereafter he would form a partnership with Henry Miller, the city's leading butcher. Clearly, Charles Lux sought out promising associations, a trait confirmed by his two real estate acquisitions: a half-interest in 1,700 acres of Rancho Buri Buri, and a "certain tract or parcel of land covered with water in the City of San Francisco known as the Outside water lot."[1] The Buri Buri property held obvious appeal. Situated just south of the city, it included prime grazing land for holding cattle before slaughter in San Francisco. The "Outside water lot," on the other hand, represented a more speculative investment in the city's future. Tracts of land such as this one fronted San Francisco Bay on the city's eastern side, and high tide made them more a part of the bay than a part of the city. Lux and his fellow "water lot" owners therefore gambled that they could successfully reclaim the property from the Pacific Ocean's tide.

Lux would profit immensely from the two acquisitions, but the land's increasing value was only part of the reason. The deals introduced Lux to John Parrott, Henry Haight, and D. O. Mills, members of an emerging San Francisco elite, whose resources and reputations unquestionably assisted Miller & Lux in the coming years.[2] Moreover, these initial contacts placed Lux within a circle of businessmen who soon managed the leading banks, law firms, and political offices of the city and state. In stark contrast to Henry Miller, Charles Lux possessed the personality and confidence necessary to operate in this circle. That Lux's introduction to the city's elite network occurred during a real estate deal was hardly coincidental. In fact, the buying and selling of California property was the primary activity of most city leaders.

Lux's land deals illustrate the contours of a larger story. Building upon these initial purchases, Miller & Lux's rapid expansion during the late 1850s and the 1860s intersected with two crucial developments in the Far West. The first was San Francisco's emergence as the nerve center for a vast, dynamic region—a position achieved through deliberate planning and organization, not simply through favorable geography.[3] As civic and business leaders organized their own markets and urban space for industrial production, such as the reclamation of "water lots" for a slaughterhouse district, their actions increasingly determined the investment patterns and industrial growth of the surrounding hinterlands. Miller & Lux's early history illustrates this capacity of city networks and markets to organize the Pacific Coast region.

Lux's interest in Rancho Buri Buri points to a second element of the firm's success and the region's development. The partners possessed an almost unnatural talent for consolidating vast stretches of land, including portions of the public domain (as demonstrated in the following chapter) and the private estates of Californio rancheros. Like others who speculated in rancho lands, Miller & Lux targeted such properties because the Mexican (and in some cases American) owners faced debt as a result of taxes, legal expenses, and the decimation of cattle herds during the early 1860s.[4] Miller & Lux acquired rancho properties—including large portions of sixteen former Mexican land grants located between San Francisco and the San Joaquin Valley—on a scale unequaled by any of its peers. By the end of the 1860s, Miller & Lux owned well over 300,000 acres of grazing land, and over half of this acreage derived from former Mexican land grants. (See map 2.) Rather than engage in land speculation for short-term profit, the firm transformed these ranchos into an integrated system of cattle production that directly supplied the city's markets.

San Francisco offered an attractive package of goods to the resourceful and well-connected entrepreneur: venture capital, natural resources, steady population growth, skilled labor, and, until the completion of the

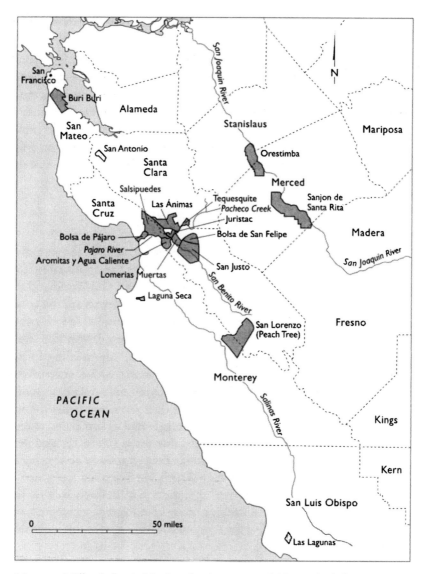

Map 2. Miller & Lux's Mexican land grant acquisitions (shaded areas).
During the 1860s Miller & Lux laid the foundation for its sprawling empire
by grabbing large portions of sixteen different former Mexican land grants.

transcontinental railroad in 1869, a two-thousand-mile buffer against
eastern markets. Miller & Lux, like other dynamic Pacific Coast firms,
used these attributes to experiment with novel forms of business modernization. The two partners developed a highly strategic sense of
landownership, nurtured a diverse cadre of agents, and connected urban
markets with rural production. The first stage in their evolution from
storefront butchers to industrial cowboys, therefore, entailed a systematic approach to city markets and western lands.

MEAT MARKETS AND "ENTERPRISING MEN"

On March 1, 1850, one month after its inaugural edition, the editors of
San Francisco's *Daily Journal of Commerce* offered an appraisal of California's business potential: "Capitalists both in the Old World and the
States, even now, have but little faith in California. They regard this country and everything relating to it as one grand bubble, liable to burst at
any moment." The *Journal*'s editors appeared pleased with this situation. "This is how it should be," they concluded; "the wealth of California is [thereby] passing into the hands of young, active, enterprising
men, who in an older country and with these same old capitalists as competitors might have worked to the end of their days, and realized but a
mere pittance."[5] The *Journal* certainly exaggerated its first claim; in fact,
eastern capitalists exhibited a mounting interest in California's mineral
markets and trade opportunities. But this exaggeration in no way inval-
idated the *Journal*'s second point: gold rush San Francisco was a veritable playground for "young, active" capitalists in all business sectors. The
rapid growth of commercial banking houses, land agents, merchants, and
trade professions attested to the economic possibilities of this makeshift
metropolis.[6]

The city's meat markets, though likely far from the editors' minds
when they wrote this article, nonetheless represented fertile ground for
capital investment and business innovation. It took Henry Miller less than
a year of wage laboring to realize the potential of the city's meat trade,
and in July of 1851 he invested his savings in a butcher shop on Jackson
Street, in the heart of the commercial district.[7] Miller sold directly to consumers, and by purchasing beef in large amounts from different slaughtering facilities he soon functioned as a middleman to butchers throughout San Francisco. Miller tailored his business to the diverse tastes of the
city's population. For instance, he supplied the French cooks with "bulls'

heads brains" because he "could not sell them meat without . . . some brains and kidney to give them."[8] Though Miller quickly learned the importance of customer satisfaction, he also grew frustrated with the limited scale of this trade, and like many other "enterprising" young San Franciscans, he searched for the means to capitalize on the city's growth.

Miller's experience with stock raising and cattle markets in his native Germany offered some ideas for innovation. He appreciated the organization of German livestock markets: strong regional systems of cattle production; decentralized slaughterhouses; constant improvements in breeding (the Neckar breed from Miller's Wurttemberg weighed thirteen hundred pounds, far surpassing most California cattle); and proper range management techniques, which allowed for high livestock density.[9] This system bred prime "killable" (or "market-ready") beef, Miller believed, yet it also stifled any form of entrepreneurship. Miller saw the exact opposite in San Francisco's regional markets: business independence, but a completely unregulated, unorganized, and grossly inefficient system of production and sales. Though showing tremendous growth potential, the city's meatpackers still awaited a market revolution.

Most cattle herds at this time, according to Miller, arrived in San Francisco "from the Southern part of California—Monterey, Los Angeles, and San Diego." With his sizeable proceeds from meat sales, he purchased small herds of Mexican cattle and placed them on rented land in the nearby Guadalupe Valley. "They varied in price," Miller remembered; "sometimes they were high and sometimes they were cheap. I took advantage of the number in the market and when cattle were scarce, I got a good price for them."[10] The variation in cattle prices, he soon realized, resulted not only from the number of cattle on the market but also from the financial instability of the rancheros, who often sold cattle below market value in order to cover their debts.[11] By purchasing the rancheros' cattle, Miller came to understand the financial plight of the state's Californio land- owners, as well as the profits to be realized by controlling San Francisco's booming meat market. Both ends of the industry—livestock production and marketing—seemed poised for takeover and consolidation.

Charles Lux's early career in San Francisco followed a remarkably similar course. He arrived in the city from New York just ahead of Miller and immediately set up shop on the bustling corner of Kearny and Sacramento Streets. Few San Francisco residents appeared more "enterprising" than Lux. His gracious smile and warm eyes, as opposed to Miller's stern visage, welcomed confidences and lured prospective customers. In

1853 he pooled resources with his English acquaintance Alfred Edmondson and purchased the Buri Buri property.[12] For three years they stocked the Buri Buri with market-ready cattle and fed the city's slaughterhouses as prices rose. When Edmondson left the partnership in 1856, Lux had more than enough capital to obtain his partner's share of the rancho. The following year Lux and Miller—by then the city's top two butchers—each contributed fifty thousand dollars toward the joint purchase of 1,600 prime Texas cattle. They drove the herd to Lux's Buri Buri grazing land, and after their cattle sold in San Francisco, Miller and Lux split the profits and briefly parted ways.[13] A similar purchase of 2,000 cattle in 1858 cemented the partnership.

In order to gain acceptance by San Francisco's financial and social elite, Lux and Miller required signs of status more visible than the strong reputations they held among the city's top merchants. Lux made his move in 1857, offering his already impressive wealth (in the place of a proper family name) to the young widow Miranda Wilmarth Sheldon.[14] The Sheldon family's assets had recently declined, but its bloodline ran back to Rhode Island's first gentry and therefore provided Lux with a powerful calling card that would admit him to San Francisco's high society. Following his new partner's lead, Miller married Sheldon's sister, Nancy Wilmarth Sheldon, in 1858.[15] When she died in childbirth the following year, Miller revealed his persistence in such matters by immediately marrying her twenty-year-old niece, Sarah Elizabeth Wilmarth Sheldon. As in the case of many nineteenth-century firms, the Miller & Lux partnership derived from personal as well as business interests.

Despite Miller's later claim that "there [was] no similarity between Lux and myself," the two German immigrants surely recognized their compatibility as partners.[16] Lux possessed a genial style that Miller lacked, and through his real estate transactions Lux had already cultivated strong ties with the city's business elite. Miller, on the other hand, was driven by the logic of capital investment and business expansion that epitomized the transformation of American capitalism at midcentury. Miller and Lux's ambitious business strategy resolved any lingering personal differences: they would control the wholesale market for meat in San Francisco by dominating the supply end. This strategy involved a simple yet innovative process of backward integration—first, they purchased as much cattle as they could stock on rented land, and soon after that they purchased the grazing land itself and produced their own cattle.[17] The partners' need for extensive rangeland placed them in a market far more complicated than the meat markets they knew so well.

SAN FRANCISCO AND
THE BUSINESS OF CALIFORNIA LAND

Few signs carried more symbolic power in the late-nineteenth-century West than the one inscribed "Land Office." Perched atop a simple clapboard house on dusty Main Streets from Oklahoma to California, the land office sign beckoned hopeful settlers and speculators alike with the dream of cheap land. This "key force of western settlement" carried out the improbable task of drawing property lines across highly contested terrain and then assigning private rights based on those lines.[18] In some instances the land office performed its work adequately; elsewhere it epitomized the fraud and folly of frontier development.

In San Francisco during the 1850s and 1860s, a group of capitalized land brokers preempted the tasks usually assigned to the U.S. Land Office, and John Parrott sat at the center of this group.[19] An American consul to Mexico and a Pacific Coast merchant during the years prior to the Mexican-American War, Parrott possessed the comforting social graces of a diplomat, along with a grifter's sense for business opportunity. He settled in San Francisco in 1848 with enough capital to invest heavily in mining companies and city lots before constructing the impressive Parrott Granite Building and Parrott Iron Building in the city's financial district in 1852. Parrott's business grew quickly, even if, as one contemporary charged, he was "most excentric [sic] in his feelings and rather slack in his moral principles."[20] Beyond money lending and mining investments, Parrott dealt in the exchange of California lands, and the four floors of his Iron Building conveniently housed the clerks, archives, and officers of the U.S. Board of Land Claims Commissioners. For all practical purposes, Parrott's building *was* the San Francisco land office.[21]

He established the Parrott & Company Banking Exchange and Agency in 1855 as the financial end of his land business, and both ventures remained profitable during a decade of boom and bust cycles.[22] He viewed land as a commodity like minerals or pork bellies, and he foresaw the need for land agents well versed in law and market conditions.[23] Parrott capitalized on the very *insecurity* of existing property rights. Throughout California and the Far West, private property in land became a site of frequent conflict (and occasional violence) because of overlapping claims, invalid grants and titles, and suspect documents. While settlers attempted to claim property through use or improvements, speculators and land-grant holders sought to secure and codify their own property rights to the exclusion of settlers.[24] Parrott, meanwhile, brought his land clients together with the financiers, lawyers, and public land officials who shared an interest in the transactions. Parrott established his reputation in this capacity, open for hire to investors like Miller and Lux.

While the vast majority of Parrott's clients resided in San Francisco, he also brokered deals for prosperous easterners that could expand his reputation nationally. In 1855, for instance, the prominent New York lawyer Samuel Barlow hired Parrott to handle his San Francisco real estate and other investments in the city.[25] Barlow had purchased valuable downtown properties during the early 1850s, just when conflicting land grants and rival claimants began to muddle city lot titles. Parrott promised Barlow to "do everything in my power to protect your interests," which included confirming the titles and thereafter selling the land. Two extremely powerful associates ultimately helped Parrott with these tasks: J. W. Mandeville, California's surveyor general, and Henry Haight, the land law attorney and future California governor.[26] By 1861, Barlow's titles were confirmed and the properties sold at a significant profit after rivals lost their claims to the land.[27] Parrott's actions on his client's behalf reveal a primary characteristic of California's business environment—the land market certainly operated through organized legal and economic institutions, but personal connections and obligations pervaded these transactions as well.

Henry Haight remained one of Parrott's closest associates throughout the 1850s and 1860s. Arriving in San Francisco in 1850, Haight established a law practice that served some of the city's major capitalists and power brokers, including William Tecumseh Sherman, Jesse Carr, Lloyd Tevis, and the Page & Bacon Bank.[28] From the beginning, Haight shared Parrott's view that California presented a unique "western phenomenon" of "resources and prospects" for landed enterprise. Yet Haight bristled over the unsettled nature of land titles. "It is confusion worse confounded," he informed his father after a lengthy description of contested claims; "almost any system [of property rights] would be preferable to the present state of things."[29] Haight quickly built one of San Francisco's most successful land law practices and he constantly expounded the need for "stability and security" in property rights.[30] The legal work of this soon-to-be California governor did not advance stable property rights in the abstract but instead advanced only the property claims of elite landowners.[31] Miller & Lux and his other capitalized clients won their claims, while Haight and his associate relentlessly attacked the claims made by "squatters" and Californios.[32]

Like Haight, many of California's leading jurists cut their teeth in the land market of the 1850s. Parrott's friend and fellow Republican S. O. Houghton entered California in 1846 with the New York Volunteer Battalion. Discharged in 1850 (though keeping his title "the colonel" for years to come), Houghton embarked on the life of an enterprising California pioneer. He spent nine months in the mining country, opened a land law practice in San Jose, married *two* survivors of the Donner Party (following the death of his first wife, Mary Donner, Houghton wed her first cousin, Eliza Donner), and served two terms in the U.S. House of Representatives (1871–75).[33] His law practice in the heart of the Santa Clara Valley catered to the property interests of San Francisco and Bay Area residents seeking properties south of the city that had been Mexican land grants. In a series of cases for large landowners (Henry Miller among others), the "colonel" established new legal precedents that shaped private property law for this new landholding class.[34] Houghton took great pride in being "one of the band" who left the east "to take possession of this [western] country," and as in the cases of Parrott and Haight, this act of "possession" necessitated the dispossession of the state's Californio landowners.[35] Californio owners lose out

Parrott's contacts in the legal community included local land law specialists as well as the top firm in Washington, D.C., Britton & Gray. Parrott could also draw upon defense attorneys who safeguarded the business and personal interests of the West's leading industrialists. California's most celebrated trial attorney of the late nineteenth century, Hall McAllister, met John Parrott in 1851, when they helped organize San Francisco's first Vigilance Committee. With Parrott's assistance, McAllister built a debt collection practice for the city's top merchants, many of whom participated in the Vigilance Committee's activities.[36] McAllister soon developed a more respectable reputation in the West's legal community through his father, who served as the first United States circuit judge for California between 1855 and 1862, and this connection drew an impressive clientele to his practice. The Central Pacific Railroad, the Pacific Mail Steamship Company, and Adolph Spreckels all benefited from McAllister's noted oratorical skills, as did Leland Stanford, who received two weeks' worth of McAllister's glowing verbiage during his closing defense in *Colton v. Stanford*.[37] Charles Lux also met McAllister at Parrott's urging, and their business relationship culminated with McAllister's successful prosecution of the landmark water rights case *Lux v. Haggin.*

Parrott's connections to leading jurists certainly assisted the Pacific Coast's land (and water) moguls, but he also helped them attain the necessary capital for acquiring property.[38] Miller & Lux provides a good case in point. Parrott brought Charles Lux together with banker D. O. Mills for the Buri Buri deal in 1853, and in the 1860s Parrott encouraged Mills and William Ralston (of the Bank of California) to finance irrigation development in the San Joaquin Valley that proved extremely advantageous for Miller & Lux. When Parrott sold his bank to the London & San Francisco Bank in 1871, Miller & Lux continued to receive preferential treatment that allowed the firm to weather the national depression when it hit California in 1875. The bank's president, Milton Slocum Latham, invested heavily in western lands, and this personal trait suited Miller & Lux's taste for a banker who understood the firm's needs and recognized land as a crucial asset for western large-scale enterprise.[39]

The business in California land sponsored by Parrott and his associates did not seek to promote and protect all large landowners. Instead, they championed the activities of ascendant economic interests that offered profitable returns and industrial progress while simultaneously undermining the rights of the previous elite. Abel Stearns, the Yankee trader-turned-large-landowner through marriage to Juan Bandini's daughter Arcadia in 1841, consolidated ownership of numerous ranchos in southern California during the 1840s and 1850s. After the gold rush Stearns extended sizeable loans to his fellow Los Angeles rancheros and picked up portions of their land grants as payment when the notes came due.[40] Stearns often received advice from Parrott on business matters, such as the marketing of cattle, the importance of crossbreeding "American bulls" with Mexican stock, and the status of his many cases before the California Land Claims Commission.[41] By the early 1860s, however, Stearns faced insolvency from a combination of legal bills, taxes, and the 1862–64 drought that decimated his cattle herds. Stearns borrowed thirty-five thousand dollars from Parrott but soon defaulted on the payments. "It might be to your advantage," Parrott suggested in 1864, "to turn over to me all your unencumbered property to prevent further trouble."[42] When Stearns refused the offer, Parrott sent his son Tiburcio to Los Angeles to issue suit against his debtor, chiding Stearns for his "procrastinating system of doing business."[43] By 1868, Stearns's property was heavily mortgaged to a syndicate of San Francisco investors.[44]

Unfortunate circumstances can account for some of Stearns's declining fortunes. Like many other rancheros, Stearns lost the ability to cover land costs during the 1860s flood and drought.[45] But Stearns's loss reveals a larger dynamic at work. Property taxes, legal fees, the Land Claims Commission, high-interest loans, and financial syndicates all represented a structured system of property rights that operated through a highly capitalized market, and that market sat in San Francisco. This new center of power forced Stearns to adjust to its business terms, whether by selling cattle to Miller & Lux, proving title in court, or turning over his property to a land syndicate. While he retained some land until his death in 1871, Stearns remained a rancher of the previous generation, an outsider to the San Francisco elite networks that controlled the new land market. *- good example of a ranchero's decline/sale to the new elite.*

MILLER & LUX: ACQUIRING MEXICAN LAND GRANTS

Miller & Lux's land acquisition during the late 1850s and 1860s symbolized many important facets of American conquest—the replacement of Mexican landowning elites by Anglo elites, the increasing influence of San Francisco over the surrounding hinterlands, and the emergence of industrial enterprises across the Far West. More specifically in terms of Mexican land grants, Miller & Lux's expansion reveals how a powerful capitalist market and its accompanying legal institutions quickly altered regional landownership patterns and social relations.[46] As former land grants were transferred intact to Anglo owners or consumed piecemeal by land-hungry settlers, the productive resources of the state became inextricably connected to that market. The gold rush had certainly propelled a market revolution in California. But this important turning point did not initiate market relations in the region. Contrary to the romantic myth of pastoral Mexican California, the Californio elite had also actively participated in market-based trade and developed their lands as private property.[47]

American rule, however, did inaugurate a radical restructuring of private property rights, and this change stemmed in part from the Land Law of 1851. The Land Law compelled rancheros to prove their land grant titles before the California Land Claims Commission in San Francisco or Los Angeles. Following the initial ruling, either the claimants or their rivals could appeal the commission's decision in district and federal courts. From beginning to end, this litigation process took an average of seventeen years, and according to most historians of the period, a majority of the 812 claimants received de jure title to their lands.[48] But Miller & Lux's acquisition of rancho lands clearly reveals that confirmation of title to the original grantees was a legal fallacy. In most cases, the claimants no longer held possession of the rancho land. Instead, it belonged to well-financed buyers like Miller & Lux, and these new American owners pushed the land claim through the confirmation and patenting process.

In marked contrast to Texas and the Southwest, where Mexican dispossession transpired more slowly, California's private lands quickly passed into American hands.[49] However, reference to the "veritable orgy" of land speculation that presumably characterized the techniques of capitalized buyers like Miller & Lux fails to describe the concerted landowning strategies they developed—strategies based on natural resources, city markets, and the emerging state infrastructure.[50] For Miller & Lux, these factors resulted in the acquisition of geographically linked properties between San Francisco and the San Joaquin Valley. The firm's acquisition and use of ranchos Buri Buri, Las Ánimas, and Sanjon de Santa Rita illustrates this process.

BURI BURI

In October of 1827, the Mexican governor José María de Echeandía granted Sublieutenant José Antonio Sánchez of the San Francisco presidio permission to "occupy" the 15,000-acre Rancho Buri Buri "for grazing and agricultural purposes."[51] Previously held as grazing land for Mission Dolores and the San Francisco presidio, Buri Buri's boundaries stretched from the San Bruno hills south into (the present site of) Burlingame, and from the San Andreas Valley east to the shore of San Francisco Bay. Sánchez and his family worked the land for the next five years, and after the Secularization Act of 1832 he filed an *expediente* (or formal petition) to legalize his title under Mexican law.[52] Sánchez had exploited the property's potential: his livestock had increased to 2,000 head of cattle and 250 horses, and with the help of his ten children and Ohlone Indian laborers, Sánchez also cultivated fields of wheat, corn, and beans.[53] Governor José Castro formally confirmed the land grant to Sánchez in 1835. Sánchez subsequently built a five-room adobe house near the road known as El Camino Real, which crossed the Buri Buri, and in the early 1840s Sánchez hired an American carpenter to construct a grain mill and mill house adjacent to his adobe.[54]

Through his occupation and cultivation of the property, José Antonio Sánchez had fulfilled the requirements of a land grantee under Mexican law. Upon his death in 1843 Rancho Buri Buri passed in equal portions to his five sons and five daughters. The eldest son, José de la Cruz Sánchez, filed petition for the property before the Land Claims Commission in March of 1852, and twenty years later on October 17, 1872,

José de la Cruz Sánchez was recorded as recipient of the 14,639.19-acre
Mexican land grant. Thus, it appeared that José de la Cruz Sánchez had
successfully passed his family's land grant through the tortuous course
of the Land Claims Commission and avoided the intrusions of squatters
and land-grabbing financiers. In fact, the Sánchez heirs owned less than
4 percent of the Buri Buri land by 1872.[55]

Like most California land grants eventually confirmed to Mexican
rancheros, the new American owners pressed the land case through the
confirmation process. These new owners, D. O. Mills, Ansel Easton, and
Charles Lux, had each purchased large portions of the property from
the heirs of José Antonio Sánchez during the 1850s, and their lawyer,
Henry Haight, secured the Sánchez title for them. High-interest loans,
taxes, legal fees, and fear of ultimately losing the property had forced
the Sánchez heirs to relinquish the family estate before an onslaught of
litigation.[56] The legal quagmire they would have faced, not surprisingly,
was a function of the property's resources and location. The Buri Buri
contained easily irrigated land with rich soils located less than five miles
from San Francisco. An 1858 boundary survey noted the land's many natural resources and improvements: "Laguna de San Bruno," "Laguna
Alta," and the "Sanchez Ditch," as well as natural streams, "oak grove[s],"
and the "San Jose Stage Road," which crossed thousands of acres of
prime grazing land.[57] More desirable land could hardly be found in California, and San Francisco's proximity only increased Buri Buri's value and
appeal.

Conflicting survey stakes on Buri Buri's acreage appeared almost immediately. Lux, Mills, and Easton represented only the wealthiest participants in this claiming race. Gold rush settlers also squatted on the
property's borders in the early 1850s and proceeded to file preemption
claims to what they considered the public domain. Demanding full use
of their property, Lux, Mills, and Easton had the land resurveyed in 1858,
and this survey clearly annexed the settlers' homesteads. Throughout the
1860s the settlers sought to enjoin the patenting of the land grant, attacking the wealthy San Franciscans as "ruthless land sharks" who had
knowingly extended Buri Buri's boundaries.[58] Even one month before
the final patenting of Buri Buri in 1872, the settlers petitioned President
U. S. Grant to "stop the issuance of the patent . . . on the ground that a
fraudulent survey had been made which included land belonging to the
government and Settlers."[59] Grant took no action on the matter.

The issue of Buri Buri's boundaries also drew a complaint from Francisco Sánchez, the owner of the neighboring San Pedro rancho. The 1858

survey incorporated Laguna Alta, an important water source on Buri Buri's eastern border. Sánchez, whose rancho shared this boundary line, appealed to the commissioner of the General Land Office, the federal office in charge of all private purchases of public land.[60] The survey, Sánchez wrote, "has done me serious injury and wrong by including within the lines of the Rancho Buriburi [sic] a portion of the rancho de San Pedro belonging to me. A greater loss than the land thus taken from me is experienced by me in the loss of ponds of fresh water [Laguna Alta] forming the chief resource for the cattle pastured upon the rest of my land." In closing, Sánchez asked for the General Land Office to respect "the line which was run on the ground by the former [Mexican] government and was binding on the parties and on the United States" by the Treaty of Guadalupe Hidalgo.[61]

Sánchez's plea for the commissioner to respect the old boundary relied on the testimony of Californio landowners Feliciano Soberanes and José María Alviso. He also gathered an affidavit from Eusabio Galindo, one of the official witnesses in 1835 when the Buri Buri's boundary lines had been set by a mounted group of fifteen Californios. The court heard this boundary dispute, but Henry Haight quickly dismissed Galindo's memory, stating that "his character for truth and veracity is so bad that he is not to [be] believed under oath."[62] The Mexican witness was no match for Haight's reputation before the commission. In the next map of Buri Buri drawn by the office of the surveyor general in 1865, the Laguna Alta was firmly included within its boundary line.

The lengthy confirmation process, therefore, allowed Mills, Easton, and Lux to acquire the Buri Buri and annex disputed property because these buyers possessed the financial and legal resources to defend their claims in court. Under the counsel of Henry Haight, the three San Franciscans pressed their case through the Land Claims Commission despite legal challenges by settlers and the San Pedro claimant. In prosecuting the case, Haight used the same political finesse that launched him into the office of California governor in 1866. The heirs of José Antonio Sánchez were simply unable to marshal such resources to retain their land.

The Buri Buri quickly became central to Miller & Lux's system of landownership and cattle production, and between 1860 and 1872 the firm doubled the acreage it owned within the former grant and leased much of the land remaining in it for grazing purposes.[63] The key to this rancho's importance lay in its proximity to San Francisco markets. With the Buri Buri constantly stocked with market-ready cattle, Miller & Lux could supply its San Francisco slaughterhouse on a daily basis and thereby keep pace with market demand. The San Jose Stage Road ran north and south through Buri Buri and served as Miller & Lux's main cattle trail throughout the 1860s. Originating in San Francisco, it passed through the Buri Buri and seventy miles later entered Miller & Lux's southern Santa Clara Valley ranchos. The San Francisco and San Jose Railroad, completed in 1866, followed the same route, with a stop at Baden Station on the Buri Buri rancho. Buri Buri therefore sat alongside San Francisco's main transportation corridor, and like other land-based enterprises in the Far West, Miller & Lux increasingly used this corridor in the coming decades. – *location!* |

LAS ÁNIMAS

In his daily letters to Charles Lux, Henry Miller always referred to Buri Buri as "your place."[64] Lux had built his country house near Baden Station in 1859, and the surrounding rancho was Lux's private estate, not Miller & Lux property.[65] Like other San Francisco elites, the Lux family retired to this country setting for most weekends and holidays. Miller, on the other hand, built his Bloomfield Farm "home ranch," which was *his* private estate, seventy miles south of San Francisco in 1863, near the town of Gilroy. The Bloomfield Farm area was previously known by stock raisers as the "center place" for its central location between southern California ranchos and San Francisco markets. According to Miller, it was "well watered, nice country, nice grass, and a nice place to camp—stockmen have a peculiar faculty for finding nice camping places—and that induced me to buy it."[66] He initially purchased only the 1,700-acre Bloomfield Farm, but he also had his eye on the 26,518-acre Rancho Las Ánimas that encompassed the farm. Over the next ten years, Miller & Lux acquired not only the bulk of Las Ánimas but also large portions of eight other ranchos surrounding Las Ánimas.[67] This region on the borders of Santa Clara, San Benito, and Monterey Counties became the "center place" for Miller & Lux's movement of cattle.

Few Californio land grants should have passed through the confirmation process as quickly as Las Ánimas. The title dated back to 1802, when Mariano Castro petitioned the viceroy of New Spain for "the tract of La Brea" (Las Ánimas), stating that it is "distant three or four leagues from any Mission or Pueblo . . . [and] will be useful as a stopping place and accommodation for the mail rider, packtrains and other travelers who traverse these spots."[68] Castro's record as a soldier in the Monterey garrison proved sufficient for Viceroy Felíz Berancuer's favor, and the following year Castro received the land grant. Castro obtained a number of other land grants in the vicinity of Monterey, and given his increasing estate, Don Mariano became a major advocate of land privatization following the Mexican Revolution of 1821.[69] Castro's cattle herds increased with his landownership. By the time of his death in 1828, the hides and tallow from his slaughtered cattle could be sold to Yankee traders in Monterey, San Jose, or Santa Clara. Mexican governor José Figueroa regranted Las Ánimas to the Castro heirs in 1835, and the property became a central trading place when merchant Thomas O. Larkin located an agent there in 1842.[70]

Perhaps anticipating the land conflicts that would occur with American rule, the Castros began selling Las Ánimas to José María Sánchez in 1846.[71] By 1850 Sánchez owned three-fourths of the rancho, and he had every reason to expect a speedy confirmation of Las Ánimas before the Land Claims Commission. But when the commission issued its patent twenty-one years later, neither Sánchez nor his heirs owned the land. Instead, three Americans, Johanna Fitzgerald, Thomas Rea, and Henry Miller, owned over 80 percent of the 26,518-acre Las Ánimas property, and three hundred individuals held the remainder in small parcels. Miller owned well over half of Las Ánimas.[72]

The conflicts accompanying Henry Miller's acquisition of Las Ánimas paralleled Charles Lux's experience with the Buri Buri. Boundary line disputes with neighboring landowners figured prominently in both cases, and settlers' preemption claims repeatedly forced Miller into court.[73] Miller hired the locally respected S. O. Houghton to press his claim before the Land Claims Commission, but appeals by settlers sent the case to federal court.[74] By 1869 the patent for Las Ánimas had yet to be issued, so Miller hired Britton & Gray, the most prominent Washington, D.C., law partnership specializing in private land claims, to examine the matter. They informed Miller & Lux that "no survey of this grant has ever been received by the [Land] Commissioner." Clearly dissatisfied with Houghton's handling of the case, Britton & Gray advised that "whoever has pretended to attend to securing [the] patent . . . has very clearly neglected the matter."[75] Miller & Lux submitted a new survey of the property, and Britton & Gray replied that the patent for Las Ánimas "should be arriving soon."[76]

If securing legal title to Las Ánimas represented one dilemma for Miller & Lux, the bustling town of Gilroy that sat inside the land grant's boundaries represented a second problem. Gilroy's boosters had ideas for the region's development that were very different from those held by Miller

& Lux. In 1854 Gilroy already had a hotel, post office, schoolhouse, a variety of merchants, and two churches to meet the needs of the surrounding population, most of whom had purchased small parcels of Las Ánimas land from the Sánchez family in the early 1850s.[77] During the 1860s Gilroy's population increased as the town became a center of trade and small-scale manufacturing. Gilroy's boosters spoke optimistically of the city's future. "The Southern Pacific RR will soon be finished as far as Gilroy," explained the *Gilroy Advocate* in 1868, and the railroad would bring San Francisco markets within "a few hours and . . . [with] little expense" to Gilroy's farmers. "Gilroy, being the great central depot[,] is destined, Ph[o]enix-like, to rise and grow in proportion to the demands of the surrounding country and the enterprises of its citizens." Gilroy's "Ph[o]enix-like" rise, however, depended on the breakup of large estates in the region. In a statement likely intended for Miller & Lux's consumption, the *Advocate* optimistically observed that "the grant owners of [these] fine lands are becoming willing to sell off farms and settle up the country."[78]

Miller & Lux, too, welcomed the Southern Pacific's advance into the southern Santa Clara Valley, but the firm had no plan to subdivide Las Ánimas for small farms. In fact, Miller & Lux was actively purchasing rancho lands around Gilroy because of the geographic proximity to the Pacheco Pass—the only connecting route between the Santa Clara and the San Joaquin Valleys. Beyond geographic concerns, Miller & Lux also sought to acquire the area's natural resources. The partnership bought the best grasslands, the choice watering holes, and the riparian land along the Pajaro River, San Benito River, Pacheco Creek, and Carnadero Creek—the same land desired by farmers.[79] Thus, contrary to Gilroy's boosters, who envisioned the land "settling up" with independent farmers, Miller & Lux viewed this region as a stopping point and resource depot for its cattle herds en route to San Francisco's markets.

Gilroy's boosters could not prevent Miller & Lux's land acquisition in the southern Santa Clara Valley, but they could affect the cattle corporation's business in a variety of ways, from the assessment value of Miller & Lux's property to the public's perception of "San Francisco land sharks."[80] In the city of Gilroy, Miller & Lux faced for the first time an organized public greatly suspicious of its landownership. Accordingly, Henry Miller attempted to shape his public image as town benefactor by contributing "gifts" to the *Gilroy Advocate* and donating land for a city park. The *Advocate* thereafter downplayed public sentiment against Miller, instead portraying him as a symbol of Gilroy's progress. Miller's

- Gilroy positive sentiment bought by Miller w/a park

grandiose Bloomfield Farm, the *Advocate* repeatedly noted during the 1870s, rivaled "in beauty some of the famous places near the metropolis."[81] The property was complete with garden and orchard, Victorian "manor-house," and stables filled with thoroughbred horses and "agricultural machinery of the latest make." The farm employed upward of a hundred skilled and unskilled workers in addition to "German and Portuguese" renters. "All business," the *Advocate* claimed, "is controlled and carried on with the regularity of clock-work."[82] Bloomfield Farm did not represent the freehold agriculture desired by Gilroy's boosters, but if divorced from Miller & Lux's rapid consolidation of nearby lands or the firm's status as an emerging corporate enterprise, Miller's farm could still symbolize the region's future prosperity.

Miller & Lux, however, used Bloomfield Farm as the heart of its expanding operations in the Santa Clara Valley, and the partners sought to develop the valley for their own needs. Immediately south of Las Ánimas, Miller & Lux purchased the most fertile portions of ranchos Juristac, Salsipuedes, Tequesquite, Lomerias Muertas, Aromitas y Agua Caliente, and San Justo.[83] In order to better utilize these grazing lands and facilitate cattle drives, Miller & Lux pushed for improved transportation routes across the properties. In 1869 the firm lobbied for the construction of a new road between the town of Hollister (then in Monterey County) and Las Ánimas.[84] The road, as laid out by the county surveyor S. W. Smith, crossed Miller & Lux's land in ranchos San Justo, Bolsa de San Felipe, and Tequesquite. It conveniently followed a portion of the cattle-driving route from the San Joaquin Valley to Miller & Lux's primary water source (Soap Lake) and eventually ran into Las Ánimas. After surveying the road, S. W. Smith left his public-sector job for a lucrative position as Miller & Lux's main surveyor.[85]

By the early 1870s, Miller & Lux increasingly relied on the railroad (rather than labor-intensive and time-consuming cattle drives) to move cattle north into San Francisco from Las Ánimas. With its large shipments every few days, Miller & Lux was one of the Southern Pacific's most valued customers. Shortly after the Southern Pacific completed its line through Gilroy—which Henry Miller assisted by granting the right-of-way across his land—Miller & Lux negotiated for a separate line with a special stop at Bloomfield Farm. In May 1872, the two parties signed an agreement whereby the Southern Pacific (SP) received the right-of-way for an extension from the main line to the west past Bloomfield Farm, and the SP guaranteed Miller & Lux "the lowest [shipping] rates charged from any regular station."[86] The SP also allowed Miller to choose the location for his loading station at Bloomfield Farm. "As soon as Mr. Miller has made his choice," wrote the SP assistant superintendent A. C. Bassett, "the work will go ahead."[87] Few Californians were given such choices by the railroad. The SP president, Charles Crocker, personally thanked Miller for "procuring the right of way for our road from Gilroy South," and to show his gratitude Crocker sent Miller a "complimentary pass" for travel on his railroad.[88]

Lobbying for roads and railroad lines illustrates the type of infrastructural improvements Miller & Lux promoted in the southern Santa Clara Valley during the late 1860s and 1870s. The firm also built costly fences around key properties, drained swampland, and dug irrigation ditches to increase and improve the rangeland. As these improvements increased the value of Miller & Lux's land, Gilroy's boosters continued to advocate "land division" to its largest "landed proprietor."[89] This plea fell on deaf ears. Some landowners who lost property to Miller & Lux addressed their complaints to the nation's capital. Landowner Hiram Wentworth asked President Grover Cleveland to support his claim against "[Miller's] ridiculous farce entitled Las Ánimas." "I wish," Wentworth angrily vented, "Mr. Miller to be thoroughly convinced that at least *once* in his life he attempted to rob the wrong man [of his land]."[90] Wentworth's attack on Miller—like the *Advocate*'s more moderate suggestion for land division—had little impact on Miller & Lux's activities in the region. Miller & Lux continued its land acquisition around Las Ánimas, and the improvements sponsored by the corporation focused on cattle production for San Francisco markets, not on the growth of Gilroy or the surrounding population. — a mistake? that will/might show later?

SANJON DE SANTA RITA

If the region around Las Ánimas served as the "center place" for Miller & Lux's movement of cattle, the San Joaquin Valley provided the vast grasslands necessary to produce and hold large herds of cattle. Here, Miller & Lux could expand horizontally and stockpile resources to offset the valley's environmental risks. Prior to American rule, few Mexican Californians had seriously considered permanent settlement in the San Joaquin Valley because of its isolation from centers of trade and population. Fear of Indian attack also kept rancheros from settling the interior valley.[91] In stark contrast to the hundreds of land grants established in California's coastal valleys, the Mexican government issued fewer than twenty grants in the San Joaquin Valley. These land grants were extremely

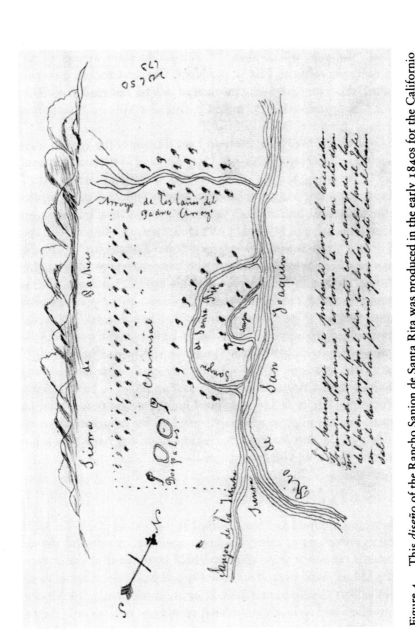

Figure 4. This *diseño* of the Rancho Sanjon de Santa Rita was produced in the early 1840s for the Californio claimant Francisco Soberanes. (Courtesy of the Bancroft Library, University of California at Berkeley.)

large—few petitioners asked for less than the maximum eleven square leagues (over forty-eight thousand acres)—and the majority sat along the banks of the valley's rivers.[92]

Sanjon de Santa Rita, granted to Francisco Soberanes in 1841, was typical in this regard. Laid out in a north-south direction, Santa Rita was bounded on the east by the San Joaquin River and on the west by the entrance to the Pacheco Pass, which led across the Diablo Range to the southern Santa Clara Valley. Within these borders sprawled eleven leagues of the finest grasslands on the valley floor. Soberanes's 1841 *diseño* (see figure 4) explains the connection between its name and its value as grazing land—two sloughs (marked *sanjon*) left the San Joaquin River and meandered across the rancho before joining the river farther downstream. These *sanjones* connected with a number of smaller sloughs, providing natural irrigation for a large portion of the land grant. The name that Soberanes bestowed on this grant was also prophetic of its future use: *sanjon* derives from the Spanish verb *zanjar*, meaning "to excavate" or "dig ditches across." Miller & Lux soon used Sanjon de Santa Rita to construct the West's largest canal system.

Francisco Soberanes had not permanently occupied Sanjon de Santa Rita between 1841 and 1853, when he appeared before the California Land Claims Commission. His family owned extensive property in the vicinity of Monterey, and this coastal estate provided a more secure livelihood during the 1840s than did the San Joaquin plains.[93] Shortly after Soberanes filed his claim with the Land Claims Commission, he began selling the property, and various portions of Santa Rita passed through the hands of twenty-one different American and Mexican owners before Miller & Lux reconsolidated the land in the mid-1860s.[94] Since Soberanes had not fulfilled the legal requirement of permanent residence on the rancho, it remains something of a mystery why the Land Claims Commission confirmed the Santa Rita land grant.

The most plausible explanation involved the financial dealings of the commissioner who decided the case, Judge Isaac Ogier. In 1861, Ogier owed John Parrott eighteen hundred dollars for an unpaid loan, and Parrott knew that Miller & Lux wanted to buy Santa Rita as soon as the commission confirmed its title.[95] Miller had viewed Santa Rita on his numerous cattle-buying trips into the San Joaquin Valley, and he appreciated its natural attributes and location. According to Miller, "The grass [was] green there nine months out of the year . . . and [it was] handy to all parts of the state. I thought [Santa Rita] was the most favorable place that I had struck yet."[96] In late 1862 Ogier confirmed the *more shady but legal dealings?*

title to Santa Rita, and Parrott most likely dropped his claim against the judge.[97]

The San Joaquin's climatic extremes played a significant role in Miller & Lux's acquisition of the property. The 1861–62 flood occurred just prior to the firm's initial two-league purchase from Thomas Hildreth, a rancher who had 10,000 cattle on his portion of the Santa Rita. Hildreth lost much of the herd when the San Joaquin River flooded the property. In debt, Hildreth sold his two leagues of Santa Rita and his cattle to Miller & Lux for ten thousand dollars in early 1863, and Hildreth moved his ranching operation to the Monterey Bay region.[98] Miller & Lux bought the remainder of Santa Rita from various parties at an average cost of four dollars an acre.[99] In the midst of the drought, Miller & Lux also gambled on the downswing in cattle prices by purchasing large herds of inexpensive cattle and dispersing them throughout its properties. William Browning, who lived near Santa Rita in the early 1860s, described the result. "While hundreds of stockmen were going broke," Browning remembers, "Miller was making a killing. . . . The entire San Joaquin Valley was strewed [sic] with the dead bodies of starved cattle. But not so on Santa Rita. Cattle could be bought for two to six dollars a head. Miller bought cattle right and left and filled the Santa Rita swamp grass fields to capacity. . . . It was commonly agreed among valley stockmen that by 1866 Miller had cleared $250,000 from the resale of these cattle."[100]

When the drought ended in 1865, Miller & Lux had gained clear title to the 48,823-acre property and had learned how to prosper during future droughts. The strategy included expanding landownership in the valley, stockpiling cattle feed, controlling the bottomlands, and protecting the firm's natural resources from neighboring landowners. Having gained a foothold in the San Joaquin Valley with the massive Santa Rita grant, Miller & Lux built its operations around this rancho over the next five years. Immediately north of Santa Rita, Miller & Lux purchased a large portion of rancho Orestimba in 1868—thereby increasing its contiguous riparian property downriver from Santa Rita.[101] South of Santa Rita, Miller & Lux began filing homestead and swampland claims to property stretching all the way to Tulare Lake, using the names of employees and relatives as "dummy" entrypersons.[102]

To the west of Santa Rita, Miller & Lux leased grazing land on rancho San Luis Gonzaga from Mariano Malarin, the prominent Californio lawyer, legislator, and banker who successfully defended his family estate.[103] Malarin received his schooling and legal training in Peru, returning to California only after his father's death in 1849. Like Miller and Lux, he thrived in the gold rush's aftermath: serving two terms in the California State Assembly, establishing a law practice in Monterey, and becoming a director of the San Jose Safe Deposit Bank and a major investor in the Madera Flume and Trading Company.[104] Clearly, Malarin represented an anomaly in the context of Californio dispossession and decline. Malarin's refusal to sell rancho San Luis Gonzaga to Miller & Lux only increased his standing in Miller's mind.

As Miller & Lux began consolidating land around Santa Rita, the firm also sought to maximize the rancho's use-value through specific improvements. Perhaps the best example is that of enclosure. Like all ranchers, Miller & Lux supported vigorously California's "free range" laws that allowed ranchers open access to the valley's grasslands. But during the drought of 1862–64, the partnership recognized that its inability to keep other ranchers' cattle away from Santa Rita's riverfront land severely hurt its own cattle.[105] At enormous expense, Miller & Lux began fencing Santa Rita in 1867. With lumber shipped in from Stockton to Santa Rita, Miller & Lux's team of builders fenced away from the San Joaquin River westward for two miles before turning south. Two years later the builders were still constructing the fence southward. In January 1869 Miller informed Lux that "the way the County is [being] plowed up and settling we are compel[led] to fenz [sic]" even farther south.[106] When completed later that year, the fence was over forty-five miles long, encompassing rancho Santa Rita and other Miller & Lux properties. One observer noted that "Miller's fence" was "the biggest construction undertaking ever attempted in the San Joaquin Valley" to date.[107]

Miller & Lux's fencing project and land consolidations in the valley indicated how the corporation viewed this region in the late 1860s. Primarily, the two partners saw the valley as undeveloped, inexpensive rangeland for their increasing herds of cattle. While the San Joaquin's distance from San Francisco markets posed a geographic barrier in getting cattle to market, Miller & Lux could overcome that barrier through a network of properties en route to San Francisco. The valley was also "settling up," as Miller often noted in his letters to Charles Lux, and this increased settlement suggested competition to Miller & Lux's land tenure.[108] Fencing therefore provided a means to consolidate property and exclude others from "their" natural resources. Inside the fence Miller & Lux not only ranged tens of thousands of cattle but also cut and stockpiled feed, dug irrigation ditches away from the natural sloughs, and experimented with alfalfa cultivation on selected parcels. Miller & Lux was preparing a vast stretch of the San Joaquin for industrial-scale cattle production.

THE URBAN-RURAL SYSTEM

Though exceptional for its integrated approach to cattle production and meatpacking during the 1860s, Miller & Lux nonetheless represented the growing movement of western firms toward business expansion and modernization. Indeed, within a five-block radius of Miller & Lux's central office on Kearny Street resided the headquarters of the West's leading firms: the Central Pacific Railroad; the Pacific Mail Steamship Company; the Bank of California; the Union Iron Works; the California Redwood Company; the New Almaden Mining Company; and the emerging Comstock syndicates headed by William Sharon, George Hearst, D. O. Mills, and the partnership of Mackey, Fair, Flood & O'Brien. Highly capitalized, ambitious, and operating in different business sectors, these firms shared a vision of western industrial development that matched the region's vast terrain. Like their eastern counterparts, western firms constructed business systems to exploit markets, resources, and regional infrastructures.

The system of production Miller & Lux set in motion by the late 1860s combined vertical integration with horizontal expansion, hinterland resources with urban markets. The system began in San Francisco's rural hinterlands, with Miller & Lux receiving large cattle herds in the San Joaquin Valley from all over California and the Far West. Some cattle arrived from as far away as Texas, Utah, and Wyoming.[109] In the month of May 1869, for instance, Miller purchased over 5,000 head from five different sellers, and he placed the new cattle on Santa Rita's extensive range. "The grass looks well and cattle are doing fine," Miller reported to Lux (in San Francisco) at the end of the month, "[but] let me know how the last cattle are killing."[110] Always attentive to San Francisco's market conditions, Miller needed to know the pace of slaughtering before sending more cattle to the city.

From the San Joaquin rangeland, a team of vaqueros would drive a sizeable herd across the Pacheco Pass to the firm's properties in the Santa Clara Valley. Only "killable" (or market-ready) cattle made this two-day trip. The cattle were then placed on one of Miller & Lux's ranchos before shipment north to Buri Buri. For instance, Miller informed Lux on June 11, 1869, that 540 "head" had just arrived at Soap Lake (near Gilroy) from the San Joaquin. "I put 40 head of Cattle on two [railroad] cars for shipment [to Buri Buri]. Ther[e] is no charge to be mad[e] for them. Also a car lo[a]d of calves for w[h]ich you will pay the [usual] price."[111] Lux, evidently, needed calves immediately for the market, but he could wait on a large load of cattle. Miller kept half of the herd at Las Ánimas and instructed the head vaquero, Tomás Díaz (and presumably two or three other vaqueros), to drive the remainder up the peninsula to Rancho Buri Buri, thereby avoiding the cost of railroad shipment. From Buri Buri, a vaquero stationed at Butchertown drove the cattle as needed to Miller & Lux's slaughterhouse on Fifth and Howard Streets in San Francisco. Slaughterhouse employees made quick work of the new arrivals, and Miller & Lux teamsters delivered the meat to dozens of city butcher shops. Thus, between the San Joaquin's rangeland and the city's killing floors, the firm's properties formed a spatially integrated system of production, and the "pull" of market demand facilitated the flow of cattle through the system.

Miller & Lux expanded its operations during the 1860s on a number of levels: cattle purchasing and meat sales, the use of lawyers and financiers, landownership, and a growing labor force. As chapter 5 will demonstrate, Miller & Lux relied particularly on Mexican vaqueros to operate the system during the 1860s—branding cattle, driving large herds to market, and separating marketable stock from "poor" stock. By virtue of their skills, the Mexican vaqueros held a unique status in the corporation until the mid-1870s, when the system of production and the role of labor radically changed. Thereafter, the vaqueros lost their skilled status and became migrant wage laborers on land that, in some cases, their families had once owned. - changes to come for labor

By the 1870s, former Mexican land grants constituted over half of Miller & Lux's 300,000 acres in California. These grants comprised the firm's initial building blocks, and the lengthy confirmation and patenting process provided an institutional means for Miller & Lux to attain the land. However, contrary to the opinion expressed by many late-nineteenth-century critics of land monopolists, California's largest landed estates did not chiefly derive from the Mexican land grant system.[112] California's "problem" of land monopoly instead developed from federal and state land laws and offices that facilitated the acquisition of the public domain by capitalized buyers. By turning its attention to the public domain and water resources in the 1870s, Miller & Lux entered the West's most contentious debate over private rights and public needs.

CHAPTER 3

Privatizing the San Joaquin Landscape in the 1870s

An anecdote familiar to most western historians involves Henry Miller and his notorious rowboat. As the story goes, Miller claimed vast stretches of public property during the 1870s by sitting in a rowboat perched atop a horse-drawn wagon that he drove across entire townships of grassland. By traversing the countryside in this fashion, Miller's cohorts could then bear witness that he had crossed the land in a boat. Such theatrics presumably allowed him to claim the property through the Swamp Land Act. Miller, evidently, covered much of the Far West in his boat. During the late nineteenth century this rural legend spread throughout California, northern Nevada, and eastern Oregon—indeed, accounts of Miller and his boat appeared everywhere the firm held property. The story's origin remains unknown, but by the turn of the century it had acquired a decidedly humorous edge. "Ol' Henry Miller," old-timers confided to greenhorns, "do you know how he *really* got all that swampland?"[1]

Such land acquisition stories amused few Californians during the 1870s. Instead, most viewed the trend toward land consolidation with increasing alarm, and the California State Board of Agriculture's 1872 report on landownership patterns confirmed their grim suspicions. Anyone unacquainted with the extent of land monopolization in California would have found the figures unbelievable. The report showed that one hundred individuals held title to a total of 5,465,206 acres, an area slightly larger than the state of Massachusetts. Consolidated landownership appeared throughout California's counties, but the most striking examples existed in the San Joaquin Valley. The valley's thirteen largest landowners each claimed an average of 238,464 acres.[2] The land reformer Henry George estimated that Miller & Lux's share of California's domain amounted to 450,000 acres, with the major portion located in the San Joaquin Valley.[3] Miller & Lux's own estimate ran somewhat higher. While the corporation had trouble tabulating exactly how much land it owned, in May 1874 Miller & Lux could account for 420,888 acres in the valley alone.[4] The firm held title to over 100,000 acres outside of the valley. Both figures grew on a weekly basis.

Californians understood the problem of land monopoly at the beginning of the 1870s through a coherent and popular set of beliefs: by hoarding private and public land, large property holders thwarted the process of freehold agrarian settlement.[5] As a result, immigration to the state had declined, ultimately affecting trade, manufacturing, and agricultural interests alike. The vociferous Henry George and the more staid speakers at the California State Agricultural Society all denounced land monopoly as the main obstacle to rural progress and fulfillment of the state's democratic potential.[6] Steeped in republican rhetoric and ideology, denunciations of land monopoly found a receptive audience throughout California because that audience was well-versed in the connection between landownership and civic virtue.[7] By the end of the 1870s, however, many residents questioned whether land monopolization alone accounted for the state's developmental problems. A new awareness slowly emerged that linked land monopoly with the consolidation of water rights, corporate growth, and industrial agriculture. Miller & Lux's activities constituted a primary reason for the public's shifting concerns.

Henry Miller and Charles Lux came under repeated attack during the decade as the state's largest land speculators. The partners, however, did not view their acquisitions in speculative terms, because they had no plans to sell off land.[8] Instead, Miller and Lux sought additional lands throughout California as a buffer against the environmental extremes they had encountered during the 1860s. This land-centered business strategy changed with Miller & Lux's initial investments in the San Joaquin and King's River Canal & Irrigation Company (SJ&KRC&ICo). Between 1870 and 1875, the canal company introduced corporate irrigation to the Far West through a plan to restructure the San Joaquin's waterscape. Initially just one of many investors, Miller & Lux soon recognized the need to control any project that threatened its land and wa-

*very important
acquisition*

ter rights. The firm's takeover of the SJ&KRC&ICo in 1878 marked a
crucial turning point in the corporation's strategy as well as the broader
effort to engineer California's waterscape. Land acquisition, Miller &
Lux realized, allowed the company to increase cattle production and
hedge bets against an uncertain environment, but water rights and irrigation systems would ultimately determine who could profit from the
valley's natural wealth.

SAN JOAQUIN HINTERLAND COMMUNITIES

San Joaquin "old-timers"—including land speculators, town boosters,
railroad builders, cattle and sheep raisers, farm colonists, and rugged skyfarmers—all sought to profit from the valley's natural wealth.[9] The true
old-timers arrived in the early 1860s, when the best lands remained un-
tilled and opportunities awaited the enterprising soul. Ed Sturgeon remembered it well. Born in Iowa, Sturgeon walked to California in 1852
and spent ten years mining and freighting in the Sierras. "I had not paid
much attention to California farming," he recalled decades later, but he
evidently thought enough of its prospects to invest his savings in two sections (1,280 acres) of Merced County land. He bought a used Missouri-
built single-bottom plow and commenced harrowing in "as much [wheat]
as possible before the winter was over." Upon seeing Sturgeon's anti-
quated plow, a neighbor nearly laughed him off the land. The neighbor
used an eight-horse team to pull a four-bottom Stockton gangplow
equipped with seed boxes and capable of "covering 32 inches at a round."
Sturgeon hurried to Stockton and purchased two new plows and a ten-
mule team, and hired two laborers for the season's planting. When heavy
rains stopped their work in mid-November, Sturgeon hunkered down in
his makeshift cabin for the rest of the winter. The warm spring and hot
summer brought a bumper harvest, he recalled: "Grain was piled [for
miles] . . . along the banks of Salt Slough and the San Joaquin [River]."
He sold sixteen thousand sacks of grain that year. Sturgeon said, "I hired
skinners and bought mules and turned my entire attention to managing
my ranch. But I never hit another bonanza like '68. They don't come
twice in a lifetime."[10]

The San Joaquin's settler society banked on the next big bonanza. But
describing the various elements that filtered into the valley during the
1870s as a cohesive "society" may be misleading. Spread out across some
11,290 square miles in six counties, most settlers saw opportunity in the
valley's vast acreage rather than in traditional forms of community life.

Like Ed Sturgeon, the new arrivals hoped for economic success above all other concerns. They invested in land, seed, and horse teams to pull the largest plows that lenders would provide. If these settlers read and supported the valley newspaper editors whose columns touted agrarian virtues, they likely spent far more time studying the adjacent market reports on San Francisco grain prices. Concerns about the coming railroad, land speculation, technology, and other forces of rural change sparked some anxiety, but only to the extent that such forces impinged upon their own abilities to prosper in the coming years.[11]

Census records reveal some of the tensions that accompanied settlement in the 1870s. The valley's overall population increased by 47 percent during the 1870s (from 44,150 to 65,290), but over one-third of these residents lived in the northernmost county of San Joaquin.[12] Only one county, Tulare, topped the statewide average for population gain during the decade, rising from 4,533 to 11,281. The valley's other counties ranked among the slowest growing in California, particularly in comparison to the booming agricultural counties of Santa Clara, Los Angeles, Alameda, Napa, and Sonoma (which almost doubled in cumulative population, from 85,611 to 158,069). The majority of San Joaquin settlers came from the eastern states, but an increasing share of residents arrived from Germany, England, Italy, and China. In the entire Central Valley, the Chinese population grew during the decade from 8,473 to 13,372, a small percentage of the total population but an extremely large target for heated racial hostility.[13] — it's *population increase in 1870s*

Closely related to the slow settlement rate was the average farm size: San Joaquin counties contained a meager share of the state's property holdings under five hundred acres and a disproportionately large share of holdings over five thousand acres. Indeed, less than 1 percent of San Joaquin landowners held almost 25 percent of the taxable property, and most of those landlords resided outside the valley.[14] As one midwestern visitor noted in 1877, "There is by far too much of a disposition to farm in the San Joaquin Valley and live in San Francisco."[15] Cattle ranching aside, both large and small landowners focused almost exclusively on planting extensive single crops during the 1870s: alfalfa and various grains (mostly wheat) accounted for 96.1 percent of agricultural production in 1879.[16] Some farmers experimented with viticulture and fruit crops on the valley's eastern side, but this sign of impending agricultural change did not lessen the annual dreams for "another bonanza."

The valley's six counties, stacked atop one another from Kern in the south to San Joaquin in the north, shared one important feature: a widely

— large farms

recognized line dividing the east and west sides.[17] The "Westside" encompassed a two-hundred-mile-long strip of land west of the San Joaquin River, from Miller & Lux's northern holdings to the valley's southern end. "Very hot desert" characterized the Westside's microclimate, a subtle but important distinction from the "hot desert" of the Eastside. The Westside not only received less rain than the Eastside but also had higher temperatures, which baked the hardpan adobe soil and created poor drainage.[18] Settlement trends replicated these natural characteristics: the Westside's permanent population (excluding migrant laborers) increased little during the 1870s, while the enormous landholdings grew still larger. Small farmers who did carve out Westside homesteads found themselves surrounded by the nation's largest landowners, an odd juxtaposition that soon found political expression.[19] The Eastside population, meanwhile, grew steadily in direct proportion to the increased number of farms and towns.

Eastsiders disdained many aspects of Westside life: the massive landholdings, lack of community growth, unruly sheep raisers, and absentee cattle kings who claimed extensive water rights. Industrial-sized wheat operations with "entire compan[ies]" of plows also appeared west of the river during the 1870s, dramatized years later in Frank Norris's *The Octopus*. "At a distance," Norris wrote, "the ploughs resembled a great column of field artillery."[20] Norris possessed little actual knowledge of industrial agriculture prior to writing *The Octopus,* so he gathered field notes during a three-week stay on one of Miller & Lux's Westside properties.[21] Eastsiders characterized Westside landowners' operations as Norris had: as massive ranching and wheat operations that bore little resemblance to any previous form of agriculture. But the Eastside clearly had its own share of large-scale farm operations; in the end the difference was one of degree rather than agricultural practice.

Eastside settlers held high expectations for prosperity as they watched developments in their part of the valley. The Southern Pacific Railroad completed construction of its Eastside San Joaquin line from Lathrop to a point outside Bakersfield by 1874, and the new railroad towns of Modesto, Merced, Madera, Tulare, and Delano materialized to provide markets and services for neighboring landowners.[22] Equally promising were the farm colonies sponsored by land speculators or investors' syndicates, including the John Brown Colony, the Alabama Colony, the Washington Irrigated Colony, and the Central California Colony (which, curiously, advertised "Better than city property—A homestead with an income!").[23] Indeed, developments on the Eastside appeared to favor the agricultural class. The railroad brought San Francisco's grain market to their doorsteps, new towns offered possibilities for economic diversification, and irrigation—how simple it seemed in theory—could resolve the valley's natural deficiencies. Hardly utopians, San Joaquin settlers held few expectations that economic and natural resources would be equally shared by all. They were far too individualistic and ambitious to entertain such thoughts. Yet they did have faith that land-consolidation trends would cease and firms like Miller & Lux would liquidate their ill-gotten gains. San Joaquin residents were sorely mistaken.

— differences in East/West side environs

GRABBING THE PUBLIC DOMAIN

In May 1873, the Merced County recorder's office began a new system of recording all public lands patented to county landowners.[24] Each land patent issued by either the state or federal government would be entered in a series of broad-sheet ledger books by the county recorder, and each book pertained to a different category of public land. Patent book "C," for instance, contained a listing of all Merced County land purchased under the Preemption Act of 1841. Book "D" recorded all entries secured with "agricultural college" scrip under the Morrill Land Act of 1862, a federal land act designed to support state agricultural colleges. Book "F" was used to record properties claimed under the federal "internal improvement" land grant; book "G" recorded properties secured with "military" (or "soldier's") scrip; book "H" listed all "swampland" entries, and so on.[25] These various books, meticulously handwritten by county recorder Jason E. Hicks in 1873, charted the disposal of a good portion of Merced County's domain.

Two widely popular objectives guided these federal and state land grants: the generation of revenue for government use, and public land settlement by American citizens. Merced County's patent books, however, suggest a profound contradiction between the two objectives. For instance, on May 28, 1873, recorder Hicks transcribed each patent for 160 acres of public land purchased with agricultural college scrip. William Chapman's seven entries covered the first seven pages of the book, and Isaac Friedlander's entries ran through page 47, for a total of 6,240 acres. The following 293 separate entries went to Miller & Lux. Using not only scrip issued for California's agricultural college but also scrip for state colleges as far away as Maine, Miller & Lux claimed 46,880 acres in Merced County.[26] For each entry, Hicks carefully transcribed the appropriate portions of the Morrill Land Act and the exact location of the

- handing out turkeys

land. For this arduous task Hicks certainly received Miller & Lux's trademark gift of a plump turkey at Thanksgiving that year.[27]

The other patent books reveal similar land disposal patterns in Merced County, and they supported Henry George's contention that aspiring farmers were rarely the recipients of the public domain.[28] Miller & Lux patented 94 separate Preemption Act claims, ranging in size from 38 acres to 6,795 acres, totaling 35,484 unsurveyed acres. Of the 500,000 acres granted to Californians for "internal improvements," book "F" shows Miller & Lux grabbed 21,796 acres in Merced County. A wide swath of property (over 13,207 acres) along the San Joaquin River went to Miller & Lux as "swampland." Finally, 59 entries of military scrip brought an additional 9,440 acres to the firm—unbeknownst to the war veterans who sold their military scrip to scrip dealers.[29] In total, between 1866 and 1880 Miller & Lux consolidated a minimum of 126,800 acres of government land in Merced County alone. Henry Miller obviously had a friendly relationship with the Merced County recorder. But this relationship stood in stark contrast to his dealings with Merced County's property assessor. "Dread him well, he is a bad egg and we must buy him," Miller informed Lux. Miller subsequently paid the assessor the high price of $1,000 for 160 acres of his land.[30]

greasing the skids

Paying off a county assessor (for low property assessments) was one way Miller & Lux diminished the cost of owning large amounts of land. But acquiring the land from the state came first, and this process required the firm to expand greatly upon its San Francisco network of operatives developed in the previous decade. For instance, in 1869 Henry Miller hired the Merced County surveyor William G. Collier to map the land surrounding Rancho Sanjon de Santa Rita. Miller's interest lay primarily in the swampland adjacent to the San Joaquin River, both north and south of the rancho. Collier completed his survey map in October, and he assured Miller "that it is the only correct [map] in existence." Surveying swampland was a tricky affair, but Collier convinced Miller he could claim a great deal more in Merced County. Referring to the fleeting character of swampland, Collier wrote, "It is a sort of three card monte [game,] now you see it and now you don't arrangement."[31]

swampland easy to manipulate

Collier's map encompassed twenty-four townships, or 864 square miles, running diagonally across Fresno, Merced, and Stanislaus Counties. Collier marked each 640-acre section he considered swampland with four small *x*'s. He then marked much of the public land that Miller & Lux had filed claims on with the initials "M & L." Collier's map showed the lands left for Miller & Lux to claim as well as the precise landownership pattern already developed by the firm. Miller & Lux, like other large landowners, had not simply "gone around and picked out the good land along the great plains of the San Joaquin and other valleys," as one critic of land monopoly charged.[32] Instead, the sections marked "M & L" (designating ownership) formed a contiguous line perfectly surrounding almost all of the swampland adjacent to the San Joaquin River. By purchasing the land in this pattern, the corporation had effectively enclosed almost all of Merced County's publicly owned swampland west of the San Joaquin River.[33]

To successfully claim such lands, Miller & Lux relied on William S. Chapman, who functioned as the firm's primary land agent from 1867 until his financial bankruptcy in the mid-1870s. Chapman organized transactions between large landowners, assisted them in filing claims on public lands, and accumulated hundreds of thousands of acres for his own speculative purposes. A controversial character throughout California, Chapman was denounced by some observers as a "scalper" of "honest settlers" and praised by others "for fair-dealing and a generosity that is often more lavish than prudent."[34] Chapman aided Miller & Lux in two important areas. First, with an insider's knowledge of land offices and land laws, he helped the corporation select and enter its requests for government land. In 1868, for instance, he informed Miller, "I have entered all the land you had selected on both sides of the [San Joaquin] River except what lays within the Railr[oa]d limits. I thought to enter [for you] the even numbered sections within the RRd but Mr. [S. T.] Nye thought as he had sent my application to Washington sometime since and soon expected a reply with full instructions, he thought best to wait until it would be received."[35]

S. T. Nye, the registrar of the San Joaquin County Land Office in Stockton, had evidently told Chapman to avoid filing claims on too much land at one time, since the federal land office might reject such petitions. The U.S. Land Office confirmed these entries for Miller & Lux.[36] Chapman, it appears, had a great facility for getting public land confirmed. He maintained strong connections with county land officers like S. T. Nye, and through his brother, Isaac N. Chapman, who was the deputy surveyor for the surveyor general's office, William Chapman gained advance knowledge of precisely what land would be opened for public entry.[37] Miller & Lux paid Chapman for these helpful relationships. — *exploiting relationship capital*

But Miller & Lux also paid Chapman for his seemingly endless supply of land scrip. Chapman was likely the nation's largest land scrip dealer, and his collection included agricultural college scrip, Valentine scrip, military scrip, Sioux Indian scrip, and many other varieties. Between 1867 and 1870, Miller & Lux's monthly payments to Chapman—often solely for scrip—averaged around ten thousand dollars.[38] Using scrip to file upon public land drastically reduced the purchase cost, since sufficient scrip for purchase of the land could be bought at a fraction of the land's normal price. Some types of scrip (also called "warrants") often assured a more "secure" title than others, depending on how government land policies and practices changed over time. In 1876, for instance, surveyor Richard Stretch instructed Miller & Lux to use "soldier's warrants" rather than "school warrants" for filing on certain public lands. "If you remember," Stretch continued, "I once warned you about [soldier's] warrants, but recent decisions at the Land Dept. decide their location good [sic], and you can save money by using them."[39]

Miller & Lux frequently consulted Stretch on what Miller referred to as "our land matters."[40] The surveyors employed by Miller & Lux mapped unclaimed land, suggested particular sections for ownership, filed "warrants" for property at the land office, and, in Stretch's case, advised the corporation on the most "recent decisions" of the U.S. Land Office. While some of the surveyors had private surveying businesses, others held public jobs at the state or county level. Stretch, for instance, was the city and county surveyor for San Francisco in 1873, a job that earned him an annual salary of $500. During that year, however, Miller & Lux augmented his government income by at least $895.46.[41]

Many large landowners supported public surveyors in this way. In January 1874, for instance, the Tulare County chief surveyor George W. Smith informed Miller that Cox & Clarke (the largest cattle and land company in Sacramento) appeared to have lost interest in a large tract of private swampland adjoining Tulare Lake. Smith, who usually surveyed for Cox & Clark, offered his survey and a "certificate of purchase" to Miller & Lux for $1,616 (this offer did not include the cost of the land itself). He added that Miller & Lux should act "as soon as possible, for the Legislature is liable to pass an act concerning all swamp land where there is no certificate of purchase." After consulting with Cox & Clarke, Miller & Lux rejected Smith's offer. "Tell him we don't want to interfere with Cox & Clarke," Lux noted on the top of Smith's letter. "The land is adjoining [their land], and ought to belong to them if they want it."[42]

This correspondence with Smith reveals an important characteristic of Miller & Lux's network. To function properly, the network included not only public and private individuals who assisted the firm in purchasing land but also other large landowners who shared information

— M & L did not want trouble w/ other large land owners

concerning the land they sought to acquire. Miller & Lux had few qualms about preempting land from settlers, but competing with Cox & Clarke was a different matter. In part, Miller & Lux sought to minimize this sort of competition, which would only raise the cost of property in the long run. Lux noted as much to Smith when he wrote that "the owners are setting M & L against C & C to get a better price."[43] Two years later Miller & Lux rejected a similar offer of four sections (2,560 acres) from the Fresno County surveyor Charles Blair. "Jeff[erson] James and [Sigmund] Selig[man] are the men to apply to," Lux suggested to Blair. "They *own* that country."[44]

Lobbyists (both public and private individuals) were an integral part of Miller & Lux's network. Horace A. Higley, for instance, had served as the first head of the California State Land Office, created in 1858 to supervise the various county land agents and thwart corruption on the local level. Under Higley and his successors, the State Land Office quickly earned its own reputation for corrupt practices.[45] By 1860 he had been promoted to deputy United States surveyor general for California, but after three years in office he faced imprisonment on charges of disloyalty for his pro-South views.[46] Following the Civil War, Higley returned to Sacramento as a private lobbyist for large landowners. Miller & Lux hired him in 1868 to lobby for passage of the Green Act—which removed all acreage limitations on the amount of school and swamplands an individual could claim—legislation of unparalleled importance to the firm. Over the next three years, Higley facilitated the corporation's petitions to the State Land Office for those public lands.[47]

Land acquisition represented a primary function of Miller & Lux's network, but these individuals also sought to influence a wide range of public policies affecting the firm's private property rights. Some of these issues might appear almost insignificant. In 1870, for example, a bill passed in the state assembly for the construction of a public road that would cross through Miller & Lux's enclosed property in Merced County. Thomas Roulhac, a lobbyist from Merced, informed Miller, "If you wish to have this [bill] stopped it can be done in the next week by delay in the Senate." Roulhac suggested that Miller run up the road's cost to Merced County taxpayers by filing for damages. Miller heartily agreed with this strategy. He instructed Lux to "defeat [it] by all means . . . as ther[e] is no need for the road at present and we shall want them to put in our Bill for Damages [in the amount of] $10,000."[48] Miller & Lux's petition for damages amounted to two-thirds of the road's cost, which forced the county board of supervisors to table the project.[49]

Halting the construction of a county road posed only a minor problem for Miller & Lux. Larger issues that held a broader base of popular support required a more concerted and costly strategy. For a corporation that owned nearly a half million acres of land by 1875, property taxes were unquestionably a source of great anxiety. The creation of the California State Board of Equalization in 1871 only furthered Miller & Lux's concern, because it sought to equalize property taxes by assessing property according to its actual value rather than its use. Between 1870 and 1872, tax assessments on land in California jumped from $227,538,127 to $636,378,114. This increase could have forced large landowners to sell off property.[50] But county residents elected the property assessors, and given the largest landowners' political clout at the local level, assessors were often responsive to their will.

In 1875, for instance, William Faymonville informed Miller & Lux that Fresno County would soon elect a new assessor and a new sheriff (who served as the official county tax collector). One of Fresno County's leading citizens, Faymonville handled much of Miller & Lux's official business in the county. Surveying the field of three candidates for the office of assessor, Faymonville instructed Charles Lux that "it would undoubtedly be to your advantage that John Stroud be elected for Assessor. He can be managed." For the office of sheriff and tax collector, Faymonville advised supporting T. J. Dunlap against the incumbent J. Scott Ashman, who "is no friend of [Miller & Lux] and never has been." Faymonville continued, "You can easily aid Mr. Stroud and Mr. Dunlap by addressing a line to Mr. Coffman who has charge of [your] canal near Firebaugh. A good many votes will be polled there, and Mr. Coffman can easily control them."[51] As the superintendent of the San Joaquin and King's River Canal & Irrigation Company, Coffman could certainly influence, if not "control," the hundreds of votes cast by company employees. With Miller & Lux's support, John Stroud won the office of county assessor, but J. Scott Ashman remained in office for two more years.[52]

Assisting the election of a "friendly" assessor constituted only one way Miller & Lux sought to improve its property taxes in Fresno and other counties. Reducing the assessment value of the corporation's land and other real property and negotiating the means of payment were the main objectives. In 1869 Faymonville helped Miller & Lux orchestrate a deal with Fresno County's treasurer whereby the corporation paid its taxes with land scrip rather than cash.[53] Faymonville became an even greater asset to the firm upon his appointment as deputy assessor for Fresno

County. Noting that some acreage assessments in the county rose as high as five dollars an acre, Faymonville assured Henry Miller that "I shall succeed in having [your] land assessed at $1 per acre, at least I have reasons to believe that the Board of Supervisors will find no fault with that." Miller proposed that Faymonville try for seventy-five cents per acre for the corporation's land, but Faymonville considered it impossible.[54]

During the 1870s individuals like Faymonville formed a crucial part of Miller & Lux's enterprise. These agents comprised a broad network that assisted the corporation in acquiring land, navigating California's legal landscape, and influencing various public institutions. For Miller & Lux, those institutions ranged from the seemingly insignificant county sheriff's office to the U.S. Congress, and together constituted a public sphere intrinsically connected to the corporation's private endeavors. The network certainly took advantage of public laws and institutions for Miller & Lux's profit, but perhaps more important it also shaped the public arena from which Miller & Lux ultimately benefited. In a region where so much depended on land ownership (such as water rights), Miller & Lux's expansion signaled, to many residents, the conflicts to come.

M & L AND "THE COMPANY WITH THE MANY INITIALS"

The winter of 1869 was decidedly wet in the San Joaquin Valley. Rain fell the entire second week of February, and the San Joaquin River quickly topped its banks and spread across the plains. T. F. Hassell, the foreman of Miller & Lux's fencing crew at Rancho Santa Rita, reported to the corporation's main San Francisco office that "the bridges [in Merced County] are all gone." Workers and cattle alike were stuck in the mud, Hassell wrote, adding that "I do not see w[h]at in the world we will do for hay."[55] Through the month of March Henry Miller and Charles Lux received similar reports from other employees. "Don't depend on cattle from here," J. C. Crocker warned from Templane. "The plains are very soft and the cattle badly scattered."[56] David Shacklefford described the San Joaquin River as "higher than it has been before this season, [and] I have been at work night and day to save the lev[e]es."[57]

Fortunately for Miller & Lux, the rains ceased in early April. Nature then did a characteristic about-face, and no appreciable rain fell in the valley for the next two years. Miller remained guardedly optimistic at the beginning of 1870. "In regard to the Drought," he wrote Lux in February, "we are better of[f] than anybody else."[58] The corporation had stocked its various properties with towering haystacks, and these provisions saved the majority of its cattle from starvation. As the drought continued through the winter of 1871, however, Miller's optimism flagged. He instructed the head vaquero Tomás Díaz to organize a major cattle drive "to the tules" in the Delta region of the northern San Joaquin Valley. When Díaz returned, Miller accompanied him on a second drive to the tule swamplands.[59] J. C. Crocker found "no grass to speak of" on Miller & Lux's recently purchased swampland in Kern County. Depressed after two drought years, Crocker confessed that "I feel as though God intends to let bad luck follow me."[60] His thought undoubtedly expressed the sentiment of countless skyfarmers across the valley floor, farmers who desperately watched the sky for signs of rain.

Rain finally came at the end of December 1871. "Everything is mud," Miller announced happily to Lux. He predicted flooding for the near future, followed by an early growth of spring grasses across the plains. Furthermore, he wrote, "the cattles [sic] will be all right [so long as] the Tulare water don't come down."[61] The Tulare "water" coming "down" was Miller's abbreviated way of describing an overflow of Tulare Lake, which during heavy storms could swell down the valley floor in a devastating flood. This did not occur in 1872, and over the next few years, nature gave San Joaquin landowners a brief respite from its climatic extremes. But the early 1870s were nonetheless an anxious period of time for the two partners. The corporation's furious land acquisition during this period was hardly coincidental. When nature challenged valley landowners with its unpredictable cycles, as it did repeatedly in the 1860s and 1870s, Miller & Lux bought more lands with varied attributes (such as riverside property or higher-elevation grasslands). If the partners could not control the region's climate, at least these lands offered their cattle a place of refuge.

The dry years of 1870 and 1871 also stimulated Miller & Lux's enthusiasm for irrigation. Throughout the West's arid parts, one historian has noted, "support for irrigation grew out of immediate water shortages, not from a desire for comprehensive water resource planning."[62] This certainly held true for the San Joaquin Valley, where irrigation demand by farmers matched the parchedness of the soil. Though hardly typical farmers, Henry Miller and Charles Lux nonetheless viewed irrigation with guarded interest. So when San Francisco entrepreneur John Bensley approached them in early 1870 with his grandiose plans for watering the entire San Joaquin Valley, Miller and Lux listened with both fascination and skepticism.

Bensley's enterprise, which he called the San Joaquin and King's River Canal Company, was not his first business venture. During the 1850s he had accumulated a small fortune in various mining speculations, organized the California Steam Navigation Company, and headed San Francisco's main water company between 1857 and 1865.[63] Like Charles Lux, his social and business connections in San Francisco included the city's top bankers, railroad magnates, and land speculators—men whose Republican Party politics were as certain as their residence in the wealthy neighborhoods of South Park and Nob Hill. Accordingly, Bensley had brought together the city's top financiers and largest landowners to bankroll and direct his canal company. In May 1871 the firm's board of directors (and major stockholders) included the Bank of California executives William Chapman Ralston, Nicholas Luning, and A. J. Pope; the Wells Fargo Company's president, Lloyd Tevis; the San Joaquin wheat and shipping magnate Isaac Friedlander, and William Chapman. Miller and Lux were curiously absent from this list of San Francisco business leaders; their absence was curious not only because they were prominent land developers but also because the first 50 miles of the proposed canal would cut across their land. The previous year Bensley had offered Miller & Lux a one-third interest in the company, but neither Miller nor Lux wanted to invest so heavily in what they considered an overly ambitious project.[64]

Their initial reluctance proved warranted. The canal company's original plan envisioned a main canal stretching 160 miles from Tulare Lake in the south to the city of Antioch on Suisun Bay. Numerous east-west ditches would cross the valley floor to a second channel on the east side of the San Joaquin. Farmers throughout the valley could expect an abundant supply of water for irrigation, with excess water sold to the valley cities that would materialize with the canal's progress. Furthermore, farmers who complained of the Southern Pacific Railroad's monopoly on crop transportation to San Francisco markets could anticipate the canal's secondary function of public transport: according to one source, the canal would "neutralize distance" between city and country, "bring[ing] the rich river bottoms of Tulare and Kern counties as near to market as many lands in the Bay district itself."[65] In essence, the canal's original design promised to restructure the geography and economy of the San Joaquin Valley. Henry Miller considered the vast scope of the project entirely unfeasible. After meeting with Bensley in July 1871, Miller summarized his thoughts succinctly to Lux: "I think Bensley will find out [that] it is no small undertaking."[66]

M & L not sold on huge canal project

Miller & Lux did recognize certain advantages to be gained by joining Bensley's investors. In all likelihood, the canal company would scale
back its loftier plans because of financial, legal, and engineering hurdles.
In the meantime, the first stage of canal construction would benefit Miller
& Lux's property in Fresno and Merced Counties by delivering water
to the drought-stricken grazing land. Investing in the company would
also allow Miller & Lux to participate in crucial decision-making, such
as who would receive the company's water and at what price. Cooper-
ating with the canal company, Miller and Lux realized during the dry
summer months of 1871, could only benefit their interests. Accordingly,
at the first meeting of company investors in San Francisco on September
9, 1871, Miller & Lux purchased eighty-five hundred shares in the renamed San Joaquin and King's River Canal and Irrigation Company
(SJ&KRC&ICo).[67] In a separate agreement, Miller & Lux granted this
"Company With the Many Initials" (as one local editor dubbed it) a right-
of-way across the firm's land in exchange for a prescribed yearly amount
of water.[68]

The first stage of canal construction proceeded quite rapidly. (Map 3
shows the initial work completed in the 1870s, while map 4 illustrates
the reclaimed area twenty years later.) During the fall of 1871 the company employed four hundred workers (with three hundred teams of
horses) to excavate the main channel from Mendota (in Fresno County)
to Los Banos (in Merced County). According to one worker, the labor
force was segregated into work crews of "Chinamen, Mexicans, Indians,
and Americans" along the forty-mile course of the canal.[69] Consulting
engineer Robert Maitland Brereton surveyed the canal in late 1871 and
measured the channel bed at thirty-two feet across, with banks four feet
deep and a grade of twelve inches to the mile. Brereton found the progress
and potential of the canal encouraging, but his 1871 report to "Messrs.
Bensley & Co." also included several suggestions and one specific warning. "Messrs. Miller & Lux own nearly all the land," Brereton emphasized, "and could therefore take all the water."[70]

Brereton's advice on irrigation systems came from a great deal of
experience. Born in England, he had spent over a decade in India working as an engineer on the Indian Peninsula Railway and studying the
country's irrigation system. The Indian government dispatched Brereton in 1871 to report on railroad construction in the United States, and
during a short stay in Victoria, British Columbia, William Ralston lured
him to California for advice on irrigating the San Joaquin Valley.[71] Evidently, Brereton viewed the San Joaquin canal as a good opportunity

to build both his reputation and bank account. A proper system of irrigation, he noted, could turn this "dusty desert" into valuable "crop land" and demonstrate the miracle of irrigation.[72] Furthermore, the enterprise's sponsors, San Francisco's business elite, would not allow the financial rewards of the project to pass them (or him) by. After writing his report to the canal company, Brereton accepted the position of consulting engineer and canal promoter with a salary of a thousand dollars a month plus company stock. Privately, he also extended an open hand to Miller & Lux, despite his earlier warning of the cattle company's powerful position in the enterprise. If Miller & Lux could eventually "take all the water," Brereton hoped to catch part of the financial runoff for himself.

Miller & Lux's relationship with R. M. Brereton, the canal company, and its prospective water users was precarious from the start. The primary tension, of course, resulted from Miller & Lux's ownership of the land slated for irrigation by the first stage of canal construction: that long swath of Merced County land mapped by John Collier, purchased with land scrip by Miller & Lux, and entered into the county land books by the recorder Jason Hicks. The most logical solution to this problem, Brereton proposed, was for Miller & Lux to sell its irrigated lands to settlers who would pay a higher rate for water than the rate guaranteed to Miller & Lux.[73] This proposal received widespread public support from San Francisco to the San Joaquin Valley; indeed, wrote one San Joaquin editor, it would exemplify the best intentions of land speculation "as a means of developing the country." After Miller & Lux and other speculators sold their land, opined the *San Joaquin Republican,* the valley "will soon teem with the golden products of the husbandmen."[74] If Henry Miller or Charles Lux ever gave cause for these hopes, their actions soon proved otherwise.

In early 1872, as canal construction progressed across Miller & Lux's land, Brereton approached the cattle company with an intriguing offer. Brereton had planned a trip to England to raise capital for the canal company's expansion, and he confidentially offered his service to Miller & Lux as a "land agent." Outlining his plan to the two partners, Brereton wrote, "I should be your general land agent in California, and should transact all your European business in connection with Emigration, and the sale and rent of your lands [in the San Joaquin Valley]. I should, in fact, be putting your lands into such shape, as to make them, with the improvements and houses upon, readily saleable at from $20 to $50 per acre—and I should be the means of bringing you the class of people you

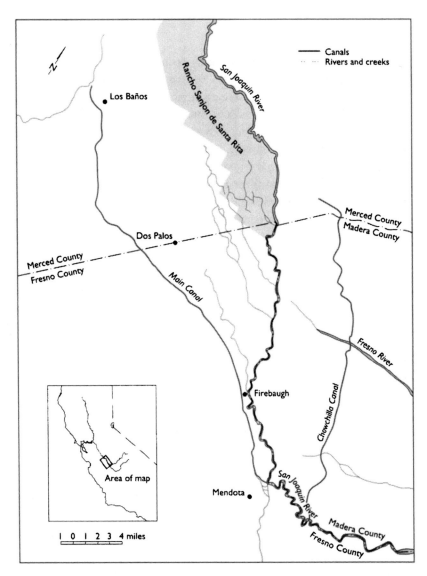

Map 3. The San Joaquin and King's River Canal, 1873. The main canal crossed over fifty miles of Miller & Lux property. The Chowchilla Canal too would soon be owned by Miller & Lux.

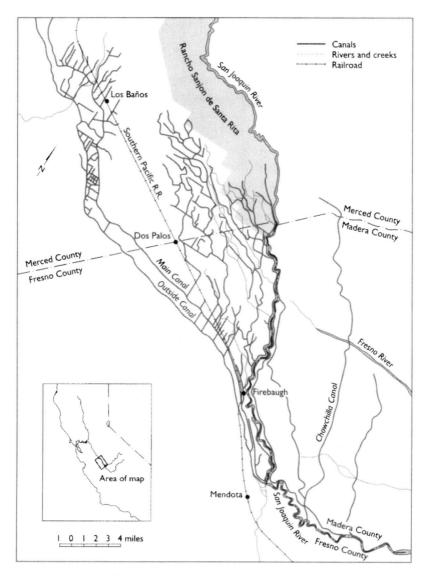

Map 4. The same landscape, twenty years later. Hundreds of miles of canals and ditches reorganized this landscape in preparation for alfalfa and cattle production.

wish, to purchase and settle on your lands. . . . Mr. Ralston and Mr. Fried-lander can tell you how much I would be giving up in India, where I am known and appreciated, as well as in my own country—if I agreed to devote my future wholly to the advancement of your interests in California."[75] In exchange for his service, experience, and "European connection and influence," Brereton demanded the following terms: a yearly salary of twelve thousand dollars "in gold," a generous expense account, 10 percent of the profits from all land sales, a house in the San Joaquin Valley, and the use of ten thousand acres in the valley for a period of five years (complete with irrigation ditches constructed by Miller & Lux).

Miller & Lux agreed to consider the offer, though Henry Miller surely bristled with anger over the terms as well as Brereton's suggestion that he could not handle properly the "country" end of the business. Two years of drought had made Miller question the feasibility of owning so much land, so he met with Brereton in early April to discuss the matter. Neither Brereton nor Miller subsequently commented upon this meeting, but relations between the two thereafter turned decidedly sour.[76] Miller moved on to the practical business of getting water on his land and, over the course of the next year, had a great deal of success. Brereton's trip to England and his search for investors, on the other hand, ended in complete failure. The canal company stock that he offered in London for seven to eight dollars a share, British investors learned, could be purchased at half that price in San Francisco.[77] By the time Brereton returned to California, Miller & Lux held a very different vision of the canal's purpose. That vision did not include selling off land to settlers, but rather, using its property (and contractual agreement with the SJ&KRC&ICo) to acquire additional water rights.

Miller & Lux began utilizing the canal company's water for irrigation in 1872, but the firm did not recognize the full potential of large-scale irrigation until the following year. The SJ&KRC&ICo had leased 6,000 acres from Miller & Lux to establish an experimental farm, and when Miller surveyed its progress in 1873, the irrigated grains and alfalfa looked promising.[78] At the Canal Farm, Miller informed Lux, "the[y are] having some very good wheat, and you would not have believed [that] some of the land would ever raise anything."[79] He suggested that Miller & Lux prepare more land for irrigation and increase its water use. But he also warned Lux about the mounting tensions between the two corporations: the canal company evidently hoped to increase its revenue by raising the water rates it charged Miller & Lux. In a blunt letter to Lux that reflected Miller's growing hostility to the canal company, he wrote, "Let the company make the canal complete and give us facility of using the water, and should the country settle up and we are benefited by the canal, we will deal with them fair."[80]

The conflict between the SJ&KRC&ICo and Miller & Lux arose from an issue much larger than water rates. At heart, the two San Francisco corporations disagreed over the method of developing the San Joaquin Valley, the means to profit from the region, and the developmental role to be played by the canal company. The trustees of the SJ&KRC&ICo remained steadfast in their original plan to build a vast canal system that would simultaneously serve the valley's need for irrigation, transportation, and hydraulic power.[81] This grand project proposed to irrigate 5,000,000 acres and promote "rapid immigration" to the valley.[82] As land values skyrocketed, the canal company's investors stood to profit considerably, since they remained the valley's largest landowners. The company also believed that all valley residents would benefit from this model project of rural development. *— grand plans for canal co.*

Miller & Lux agreed with certain aspects of this plan but viewed such grand schemes with caution. The depression of 1873 had begun to shake eastern markets, and Miller & Lux was already preparing for the coming economic reverberations.[83] Miller & Lux also held larger concerns about the valley's development and the canal enterprise itself. First, the corporation sought to control the pace of growth and change in the San Joaquin, particularly in areas that threatened to infringe on its property rights. The *uncertainty* of a future in which land values, taxes, and population would all rise and valley farmers (with irrigated land) would contest Miller & Lux's power was unsettling, to say the least. Second, Miller & Lux considered the canal company's comprehensive design as fundamentally flawed—economically, structurally, and ecologically, the project would never succeed as planned.[84] *— canal a threat to M & L*

By the end of 1873, Miller & Lux's evaluation of the project's financial instability proved correct. Brereton's attempt to raise capital from his "English friends" had ended in failure, and the canal company's vigorous lobbying for a federal land grant subsidy (totaling 256,000 acres) was stalled in the Senate Committee on Public Lands, pending the results of a Central Valley irrigation survey led by General B. S. Alexander of the U.S. Army Corps of Engineers.[85] After a year of study, the Alexander Commission refused to endorse a land grant subsidy for the SJ&KRC&ICo. The historian Donald Worster's sardonic conclusion to this episode—that "Congress was in a railroad mood, not a water mood, when it came to giveaways"—partly explains the trouble faced by the canal company in gaining federal support.[86] Perhaps more important, the federal government during the 1870s had no idea how to approach irrigation in the West and little imperative to act. With no government assistance on the horizon at the end of 1873 and four hundred thousand dollars already spent on the project, the company's trustees actually asked the state of California to purchase the canal. Governor Newton Booth was not interested.[87]

"DO CORPORATIONS MAKE KIND MASTERS?"

Public response in the San Joaquin Valley to the canal company rested on the delivery of its promises. If those promises seemed far-fetched—including a canal navigable for crop transport and the notion that "development" would allow the valley to gain political and economic power—most San Joaquin boosters were willing to give the canal company some leeway. San Joaquin farmers and developers needed water, and they appeared willing to support any project capable of fulfilling that need, even one financed and promoted by San Francisco capitalists. Above all, valley farmers wanted their faith in irrigation confirmed: that irrigation substantially benefited agriculturists in this arid region, and that it would induce land speculators to liquidate their vast holdings.[88] Clearly, San Joaquin residents had a particular type of agricultural speculator in mind, one akin to the midwestern landlord John Scully, who amassed over 220,000 acres in Illinois, Missouri, Kansas, and Nebraska during the late nineteenth century. But Scully leased his land to aspiring farmers, while Miller & Lux had a different agenda for the San Joaquin's land and irrigation resources.[89]

Between 1871 and 1875, the SJ&KRC&ICo continually expressed optimism for the canal's future and irrigation's promise. In 1872, 1873, and 1874 the company published lengthy stockholders' "reports" trumpeting the canal's progress and its great potential. The reports prominently displayed the names of stockholders and trustees to assure the public of its support by visionary men. The company's 1873 *Prospectus*, in particular, emphasized that San Francisco "capitalists" were not the only participants in this large-scale enterprise. The project was a "result of . . . *co-operation* on the part of capitalists, land-owners, farmers, and the Federal Government," the *Prospectus* stressed, and would promote "rapid immigration to this immense valley, and the settlement of the public land by an agricultural and permanent class of citizens."[90] Newspapers from San Francisco to Bakersfield reprinted sections of these reports, and for the first two years of the company's operation they shared its spirit of cooperation and rural development. – hope !

In 1871, for instance, the *San Joaquin Republican* waxed eloquently on the approaching "consummation" between "capitalists in San Francisco" and the San Joaquin Valley's farmland. The San Joaquin, suggested the *Republican*, would soon be "one of the richest and most extensive agricultural regions in the world. . . . The scheme is one of mammoth proportions and at first glance impresses one with the idea that its immensity renders it impracticable, but when we read further and learn the names of the incorporators of the San Joaquin Valley Canal and Irrigation Company [*sic*] we are reassured, and we lay down the paper with the idea dawning upon us that those men are capable of performing anything they undertake."[91] San Francisco's *Alta California* was equally impressed with the company's intentions and progress. In its regular column "Industrial Conditions of the State," the *Alta* noted the canal's daily progress (two-thirds of a mile per day), size of the labor force (four hundred workers), and various details about the canal's capacity for transporting crops. By the end of 1872, the *Alta* predicted, "facilities will be provided for irrigating 500,000 acres."[92] While this figure clearly stretched the truth, it revealed that public speculation about the canal's potential (and irrigation in general) blended both fact and enthusiasm. This report's appearance in the *Alta*'s "Industrial Conditions" column also suggests that San Francisco business leaders closely watched agricultural developments. Irrigated agriculture, when sponsored by monied interests, represented a promising industrial enterprise.

But as San Francisco leaders grew increasingly curious about corporate irrigation, valley residents began questioning the canal company's right to control the means of agricultural production. A number of events inspired this change in attitude. First, the canal company's lobbying for a federal subsidy struck many observers as unjust. "This is the worst kind of subsidy," argued the *Sacramento Daily Bee*, "worse a thousand times than any railroad subsidy ever given, for it enables a company to monopolize not business, but the main elements of all life." Rather than allow "a San Francisco Co[mpany]" to become "the owners of the water," the *Bee* proposed, federal money should subsidize the farmers' acquisition of the canal for themselves. "This," the *Bee* concluded, "would prevent all monopoly."[93]

The organization of California's Grangers (officially known as the Patrons of Husbandry) in 1873 constituted a second focal point of opposition to the canal company. Like its rural brethren across the country, California's Grange drew its membership from those small farmers most threatened by the economic crises of the 1870s. While the Central Pacific Railroad (and specifically its freight transport rates) was certainly a main target of all western Grangers, Central Valley Grange societies focused much of their attention on land and water monopolies.[94] As a San Francisco–based firm funded by bankers and land monopolists, the canal company represented the gravest of threats to a group whose ideology explained the dislocation of rural life precisely as a result of such money interests. Writing to the *Sacramento Union* in 1873, a Stanislaus County Grange member directly attacked the SJ&KRC&ICo's proposal for a federal subsidy as "a most infamous scheme": "Why do you presume to make such outrageous propositions as those embodied in your 'contract for subsidy' to the people of an intelligent community? Why, sirs, would you own us, we would be but your serfs, beholden to your mercy for the bread we would put in our children's mouths. . . . What do you take us for? Fools outright? Slaves from some foreign lands, used to despotism, and ready and willing to bow our necks for the yoke of the burden you would place upon us?"[95] This plea from a self-described "San Joaquin Farmer" expressed the increasing outrage of many potential irrigators as they recognized the implications of land and water monopoly.

Miller & Lux's role in the canal company provided the most important catalyst for the public's changing perception of the enterprise. The first stage of canal construction ran directly through Miller & Lux's property and could potentially irrigate some 200,000 acres of the firm's land. Had Miller & Lux immediately partitioned and put this land on the market for sale, as countless individuals suggested, it could have created a ground swell of popular support for the canal company and corporate irrigation in general. But Miller & Lux, as the *San Francisco Chronicle* noted in early 1873, had other considerations: "Miller & Lux, having their lands assessed at a very low rate, and having waters free for the use of their cattle, have not cared to go to the trouble and expense involved in irrigating and dividing into farms the lands that could be watered by these forty miles of canals. They have all the pasturage they require for their present profitable business, and prefer to go slow in the matter of improving and settling their lands."[96] Rather than "go[ing] slow" at "settling their lands," the firm was actively purchasing more property along the San Joaquin River and consolidating the valley's most extensive water rights.[97]

By 1874 the canal trustee William Chapman observed that public opinion throughout the San Joaquin Valley had turned decidedly against the enterprise.[98] In a last-ditch effort to gain popular support, a federal subsidy, and private investors, the company organized an "irrigation excursion" to the site of the "Great Canal." Included in the forty-person entourage were Leland Stanford (whose Southern Pacific Railroad provided a private train from San Francisco to Merced); B. S. Alexander and other members of the Army Corps' Alexander Commission party; the Bank of California's president, William Chapman Ralston; the canal company trustees Isaac Friedlander, William Chapman, and Charles Lux; John Hittell of the *Alta*; and A. D. Bell of the *Evening Post*. As a writer for the *San Francisco Evening Bulletin* wryly noted, the canal promoter R. M. Brereton rounded out the guest list with various "gentlemen of capital" from San Francisco whose "cooperation" he sought to enlist.[99] Between stops for cigars and French brandy, the group observed the results of irrigation on the canal company's experimental farm and questioned a few land renters about crop yields. However, few participants lost sight of the fact that this region bore the Miller & Lux stamp: outside the perimeter of the 6,000-acre experimental farm roamed 10,000 cattle, all carrying Miller & Lux's distinctive Double-H branding mark.[100]

In practical terms, the excursion provided no new investment capital for the indebted canal company, nor did it persuade the Alexander Commission to recommend the SJ&KRC&ICo for a federal subsidy. But for those in the valley who opposed the canal company, this invasion of the dusty plains by a trainload of large landowners and wealthy urbanites was highly symbolic. Summarizing the sentiment of farmers throughout the San Joaquin Valley, one newspaper wrote, "While Lux & Miller own the land there can be no oppression, for there will be nobody to oppress. Two cattle-dealers with a frontage of 28 miles of land cannot be starved by a water company . . . but [even if] the cattle of Miller & Lux [are] replaced by Christians, what then? Whose Christians will they be? The Water Company's, we think. The San Joaquin and King's River Canal and Irrigation Company, a corporation, will own them, body and soul. Do corporations make kind masters?"[101] The SJ&KRC&ICo now embodied the worst fears of many valley residents. Monopolies of land would likely not disappear in the face of corporate irrigation, but if they did, farmers would still remain powerless under the rule of a water corporation. Corporate profits would then dictate the allocation of water resources in the valley. This newspaper did not even suggest a third option: what if Miller & Lux, the land monopoly, gained control of the entire irrigation enterprise?

— common farmers worried

THE ALLOCATION OF RESOURCES
IN AN ARID COUNTRY

On October 11, 1878, six months after John Wesley Powell submitted to Congress his monumental *Report on the Lands of the Arid Region of the United States,* Miller & Lux did indeed gain control of its first subsidiary operation: the largest irrigation company in the American West.[102] Though unrelated, the two events responded to the same question: how should settlement proceed in the "arid regions" of the American West? Both Powell and Miller & Lux recognized the centrality of irrigation to the region's development, and both parties also viewed farmers' expectations for irrigation resources and technology as unrealistic. Powell's "program" called for an alliance between the federal government and local communities, with the government providing scientific information to farmers but leaving the farmers responsible for building and controlling the irrigation systems. Local control and cooperation were key to Powell: whoever "redeemed" the arid regions would ultimately control the land's productive resources and determine their use. The federal government, Powell believed, should not dominate this important task, and large-scale capital would only monopolize water resources as they already monopolized large portions of western lands. As he finished a draft of his *Report* in 1877, Powell unknowingly laid out the logic behind Miller & Lux's next move.

Miller & Lux had begun buying up the canal company's stock in 1876. Miller had grown increasingly frustrated with the company's trustees since 1874, and when they attempted to raise Miller & Lux's water rates (from $1.25 to $2.50 an acre) he became furious. "We can't get along in this present state of affairs," Miller wrote to Lux in the late spring of 1876.[103] He asked Lux to inform the SJ&KRC&ICo that "we shall not irrigate one acre this season" if charged higher rates, to which the canal company responded by temporarily cutting off Miller & Lux's water supply.[104] Miller became irate, and reportedly took an ax to one of the wood floodgates, releasing water from the canal onto Miller & Lux's pasture land.[105] The tension diffused between the two corporations in 1877, but Miller remained anxious about the canal company's control of what he considered "our" canal. "I see every day more the necessity of owning the controlling interest [in the SJ&KRC&ICo]," he wrote Lux in August. "By having control of the water we could make all the grass needed in a dry season. The water is nearly all tak[en] out of the River by us . . . and should the canal be extended further north, it would create a scarcity of water this time of year."[106] Miller asked Lux to find the thirty-three thousand shares of company stock necessary to give Miller & Lux control of the SJ&KRC&ICo, and by October 1878 Miller & Lux had gathered from various shareholders just over 50 percent of the available stock.[107] Validating John Wesley Powell's fear of what could happen to irrigation throughout the West, the cattle corporation now owned the region's largest irrigation enterprise.

Miller & Lux's takeover of the SJ&KRC&ICo coincided with the national depression that eventually hit the Far West two years later and temporarily closed the Bank of California. Under William Chapman Ralston's direction, the Bank of California had extended large loans to a number of canal investors. Ralston also speculated in San Joaquin Valley property for himself, using bank funds to finance this activity. Following the Bank of California's collapse and Ralston's death (apparently from suicide) in August 1875, the bank's board of directors called in the loans given to some of the largest landowners in California.[108] Isaac Friedlander owed the Bank of California over $500,000 for his land speculations, and William Chapman's debt to the bank amounted to $214,000.[109] John Bensley, the canal company's founder, faced financial ruin as well, although he remained solvent until 1877. Miller & Lux picked up his large bloc of canal company stock, in addition to the shares held by Friedlander, Chapman, and R. M. Brereton.[110]

How did Miller & Lux survive this economic crisis, and even expand its operations and overwhelm its rivals? First, Miller & Lux dominated a regional, relatively consistent market for cattle and wholesale beef, unlike Friedlander and Chapman, whose incomes were tied to depressed, export wheat markets. Even when prices declined during the mid-1870s, Miller & Lux retained a steady monthly income to cover its labor expenses and investments in cattle and land. The firm also viciously battled its competitors in San Francisco. When the city's second-largest meatpacker, Dunphy & Hildreth, asked Charles Lux to slow his slaughtering rate, Miller told Lux to stand firm. "About [Dunphy &] Hildreth wanting you to kill less," Miller instructed Lux, "don't you do it. Let each look out for themself. If the[y] have cheap cattles they would not come to you and want [you] to kill less and us to join them."[111] Like thousands of companies across the nation that lost market share in the new competitive environment, Dunphy & Hildreth closed shop by the decade's end.[112]

Equally important, however, was the fact that Miller & Lux had not tied its fortunes to Ralston's Bank of California. Throughout the "terrible seventies" Miller & Lux's investments were backed by the foreign-owned London & San Francisco Bank, and John Parrott's influence in this bank allowed Miller & Lux to continue operations despite a monthly deficit.[113] In April of 1876, the Miller & Lux accountant John Bolton had told Miller that the corporation was overdrawn by $42,636 to the London & San Francisco Bank. Lux cautioned Miller against buying more land and livestock, but Miller remained confident that a business strategy of constant expansion was the best way to survive the economic crisis. Responding to Lux's caution on one occasion, Miller wrote, "I know we are in debt and [I] want to get out as bad as you do. But there are times when you can't let a good [purchase] go by just because you can't spare the money."[114] This risky business strategy could have spelled disaster for the firm, yet it ultimately allowed Miller & Lux to acquire the canal company and strengthen its grip on the valley's water resources.

San Francisco meatpackers and rival land barons constituted one type of competition. A very different challenge to Miller & Lux's power also appeared during the mid-1870s, this one on the political front. The San Joaquin Grangers, who had pushed for statewide water reform legislation since 1874, proposed a locally controlled "West Side Irrigation District" plan two years later. Irrigation districts offered an approach to water development quite similar to that envisioned by John Wesley Powell, in that all local landowners would share the costs and benefits of a given irrigation district.[115] The Westside bill envisioned a massive district from Tulare Lake to Contra Costa County, financed by a $4 million tax measure. It essentially copied the canal company's irrigation plan, and would in fact condemn the canal company's water rights "for the greater good" of all valley residents.[116] Questions as to the legality of condemning water rights were avoided as the Westside bill passed through legislative committee in early 1876. One week before the bill came up for a vote, the Miller & Lux lobbyist Jeff Shannon (who also served as the Southern Pacific's land agent in the valley) reported that "prospects look good to defeat the whole works. The more [the Westside bill] is ventilated the worse it looks."[117] Shannon had overestimated his lobbying skills. The Westside bill passed the Senate on March 23 and was signed into law the next week.

Miller & Lux had prepared for this eventuality. In conjunction with other large landowners on the Westside, the firm sponsored supplemental legislation (to the Westside bill) that required a thorough irrigation survey of the district prior to the election of district officials.[118] The corporation banked on two possible ways to defeat the irrigation district: the first possibility was that valley residents would decide against the district tax measure as soon as ample rain returned (1876 was one of the driest years on record); and the second was that Miller & Lux could get its land and canal withdrawn from the boundaries of the district. Rain did not return to the San Joaquin Valley in 1877, and after Henry Miller attended an irrigation meeting in the Granger-stronghold town of Grayson in April 1877, he wrote to Lux that "every one seems to think a Canal is the[ir] only salvation."[119] Perhaps *some* canal would be the farmers' "salvation," but Miller & Lux would not help pay for it. In late 1877, the corporation won an injunction suit against the West Side Irrigation District, charging that its land must be removed from the district or $1.3 million paid for Miller & Lux's land and water rights.[120] Subsequently, the 1878 legislature excluded Miller & Lux's land and canal from the irrigation district, and the bonds that would finance the district failed to sell. Rain had returned to the San Joaquin Valley in 1878, and farmers looked forward to a bonanza crop of wheat without irrigation.

Miller & Lux's bitter opposition to the West Side Irrigation District came as no surprise to observers in San Francisco and the San Joaquin Valley. As early as 1874, the *San Francisco Evening Bulletin* had prophesized that "the greatest danger" of land and water monopolists was their "influence . . . in shaping legislation upon the question" of irrigation resources. "If they will it, they can not only prevent the people from carrying out the district system—in our judgment the only just and wise one—but they can cause legislators to continue the present laws of corporation and appropriation in force, and thereby go on and secure and hold, as we fear they will do, all the water-courses and [water]sheds in this State, and reduce them to the control of corporations, of which a half-dozen wealthy men shall be the proprietors."[121] Corporate control of water resources was clear by 1879: Merced County, with only nine "ditches" in operation, led the state in the number of acres irrigated. Miller & Lux governed those ditches, revealing the extent to which corporate irrigation reigned in the valley.[122] The decade-long conflict over land and water created the need for a thorough examination of the links between monopoly, capitalist enterprise, and the allocation of natural resources. The 1878–79 California Constitutional Convention provided just such an opportunity.

CONCLUSION: THE POLITICS
OF MONOPOLY AT THE END OF THE DECADE

The delegates who convened in Sacramento in 1878 to rewrite California's constitution arrived with various goals. Like those who gathered at constitutional conventions throughout the nation, most of California's delegates hoped to regulate the railroad and curtail the power of other large corporations in the state's economy and legislature.[123] Other delegates, primarily those representing Central Valley counties, sought land and tax reform as a way to force land monopolists into selling off land. Circumscribing the rights of Chinese residents topped many delegates' priority lists, particularly the large bloc that represented Denis Kearney's Workingmen's Party of California (WPC).[124] The WPC had won all thirty of San Francisco's elected seats and comprised a main force behind the convention itself.[125] While many observers denounced Kearney's radical rhetoric as "incendiary and revolutionary," his account of the state's problems nonetheless found widespread acceptance.[126] Unemployment, Chinese labor, the railroad, and political corruption explained a great deal to Californians about their economic problems. Influenced by these real and imagined ills, the Constitutional Convention also represented a fledgling attempt to curtail the worst aspects of modern corporate capitalism.[127]

Antirailroad sentiment ran high at the convention, and a coalition of WPC and Grange delegates ultimately did pass a resolution creating a railroad commission to regulate the state's most notorious monopoly.[128] Land monopolies also received great attention, and Miller & Lux was attacked with particular fervor. Miller & Lux, proclaimed one delegate, "the great land monopolists of California, have succeeded in owning, or controlling . . . the great valley of the San Joaquin from San Francisco to Los Angeles. They can drive their cattle from one end to the other upon their own ground. The public cannot do that. If we don't solve this question, it is useless to deny that we will have a bloody revolution in this country."[129] Another delegate, James O'Sullivan of San Francisco, outlined the methods by which Miller & Lux had "robbed the people of that [land] which rightfully belongs to all." First they acquired Mexican land grants, and then they used the " 'dummy' system" and "rings" (or networks) of "agents" to file on the public domain. In the process, O'Sullivan argued, the people of California had become "landless— disinherited through land monopoly." He calculated that the dissolution of land monopolies would increase family farm ownership by over 400 percent in the state.[130] If land monopolists like Miller & Lux were not stopped, added William P. Grace of San Francisco, they would "form themselves into an aristocracy which will be worse than was ever seen in England. By means of Chinese labor they will soon crowd the laboring man and the farmer to the wall."[131]

The most strident land monopoly critics ultimately supported the "minority report" of the Committee on Land and Homestead Exemptions. This report proposed limiting landownership to 640 acres per person and outlawed the inheritance of land in excess of that amount. It also required the "actual occupation and continuous use" of land, the abolition of land scrip, and a new 160-acre limit on all public land grants.[132] It was a radical statement of land reform, but it received only minority support. The majority's report offered a decidedly less radical vision. "The holding of large tracts of land," read the final version, "is against the public interest, and should be discouraged by all means not inconsistent with the rights of private property."[133] The first article of the new constitution assured the "rights of private property," and that right was the primary concern for Miller & Lux and other large landowners.

The most curious aspect of this debate was not the zeal with which delegates lambasted large landowners but the way a red herring debate on "land limitation" confined the discourse. The idea that California's climate and natural environment posed distinct barriers to "small" farms; the glaring fact that agriculturalists needed water rights; and the possibility that natural resource management offered a promising (and not unprecedented) area of state jurisdiction—all of these issues were essentially obfuscated by simplistic denunciations of land monopolists. In a statement that revealed the limits of this debate, Thomas B. McFarland of Sacramento County charged, "I would like to know what business a man has to [own] more than 640 acres of land? If a man cannot live on that, he ought to die."[134] In late-nineteenth-century California, few farmers could honestly deny the aspiration to own more than 640 acres.[135]

An obvious extension of the land monopoly debate could have encompassed the control of irrigation resources in the state. Miller & Lux's recent takeover of the SJ&KRC&ICo provided a readily available example. The delegate Patrick T. Dowling in fact suggested the necessity of a "State system of irrigation" that followed the lead of Mediterranean nations. But this suggestion came as a mere afterthought to his racialistic assertion that "California is Asiatic in climate, it is Asiatic in soil, and it is too much Asiatic in the character of its people."[136] Few delegates to the convention made anything but cursory remarks about water as a shared resource. Interestingly, the two paragraphs devoted to water and water rights in the 1879 constitution did declare the use of water to be a "*public* use, and subject to the regulation and control of the State."[137] However, the "State" in this instance referred to local officials, not a centralized (and possibly more autonomous) state authority or irrigation commission.[138] At least for the time being, Miller & Lux had little to fear from local officials.

Clearly, the delegates from the San Joaquin Valley had no way to assess or direct the rapid changes brought upon their region by large-scale capitalist enterprise. Miller & Lux was not just a large landowner but a multilayered corporation based in San Francisco that held land throughout the state. This description contains a variety of issues that were intrinsic to the valley's development and autonomy: urban ownership of hinterland resources, the relationship between private irrigation and the "public good," ranching versus agriculture, and above all, the power of accumulated capital. But formulating a coherent critique of what amounted to industrial agriculture, without curtailing the rights of private property and individualism, proved difficult.[139] In place of this critique, land monopoly still resonated with meaning for most convention delegates and San Joaquin residents.

During a decade of severe economic dislocation across America, Miller & Lux survived and ultimately thrived. The corporation expanded its landownership by using a broad network of agents who helped the firm navigate California's institutional landscape. Miller & Lux subsequently used its land and property rights to gain control of California's first major irrigation project, the San Joaquin and King's River Canal & Irrigation Company. In the process, the two partners scuttled plans for the West Side Irrigation District, at least temporarily delaying the movement toward locally controlled irrigation. Irrigation, Miller & Lux realized during the 1870s, was the future of the San Joaquin Valley. However, successful large-scale irrigation first required engineering the landscape's natural systems.

At the close of the 1870s, John Wesley Powell had also turned his attention to engineering the arid regions of the American West. Powell's *Report* suggested not simply a series of proposals for the western landscape but a decree of what "must" be done to rescue "these lands . . . from their present worthless state."[140] The language employed by Powell accurately reflected the urgency felt by hopeful irrigators throughout the West. "The redemption of the Arid Regions involves engineering problems," Powell wrote, "and the engineering problems involved are of [a] diverse nature."[141] Powell's statement was correct in more ways than one. As the next chapter illustrates, irrigation and reclamation presented a variety of engineering problems to irrigators, legislators, and courts. But "redeeming" the land also entailed confronting the diversity of nature itself. Before the land could be irrigated, it had to be simplified, and simplifying nature proved a difficult task. *good finish*

CHAPTER 4

Lux v. *Haggin*

Reclaiming the San Joaquin from Nature

Late-nineteenth-century Californians had few reservations about exploiting their natural resources to the greatest extent possible. Timber
companies clear-cut nearly all the redwood forests within fifty miles of
San Francisco Bay during the 1850s and then rapidly moved up the
northern coast in the following decade. Miners and mining firms tore
and blasted apart the Sierra hillsides during one of the largest mineral
rushes the world ever witnessed: $500 million in minerals poured from
the mining districts in less than a decade.[1] Agriculture, irrigation, and
land reclamation offered slower economic returns, but industry leaders
showed no lack of resolve for transforming the agricultural landscape.
"Nature is obstinate here and must be broken with steam and with
steel," wrote the journalist Stephen Powers in 1869. "Until strong men
take hold of the State this way and break it in . . . its agriculture will
be the merest clod whacking."[2] The writer Frank Norris clearly agreed
with this sentiment. His 1901 novel, *The Octopus*, depicted the land-
breaking process as a carnal act: "Everywhere throughout the San Joaquin . . . a thousand ploughs up-stirred the land, tens of thousands of
shears clutched deep into the warm, moist soil. . . . The heroic embrace
of a multitude of iron hands, gripping deep into the brown, warm flesh
of the land that quivered responsive and passionate under this rude
advance, so robust as to be almost an assault, so violent as to be veri-
tably brutal."[3] Celebrated by Norris for their valiant conquest of the
land, California agriculturalists viewed their task in terms of bringing

order and productivity to the soil. Land reclamation practices exemplified these goals.

Reclamation changed the American West's landscape more than any other human enterprise. Practiced for thousands of years by southwest Indian communities, legally codified by Spanish settlers, and sanctified by Brigham Young's assemblage of desert saints, land reclamation rapidly accelerated in California under the direction of capitalized enterprises like Miller & Lux. Reclaiming western lands by means of irrigation received endorsement from every segment of western society. Even John Muir did not hide his enthusiasm for San Joaquin reclamation work. In 1874 he announced "irriguous revivals are breaking out all the glad plains."[4] Muir referred specifically to irrigation's advance, and irrigation was only part of land reclamation's larger agenda. *Irrigation* referred to watering dry land, extending agricultural acreage, and increasing the land's productivity. *Irrigation* conjured up images of production and reproduction: maximizing crop production for economic exchange and profit, as well as the reproduction of independent farming communities that existed in the East without irrigation.[5] *Reclamation,* on the other hand, signified a broader process that included draining wetlands, engineering waterways, preparing the ground for irrigation, and simplifying ecological communities. While agriculturalists often used the terms *irrigation* and *reclamation* interchangeably, reclamation nonetheless contained distinct ideas about the land and, ultimately, about nature itself.

"Reclaiming" the land implied an act of recovery or rescue: to "reclaim" the land from its current or natural condition. Nature's reclaimers attempted to alter specific natural characteristics as they simultaneously sought to regulate nature's underlying disorder. Rivers that shifted course through recurrent floods; soils and plant communities that exhibited remarkable variation from one 640-acre section to the next; wetlands that teemed with biodiversity but impeded single-crop production—such conditions had no place in the orderly "garden" envisioned by those who would reclaim western lands. To these reclaimers of the land, nature's complexity and disorder proved its need for redemption.

Few places in the American West better illustrate the confrontation between a natural landscape and a society dedicated to its reclamation than the Tulare Basin, located at the southern end of the San Joaquin Valley. Between 1875 and 1890, the Tulare Basin became a locus of controversy not over reclamation itself—since that goal received widespread support—but over the legal, social, and environmental fallout from reclaiming the landscape. *Lux* v. *Haggin* (1881–86), California's landmark water battle between Miller & Lux and James Haggin, served as a public forum for the conflict. Throughout its district court appearance and two appeals in the state supreme court, *Lux* v. *Haggin* raised attention to California's mounting conflict between riparian water rights and appropriative water rights; in short, between landowners whose property bordered a river, and those who appropriated a river's flow for irrigation. But *Lux* v. *Haggin* revealed more pervasive tensions than just conflicting water rights doctrines. Agriculturalists who lacked capital and the power to reclaim their own land struggled against urban capitalists who controlled property and production. Rural communities pondered the conflicting goals of economic development and local autonomy. Society as a whole attempted to transform both desert and swampland into a contained, productive garden. In the Tulare Basin, these various forces converged in the years surrounding *Lux* v. *Haggin*.

THE TULARE BASIN AND ITS RECLAIMERS

How nature actually functioned must have perplexed those nineteenth-century Californians who scrutinized their surroundings. On the one hand, they had inherited a centuries-old "mechanistic" view of the world as a vast machine: it was predictable, orderly, and it followed prescribed natural laws.[6] The task for scientists, engineers, and even agriculturalists lay in revealing nature's order through observation. By *knowing* the order of plants, animals, climate, rivers, and other entities, people could manipulate nature toward productive ends. On the other hand, Californians lived in a world of profound natural disorder. Earthquakes shook the ground and turned buildings to rubble. Periodic floods inundated the inland valleys for months at a time, while drought radically altered flora and fauna communities. Small changes to natural ecosystems produced complex consequences that followed no discernible laws or patterns.[7] The landscape's very appearance transformed from one year to the next, suggesting to the careful observer (recall William Brewer's experience in the early 1860s) that nature held a great capacity for unpredictable innovation.

The logic of reclamation embraced both perspectives on nature. It sought to reveal and utilize a landscape's perceived order while attempting to control the essential disorder that necessitated reclamation in the first place. For Tulare Basin residents, the landscape's formation and composition confirmed the need for reclamation.[8] A heavy sediment load carried down from the Sierra Nevada by the King's, Kaweah, Tule, White, and Kern Rivers continually reshaped the basin floor. Since the basin lacked an outlet to the Pacific Ocean, spring runoff from the mountains created a series of shallow lakes: Tulare, Buena Vista, Goose, and Kern Lakes. In wet years, the four lakes could form one continuous water mass stretching across the entire valley floor. On average, however, the Tulare Basin received less than ten inches of rainfall a year. Of course, the *average* usually suggested what would least likely occur in this Mediterranean environment.[9] Climatic extremes were the norm, and they affected the basin in numerous ways. Extremes gave the region's meager watercourses an unparalleled importance to human settlements; they shaped a variegated landscape from boggy swampland to desert alkali flats and fashioned four distinctly different soil types that added to the basin's natural diversity.[10]

The Tulare Basin appeared to mock the notion of a definable and orderly landscape. Recounting in 1886 the impetus to "redeem" the Tulare Basin, U.S. Senator Aaron A. Sargent wrote, "When our people began to settle the valleys of this State, they found these swamps and swampy lakes, which Nature had already fashioned. In the progress of settlement, the question has arisen, Is it necessary or right to keep forever these polluting areas, or can engineering science and public necessity obviate them?" Nature should certainly be changed, Sargent answered, especially when "enterprise stands ready to create taxable property there." While nature may have ordered the landscape in a particular "fashion," its imperfections clearly bothered Sargent: "Our streams must be taken from their useless and shifting beds and given the widest scope. Then we may create an empire here, of health, prosperity, and development."[11]

Sargent and many others possessed a strong belief that "engineering science" could order the unwieldy environment. By rationalizing the landscape—measuring river flows, assessing soil components, comparing irrigation practices, and analyzing patterns of precipitation—nature's engineers could quantify these variables and reclamation could proceed with scientific certainty. To this end, the 1874 Alexander Survey compiled data to illustrate how the San Joaquin Valley actually functioned as a natural landscape. Alexander surveyed the valley's "catchment" area (including twenty-three rivers) and estimated that 8.5 million acres "may be readily irrigated."[12] He studied the placement of existing canals and proposed sites for future ones. Alexander's *Report* concluded that the "damage" caused by natural flooding undermined the "wealth of California," and it was therefore the "duty of Government" to assist the people with a "rational" reclamation policy.[13]

The Tulare Basin's reclamation proceeded during the 1870s with little regard for rational organization. Individual water claims to the Kern River by private canal companies, for instance, far surpassed the river's maximum flow and the canals' maximum capacity. Thirty-two separate canal projects claimed a combined total flow of 11,887 cubic feet per second, while the maximum capacity of those canals amounted to only 7,262 cubic feet per second. "Maximum" capacity, furthermore, indicated the breaking point of any given canal. Ambitious private agendas had clearly trumped any attempt at rational organization. By the end of the decade, the state engineer William Hammond Hall concluded that a chaotic "free-to-all rule" of land reclamation had "br[ought] trouble to all" participants.[14]

John Muir had seen no such trouble six years earlier. On assignment for the *San Francisco Bulletin* in 1874, Muir described the zeal with which Tulare Basin landowners hoped to "strike it rich" through land reclamation. "It appears," he observed, "that all th[eir] physical and moral brightness flows directly from a[n irrigation] ditch." He studied swampland drainage and canal construction just long enough to announce his endorsement. Irrigation, Muir suggested, essentially mimicked the natural flooding process, whereas leaving the land unchanged ultimately "degraded" it "by atmospheric weathering." Muir, who later championed the preservation cause, here supported a reclamationist logic that linked social progress with natural engineering. By reclaiming the landscape, Muir concluded, the basin's "cheerless shanties" would be "displaced by true homes embowered in trees and lovingly broidered with flowers."[15] The redeemed landscape would soon sprout a perfect rural order.

Muir and others who publicized the reclamation cause drew heavily on domestic imagery to express their family-farm ideal. Fresno County's irrigation colonies (immediately north of the Tulare Basin) often served as the model. "On the broad Fresno plains," claimed George E. Freeman in the *Overland Monthly*, "the work of irrigation is so light, that women who have bought their twenty or forty acre tracts in some of the colonies, enjoy guiding the small streams from furrow into furrow, and one often sees a sunbonneted figure, hoe in hand, watering the strawberry garden."[16] The "garden" image, symbolized by the presence of women and families, proved extremely powerful in the Tulare Basin. During the early 1870s, local papers cheered the arrival of families in the region and predicted a rapid increase in the number of female "sunbonneted figures" on the surrounding plains.[17] But if the growing numbers of women and children revealed a trend toward family-centered agriculture, the trend was short-lived.[18] Land and water consolidations by San Francisco–based enterprises signified a more powerful force in the Tulare Basin, and their reclamation projects halted any trend toward independent family farms. — *Big Ag from the start of industrial age*

RECLAIMING THE "GREAT TULE SWAMP"

In late 1878, the *Gilroy Advocate* published a series of letters from "Pioneer," an "oldtime" Gilroy resident currently visiting the Tulare Basin. This trip, Pioneer enthusiastically wrote, allowed him to observe "the grand scheme to reclaim the great tule swamp between Buena Vista and Tulare lakes."[19] Such traveler reports appeared frequently in California newspapers, but Pioneer's letters contained a note of particular interest for Gilroy's readers. The grand reclamation "scheme," though two hundred miles away from Gilroy, was directed by the town's largest landowner, Miller & Lux. The firm had begun purchasing Kern County lands in partnership with a local rancher, James C. Crocker, in 1868. Crocker knew the country well. He located the best swamp and desert lands along Buena Vista Slough, cultivated relationships with the county land officials, and convinced Miller & Lux that this undeveloped San Joaquin range could produce prime cattle for its northern ranches. Crocker moved quickly. In 1870 he "secured twenty miles fronting the tulies [*sic*] [along Buena Vista Slough]," he wrote Miller, "and with this tule land we will have the best stock rancho in the state. [It] will keep 20,000 head [of] cattle."[20] Under Miller's direction, Crocker continued to acquire Kern County property, and by 1879 the firm owned 78,908 acres along Buena Vista Slough. That acreage would double in the following decade.[21]

Buena Vista Slough seemed a perfect site to carry out the firm's reclamation agenda. The slough meandered through fifty miles of tall tule grasses that made it nearly impassable in dry and wet years alike. The writer and naturalist Mary Austin lived near the slough during the late 1880s and concluded it was "full of mystery and malaria," a characterization likely seconded by Pioneer, who spent much of his Kern County vacation in bed "prostrated with [malarial] fever."[22] Early cartographers depicted the slough in different ways. George Derby's 1852 Tulare Basin map showed the slough as a small and contained watercourse connecting the two lakes. But William Blake's 1853 map presented an expansive and undefined slough along its course to Tulare Lake, and the lake itself spilling out across the valley floor into a vast marshland.[23] Derby drew his map in a dry year, while Blake's rendering reflected the 1851–52 flood. Taken together, the two maps reveal Buena Vista Slough's most important characteristic: while it changed on a yearly basis, it remained a watered oasis in the midst of a dry desert.

Reclaiming this region came with certain risks. During the dry season Miller & Lux's horse-drawn scrapers could clear and level the surrounding land, uncovering a sandy loam soil high in alkalinity.[24] A main canal could then divert the Kern River away from Buena Vista Slough, allowing the swampland to dry. Irrigation could next proceed across the rectilinear sections surrounded by earth levees. Despite such engineering, however, Buena Vista Slough would still remain the floodplain's natural artery, and a single flood could destroy the expensive reclamation work. For this reason, Miller initially opposed the cooperative reclamation enterprise proposed by Crocker, Charles Lux, and the neighboring landowner, Horatio Livermore. Miller questioned the project's overall feasibility, while the "preliminary steps of [corporate] organization" that Livermore suggested during the summer of 1876 struck him as premature. With Miller vacillating, Lux took the initiative and organized the Kern Valley Water Company to reclaim the "great swamp."[25]

For the next several months, Miller distanced himself from the reclamation project. "Do just as you like," Miller wrote Lux in January 1877; "[it is] your reclamation work."[26] But when no rain fell during the next two months, Miller saw the necessity of reclaiming what he now called "our swamp."[27] The reclamation project proceeded with remarkable speed, due in large measure to a massive workforce recently laid off by the Southern Pacific Railroad, which had finished its line connecting Kern County with northern California. According to Pioneer's report, Miller & Lux engaged between 200 and 300 manual laborers at $30 a month, plus carpenters, blacksmith, and foremen at $45, $50, and $60 a month, respectively. Miller & Lux supplied both food and housing. Over 25,000 pounds of beef (slaughtered on site) was served in one month by "3 Chinese cooks, 6 waiters . . . [and] a boss Chinaman to superintend them." Pioneer noted that "these were the only Chinamen employed by the company," an important assurance to his readers in Gilroy, where "anti-coolie" clubs had formed to protest the use of Chinese workers by large employers.[28]

To reclaim the swampland that measured fifty miles in length and several miles across, the Kern Valley Water Company diverted the Kern River's course away from Buena Vista Slough and into a main canal that measured 250 feet in width and 21 miles in length. Specially designed

first mention of a large workforce

one-ton "Fresno Scrapers" pulled by fifty-horse teams excavated this canal bed by making a series of long cuts. Twelve-foot-high earth levees lined each side of the main canal, which sank twelve feet into the ground. Cross-ditches fanned out from the main canal in order to channel the water into large "checks" of flat land. (See figure 5.) For those readers uninitiated in the practice of modern, hydrological engineering, Pioneer described how the process *should* work: "The water comes flowing from the canal and continues till this great reservoir is completely filled; then the weir is opened, and the water continues pouring in towards the next cross levee 6 miles distant, where there is a weir and a headgate as before; and when this great reservoir is filled the weir is raised, and another reservoir filled up to the cross levee, 2 miles away, and so on to the next cross levee, 7 miles distant; and the water then flowing 2 miles further to the bed of the levee and works, spreads as now over the great tule swamp towards Tulare Lake. The water [fills] in each of the great reservoirs, which you can see at a glance are in reality lakes of no mean magnitude."[29] Pioneer imagined a perfectly ordered waterscape created by corporate capital and labor. Small landowners surely could not engineer the waterscape on this scale.

The only feature it lacked during the winter of 1877 was water. In March, Miller had ridden up the valley's Westside in search of grazing land and found virtually no grass. "The whole country is burned up," he wrote Lux. "It don't seem possible, but it is the plain truth. Even on the low land . . . there is nothing. It is not yet known how bad [the drought will be], but a great deal of stock will be lost [unless] we kill them off to keep them from starving."[30] Miller's forecast proved correct. Close to 10,000 head of Miller & Lux cattle perished that year from starvation along Buena Vista Slough. But the lack of water in the slough also resulted from upstream diversions by Kern County's other great landlord, James Haggin. Crocker had warned Miller & Lux that Haggin's appropriations from Kern River would soon endanger the firm's own reclamation project, but neither Miller nor Lux appeared to believe Crocker.[31] With their water supply now threatened by a rival corporate interest, reclaiming the Buena Vista Slough region became both a legal and an engineering challenge. Ironically, Miller & Lux's group had to divert the slough's flow while protecting their legal right to that slough: they were caught in the contradictory position of asserting riparian rights to a watercourse that would no longer exist if their reclamation project succeeded. — *irony*

Such legal gymnastics required organization, so in late 1878 Miller

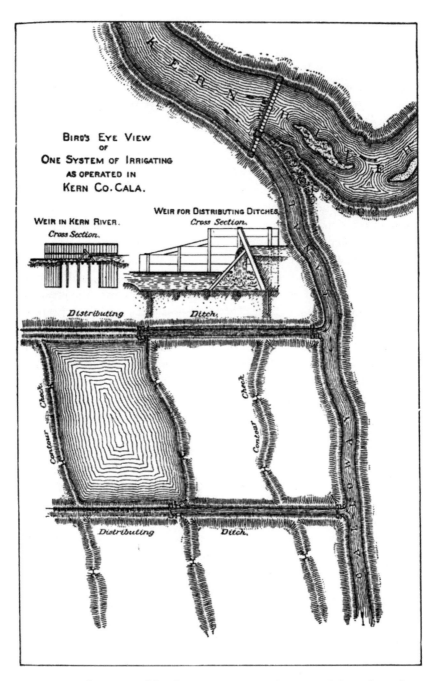

Figure 5. The system of flood irrigation in Kern County and throughout the San Joaquin Valley diverted a river's flow into a canal; cross-ditches delivered the water into a series of rectilinear fields, or checks. (Courtesy of the Bancroft Library, University of California at Berkeley.)

& Lux organized the Riparian Suits Association to function as the legal arm of the Kern Valley Water Company. Besides Miller & Lux, the Riparian Suits Association's membership included Horatio Livermore, John H. Redington, George Cornwell, L. H. Bonestell, Horatio Stebbins, and the Sacramento-based ranchers Cox & Clarke.[32] Their "Statement of Principles" read as a trial balloon for *Lux* v. *Haggin;* it expressed their "common interest in the assertion, preservation, and maintenance of the 'Riparian Rights'" to Buena Vista Slough. They threatened legal action against those "parties who are illegally diverting the said waters [of the Kern River] and preventing their natural, and heretofore continuous, flow through [Buena Vista Slough]." The members agreed to divide legal costs and "campaign expenses" (political lobbying) as they had divided the slough itself—by the numbers of acres owned by each party.[33] Miller & Lux's share of the swampland and expenses, however, quickly increased from 36,644 acres (or 37 percent) to 78,908 acres (or 80 percent) when the corporation bought all the land owned by members Redington, Bonestell, and Livermore, and one-third of that owned by Cox & Clarke.[34] Miller & Lux clearly determined the group's "common interest." Over the next five years, the Riparian Suits Association filed eighty-four lawsuits against upstream appropriators. *Lux* v. *Haggin,* almost the last on this list, would be the test case for control of the Kern River.

JAMES HAGGIN: THE "GRAND KHAN OF THE KERN"

James Ben Ali Haggin ran the gamut of western business enterprises before staking his claim on the Tulare plains. Born into a Kentucky slaveholding family, Haggin followed the gold seekers to San Francisco in 1850 and set up a law practice with his brother-in-law, Lloyd Tevis. Together they launched a series of profitable ventures in transportation, banking, urban development, manufacturing, and most generally, the building of San Francisco.[35] These business dealings planted Haggin among the city's elite, and his fortunate mining investments in Nevada and Utah soon made him truly wealthy. During the 1870s Haggin and Tevis joined George Hearst's Homestake Mining Company and relieved South Dakota's Black Hills of its gold deposits, and they followed this venture by helping Hearst organize Montana's Anaconda Copper Mining Company.[36] Somewhere between the San Francisco projects and the mining ventures, Haggin and his associates began adding large tracts of California land to their business portfolio. Like other industrial cowboys, Haggin centered all his investments on exploiting western lands.

Haggin also matched Miller & Lux's skill for manipulating state land laws and officials. Haggin secured close to sixty thousand acres of Kern County railroad lands during the 1870s through an alliance with William B. Carr, a prominent Republican Party leader known as the "political Napoleon of the [Southern Pacific] Railroad Company."[37] Previously withheld from settlers, these lands comprised some of Kern County's most valuable real estate.[38] Haggin next followed Miller & Lux's lead by seeking out public lands. With the assistance of California's Senator A. A. Sargent, Haggin and his cohorts orchestrated the passage of the 1877 Desert Land Act, an act perfectly designed for acquiring Kern County's dry acreage.[39] During the first month of the act's operation, Haggin paid hundreds of San Francisco residents to file "dummy" claims on Kern County's desert lands. He particularly sought the even-numbered sections to match his odd-numbered railroad lands. In this manner, Haggin claimed over a hundred thousand acres north and south of Bakersfield. While the *San Francisco Chronicle* and other newspapers lambasted this premeditated grab of Kern County real estate, Haggin defended his actions with the promise to reclaim and offer the land at public auction. He would turn "wasteland" into farmland, Haggin wrote, and "divid[e his acreage] into small tracts and [sell] them out to farmers, with the water-rights necessary for irrigati[on]."[40] The small-farm ideal evidently justified his exploitation of the Desert Land Act, or so decided a subsequent investigation by the U.S. Department of the Interior. Reclaiming western lands "could not be done by a single person," the investigation concluded, but rather required large-scale organization and the promise of land sales. Haggin's fortunes rose with this promise.[41]

gobbling up lands for the public good

To water his desert lands, Haggin began purchasing the surrounding land and water rights claimed by early settlers, as well as the controlling interest in many small irrigation canals.[42] By 1877, when Miller & Lux's water supply disappeared, Haggin had gained control of almost every irrigation ditch diverting the Kern River's flow. While Haggin's land and water consolidations angered some local landowners, he convinced many others that his deep pockets could reclaim the desert and bring thousands of settlers to the region. Haggin also stymied local criticism through his control of the ditches upon which farmers relied for irrigation.[43] This "Grand Khan of the Kern" could easily decide not to provide a particular farmer with water. Finally, his Kern County Land Company, organized in 1875, was the largest employer in the county, and few small farmers could bypass the opportunity for off-season employment.[44] Most Tulare Basin residents had some connection to "the Com-

h2O control meant power

pany," as the Kern County Land Company came to be known in the 1880s. Years later, one paper convincingly argued that the "development of Kern County is so closely allied with the growth of the Kern County Land Company that the story of one is the story of the other."[45]

The two San Francisco corporations rationalized their property consolidations on the basis of their belief that the Tulare Basin landscape was fundamentally flawed and its best hope for redemption lay in capitalized, private ventures. Summarizing this philosophy in 1878, the *Visalia Delta* remarked, "All that is desired is that these barren plains should be made to blossom as the rose. And all that is necessary to make them bloom is to give them away in chunks."[46] The recipients of those "chunks"—wealthy San Francisco developers—possessed the means to fertilize the "barren" land and maximize its economic potential. This developmental approach to the landscape clearly intersected with ascendant legal ideas concerning private property, natural resources, and water use in particular. By the mid–nineteenth century, an instrumental approach that sanctioned industrial development had emerged in American water law.[47] From New England's textile industries in the 1830s to California's reclamation projects four decades later, this instrumentalism increasingly sanctioned corporate attempts to put rivers to their maximum use. While both sides in *Lux* v. *Haggin* agreed with this legal shift, difficult questions still remained unanswered. What constitutes a river? How should private property rights deal with environmental change, such as a shift in a river's location? Is nature inherently stable and orderly or random and chaotic? - *enviao unpredictability incorporated into law —> water rights etc,*

WHEN IS A RIVER NOT A RIVER?

From the beginning of litigation in 1879, *Lux* v. *Haggin* served as a public forum for many tensions in the San Joaquin Valley and the Far West: the relationship between landed corporations and small farmers, San Francisco's control of hinterland resources, and riparian versus appropriative water rights.[48] While these highly politicized issues turned *Lux* v. *Haggin* into a case with different meanings for different audiences, a basic question nonetheless remained for the court to decide: What is a watercourse? In order for Miller & Lux (and coplaintiffs) to establish its riparian water rights, the firm had to prove that Buena Vista Slough, which crossed its swampland, was in fact a watercourse. If it was ruled a watercourse, then Miller & Lux was a riparian landowner. Conversely, if Buena Vista Slough was indistinguishable from Buena Vista swamplands—

*- what is a river/watercourse?

if no watercourse existed as Haggin and the other defendants contended—then Miller & Lux had no riparian rights to protect. A river's legal definition therefore stood at the center of *Lux* v. *Haggin*.

Buena Vista Slough's legal status quickly drew all participants' attention, including that of the large entourage of corporate attorneys, newspaper reporters, and public observers who filled district court judge Benjamin Brundage's courtroom in Bakersfield for seven weeks in the spring of 1881.[49] Whereas Haggin's attorneys argued that Miller & Lux could not assert riparian rights because Buena Vista Slough was indistinguishable from the surrounding swampland, Miller & Lux counsel Hall McAllister sought to establish the watercourse's existence as the backbone of the partnership's complaint against Haggin (see maps 5 and 6). Buena Vista Slough, McAllister claimed, "had run from *time immemorial* . . . watering and refreshing these lands and conferring upon them their entire vitality and value."[50] McAllister called witness after witness for Miller & Lux, and they all testified to the slough's permanent characteristics—specifically, its bed, banks, and water flow. They all conceded that Buena Vista Slough traversed a vast swampland, but the swampland, McAllister argued, did not negate the slough's existence. "The swamp district is not a quagmire," he contended, it is orderly and consistent, "traversable both by man and beast."[51] Indeed, the slough was *the* primary component of that natural order.

This theme of nature's inherent order and consistency ran throughout Miller & Lux's case, because the attorneys believed that riparian rights hinged upon a river's fixed location. If a watercourse changed location, so changed the property rights associated with that watercourse. Nineteenth-century American water law, as forged in the humid eastern states, appeared to support such reasoning. A river's legal characteristics seemed clear. "A watercourse consists of bed, banks, and water," wrote Joseph Kinnicut Angell in his prominent *Treatise on the Law of Watercourses.*[52] McAllister cited Angell's definition of a river, noting Angell's important qualifier that "the water need not flow continually; and there are many watercourses which are sometimes dry."[53] Eastern water law spoke to other characteristics of western rivers. The Massachusetts case *McComber* v. *Godfrey* concluded that a river's "well-defined channel" could "spread out over the surface on the defendant's land" to a point where "there was no defined channel." Similarly, the New Hampshire case *Swett* v. *Cutts* separated "boggy or swampy lands" from actual "streams and rivers."[54] In New Hampshire, the latter constituted a legal watercourse; the former did not. Eastern legal precedent therefore

— watercourse defined

recognized the existence of a variety of water systems, from "boggy" places to rivers with well-defined banks. But a *"natural* stream of water" remained fixed in the one location nature had bestowed upon it.[55]

If nineteenth-century water law failed to codify disputes arising from a river's changing its location, the law certainly recognized the ways economic development would impact the nation's rivers. Productivity, maximum use, and private control—these ascendant values underlay the shifting legal terrain governing waterways.[56] Eastern courts strongly endorsed changing the landscape's natural features for manufacturing purposes, and the courts also narrowed the range of compensatory injuries to developers for their actions.[57] Redefining water law for eastern manufacturing purposes only begins to suggest the law's instrumentality in California, where irrigated agriculture emerged as a leading economic sector that was based on the transformation of ecological communities.[58]

Miller & Lux could easily illustrate its need for the river's flow to increase production, but McAllister still had to prove Buena Vista Slough's existence and permanence. To make this case, McAllister described the location of the slough within the entire San Joaquin watershed. Waters "descended" from the Sierra range past Bakersfield "along the course of Kern River, by Buena Vista Slough . . . to Lake Tulare," and eventually flowed into the San Joaquin River.[59] Buena Vista Slough was thus central to this watershed system, and not, as Haggin proposed, simply the overflow of Buena Vista Lake. The slough flowed naturally, McAllister emphasized, and "it [came] annually and regularly."[60] While McAllister argued for Buena Vista Slough's consistency, he explained that nature as a whole was also guided by order. "Nature," McAllister argued, "appropriated these waters long before California was settled [and] *she* fixed the appropriation by the physical features of the country. . . . The whole question is this: Shall this river and this flow of water be left as Nature left it?"[61] Nature, McAllister intimated, was no capricious mistress: "she" did not change her handiwork once completed. Yet the reclamation process by definition altered nature. In fact, it "reclaimed" land from an errant and chaotic nature, from nature gone awry. *—> the flaw in the argument*

In order to resolve this apparent dilemma between reclamation and natural order, both sides in *Lux* v. *Haggin* argued for the superiority of their respective reclamation efforts. McAllister presented Miller & Lux's reclamation as a project that actually *preserved* the integrity of Buena Vista Slough. "You can reclaim this swamp land district," he stated, "without affecting Buena Vista Slough in any way, shape, or manner." Meanwhile, McAllister contended, "the course pursued by [Haggin], as

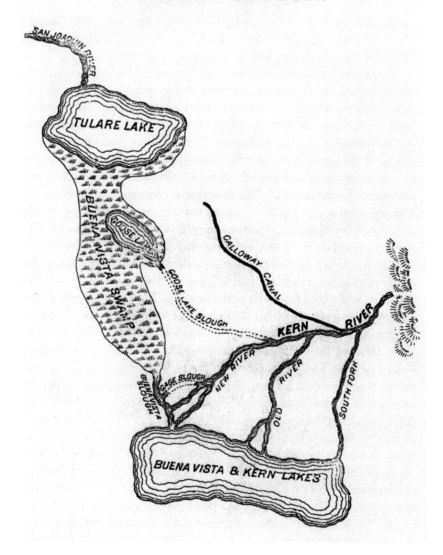

Map 5. *Lux* v. *Haggin* evidence map for the defendants, 1884. Haggin's attorneys depicted Buena Vista Slough as a vast and undefined swampland. Without a defined watercourse, the defendants argued, Miller & Lux could not claim any riparian water rights. (Courtesy of the Bancroft Library, University of California at Berkeley.)

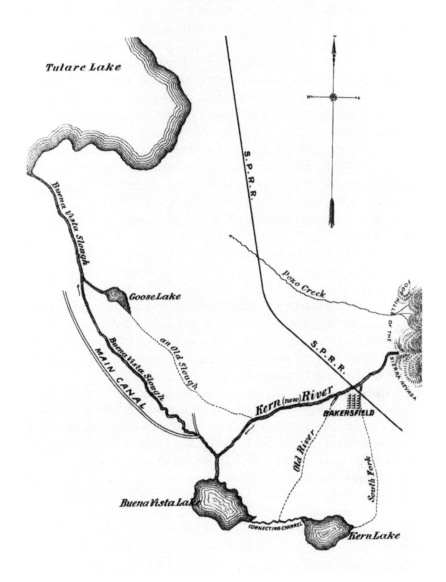

Map 6. *Lux* v. *Haggin* evidence map for the plaintiffs, 1884. Miller & Lux represented Buena Vista Slough as a clearly defined waterway that connected the Kern River and Buena Vista Lake to Tulare Lake. (Courtesy of the Bancroft Library, University of California at Berkeley.)

the testimony shows without contradiction, goes to destroy the Kern River. It goes to fill up the river with sand-bars. It goes to make a growth of willows across the river; it goes to the substantial destruction of the river, and that seems to be the thoughts and intentions of defendants. . . . It will take only a few years to destroy the whole river."[62] McAllister concluded that Miller & Lux's reclamation project would actually preserve the river's location, while Haggin's would fundamentally destroy the watercourse.

James Haggin's co-counsel, John Garber, sought to discredit this preservationist attack. Haggin's appropriations did not destroy the Kern River, Garber argued; the Kern would continue to flow and Haggin's appropriations would assist the "industrious citizens who have thus built up the resources of the State, fertilized its desert wastes, and turned what was a wilderness into a garden spot." It was Miller & Lux's wasteful swampland, Garber argued, that "squander[ed]" the Kern's flow.[63] Denying that any "tangible" stream even existed on Miller & Lux's property, Haggin's other counsel, George Flournoy, stated that "it will not do to regard" such "imaginary channels through low ground and swampy places" as having rights or at least the same rights as those attributed to "a real water course" such as the Kern. Without a "defined, tangible, [and] provable" river, Flournoy concluded, Miller & Lux had no riparian rights for the court to respect.[64]

A series of questions about nature thus stood at the center of this highly politicized water rights battle. What is a watercourse? At what point does a river, stream, or swampy slough cease to be a watercourse? Does nature, furthermore, confer certain rights upon a watercourse or landscape that humans must respect? If the litigants in *Lux v. Haggin* had little concern for preserving nature, they had great concern for how these questions influenced property relations and legal expediency. Neither Lux nor Haggin was suggesting that reclamation—this nineteenth-century crusade to engineer the landscape—should be impeded by notions of nature's autonomy. Nobody believed that a river actually possessed "riparian rights" of its own, as McAllister had rhetorically suggested, least of all Judge Benjamin Brundage. On November 3, 1881, Brundage ruled that "no continuous or defined channel" existed in Buena Vista swamp, and therefore Miller & Lux was not a riparian landowner.[65] Furthermore, Brundage wrote, "the doctrine of riparian law[,] . . . if enforced in the State of California, would condemn to perpetual barrenness nearly the whole of its great interior valleys, and would carry widespread disaster and ruin to many prosperous communities." Irrigation by means of appropriation, he concluded, was "a natural necessity."[66] Haggin had won *Lux v. Haggin*'s first appearance, and his desert must be made to bloom.

Perhaps it should come as no surprise that both sides in *Lux v. Haggin,* as well as the court itself, represented the San Joaquin plains as a consistent landscape, unchanged since "time immemorial." All parties to this conflict were deeply invested in a legal process that recognized absolutes. A person was either a riparian landowner or not a riparian landowner; either a river existed or it did not. The law appeared to have little room for nature's complexity. American jurisprudence, as Hall McAllister had concluded, "is but the refle[ction] of that greater and higher law which controls all nature," and that "higher law" was one of order, not chaos.[67] Accordingly, the Kern County landscape depicted in *Lux v. Haggin* reflected ideas of natural stasis, not natural change.

A closer examination of the Tulare Basin, however, suggests not only that natural change typified this landscape but also that a disorderly nature significantly contributed to the conflict between Miller & Lux and James Haggin. For instance, in 1860 the Kern River ran due south from Bakersfield and emptied into Kern Lake. The overflow of Kern Lake then moved in a northwest direction into Buena Vista Lake, through the Buena Vista Slough swamplands, and eventually into Tulare Lake. But the great flood of 1862, which turned the entire San Joaquin plains into a vast inland sea, also changed the course of the Kern River in a northern direction away from Kern Lake. The Kern River now flowed into the connecting channel between Kern Lake and Buena Vista Lake. The Kern River had not yet completed its northern meanderings. During the winter floodwaters of 1867–68, it again shifted to a different channel that local residents called "New River," and the Kern River's "newest" path emptied into Buena Vista Slough.[68] Like other waterways in the San Joaquin Valley, Kern River altered its course on an episodic basis and had done so from "time immemorial" (in contradiction to Hall McAllister's point). If Miller & Lux's swampland along this slough was riparian by right of its direct connection to Kern River, that riparian status reflected only the most recent incarnation of a constantly changing waterway.

The shifting course of the Kern River was only the most noticeable symbol of the Tulare Basin's dynamic complexity. The landscape's flora and soils, for instance, developed in highly irregular patterns. The wetlands grew thick with a variety of grasses: bulrush, cattail spike rush, sedges, and the tall tule grass from which "tule land" received its name. The remnants of indigenous riparian forest surrounded these wetlands, including trees such as California sycamore, Oregon ash, cottonwood, and willow. As the land transitioned into desert away from the swamps, the plant composition gave way to saltbush and naked alkali soil.[69] An 1880 report on California's irrigation resources by the state engineer William Hammond Hall noted in particular Kern County's diverse soils and plant life.[70] Miller & Lux understood this fact of soil diversity all too well. One of the firm's canal superintendents later testified that Kern County's soils changed radically within a single acre. "Sometimes," he added, "a hundred feet will make a difference [in soil composition]."[71] Thus, rather than a uniform and static landscape, Kern County encompassed a shifting mosaic of plant life, animal communities, waterways, and soils.

When the riparianists took their appeal to the California Supreme Court in 1884, Miller & Lux's lawyers again presented its reclamation enterprise as sanctioned by nature. According to McAllister, Haggin and his appropriators wanted to "carry [the Kern River] thirty miles off ['from where God and nature have placed it'] to make a garden of what nature has made a desert, and to make a desert of [the] plaintiffs' swamp land."[72] Such an appropriation, McAllister argued, violated nature's laws and surely undermined the basis of private property rights. The court moved quickly. Concerned primarily with the urgent question of property rights, the court agreed with Miller & Lux's appeal for riparian rights and overturned the lower court's decision. A rehearing by the supreme court two years later upheld that reversal.

In the supreme court's final decision, Justice E. W. McKinstry affirmed Miller & Lux's riparian rights along Buena Vista Slough, but he also gave hope to appropriators by acknowledging the "public use" of irrigation. Irrigation companies or irrigation districts, he conceded, could condemn riparian rights with just compensation.[73] Engineering the landscape by whatever means most expedient served society's best interest. But what did the court decide concerning that deceptive slough on which so much of this case centered? According to Justice McKinstry, the supreme court "deemed it unnecessary to consider the suggestion . . . that there cannot be a watercourse through swampland."[74] Sometimes a definable watercourse existed, other times not. For McKinstry, it was good enough that Buena Vista Slough *could* have existed at the time of the complaint. "The effect of the evidence," McKinstry wrote, "must depend upon the permanent or transitory nature of the thing itself. . . . We cannot say how long a channel for water will continue."[75] McKinstry all but refuted both litigants' depiction of an orderly landscape.

Nature, McKinstry suggested, did not necessarily reflect the judicial system's desire for stability and permanency. But then how should the legal system mediate competing demands on a river's inconsistent flow? McKinstry sided with the riparian owner. "The right to a watercourse," McKinstry wrote, "begins *ex jure nature,* and having taken a certain course naturally, it cannot be diverted to the deprivation of *the rights* of the riparian owners. . . . The right to the flow of water *is inseparably annexed to the soil,* and passes with it . . . *as a parcel.*"[76] Nature, through its divine plan, had thus decided who would receive its bounty. And as nature changed the Kern River's course, it rewarded those who obtained it "as a parcel" with their land. On the one hand, *Lux v. Haggin* recognized natural change as an unpredictable phenomenon that rewarded some landowners and injured others. But the court also sanctioned the massive engineering project by one of the state's largest landowners, thereby supporting those interests intent on restricting all future natural change. ✱ - a complicated case

Throughout *Lux v. Haggin,* both sides enlisted nature as a witness to defend their water claims on the Kern River. Haggin's counsel contrasted his use of the "real" watercourse to the plaintiffs' "imaginary" one; Miller & Lux argued that it sought to preserve the Kern River "as Nature left it," while Haggin's work would ultimately "destroy the whole river."[77] The most compelling aspect of this discourse—besides its hollow appeals for natural preservation—was the persistent attempt by both sides to construct an intrinsically static model of nature. A river arose from a "permanent source," it flowed "continuously" through "unchanging" banks, and its course remained the same "from time immemorial." The court's decision notwithstanding, this constructed nature proved advantageous for a legal landscape that recognized absolute rights of property and resolved disputes between claimants in the most expedient manner. A stable nature also mirrored and reinforced the plans held by the valley's landscape engineers, who increasingly sought to control natural forces in the coming years. While this view of an orderly nature misrepresented the actual landscape, it did presage the direction that would be pursued by industries built on the land.

THE RECLAIMED LANDSCAPE:
SALINITY, RABBIT SLAUGHTER, AND TULE ELK

In the year following the *Lux v. Haggin* decision, Henry Miller and James Haggin negotiated a private agreement later described by the *Bakersfield Californian* as Kern County's "irrigation bible."[78] This contract guaranteed Miller & Lux a consistent water supply from the Kern River, gave the remaining flow to Haggin and the Kern County Land Company, and the two sides shared the cost of building a holding reservoir.[79] Various factors made such an agreement possible between the courtroom rivals. First, Miller & Lux could not use all of the Kern River's flow. In fact, the river's unrestricted flow during a wet year threatened to devastate the firm's reclamation project. "Such rivers refuse to be governed by the decrees of courts," noted one observer, so the Miller-Haggin agreement attempted to govern a river where court decrees had failed.[80] Second, both sides (and most valley residents) agreed on the fundamental issue of reclamation, because only through reclamation could Californians break "obstinate" nature.[81] Perhaps most important, the Kern County Land Company and Miller & Lux shared a vision of the valley's development. The two San Francisco firms wanted to control the hinterland's agricultural production through landscape engineering, and cooperation between the companies offered the best strategy toward this end.

Engineering the land changed the Tulare Basin in ways that radically altered the landscape's complexity and sustainability. Water diversions from the Kern River and Buena Vista Slough had all but dried out the thirty-mile stretch of wetland that fed Tulare Lake. Once the largest freshwater lake west of the Mississippi River, Tulare Lake evaporated in the following decades.[82] Irrigated fields of alfalfa and grazing cattle, most bearing Miller & Lux's branding mark, replaced the natural diversity that characterized this wetland habitat. The levels of Kern and Buena Vista Lakes also dropped precipitously as a result of land reclamation. Eugene Hilgard, a University of California professor of agriculture, described the effects of such environmental alterations in 1882: "About eighteen months before [I viewed Kern Lake] all the fish and turtles in the lake had suddenly died, creating a pestilential atmosphere by their decay, and even the mussels were mostly dead, a few maintaining a feeble existence. A strong alkaline taste and soapy feeling of the water fully justified their choice of evils. The tule marsh, laid dry by the recession of the lake, was thickly crusted with alkali, and the tules dead. . . . Buena Vista Lake was stated to be in a similar condition, but not yet quite so far advanced in evaporation and still maintaining some animal life in its water, having lost its connection with the river more recently."[83] Kern Lake contained twenty-six times the amount of salt found in "average river water," Hilgard observed, which accounted for the lake's "deadliness."[84]

Presaging one of Miller & Lux's major dilemmas, salinity became a serious problem on the land itself. When levees were constructed for reclaiming swampland or irrigation ditches, the turned-over soils brought extremely high amounts of alkali to the surface. Some of these embankments, Hilgard noted, "appear as though covered with snow, and the alkali can be bodily picked up by the handful." He warned that "the slightest increase" in soil alkalinity posed a distinct danger to the land's productiveness.[85] Many observers who studied the Tulare Basin now cautioned against *overirrigation*, which raised the water table and brought additional salinity to the surface. Such was the problem in Fresno County by the end of the 1880s. According to the state engineer William Hammond Hall, "Water stands on the surface [of the land in Fresno County], rushes grow, mosquitoes breed, malarial fevers abound, and the people are crying for drainage. . . . If irrigation keeps on, the time will come when the whole country will require draining."[86] By 1900, the head of the Office of Irrigation Investigations, Elwood Mead, reported this same problem throughout the Tulare Basin.[87] Some sections appeared as dry as a desert, while salty water inundated other sections.

Swampland reclamation eradicated close to twelve hundred square miles of sloughs, shallow lakes, and marshes in the Tulare Basin. These wetlands had constituted a principal wintering habitat for waterfowl and shorebirds on the Pacific flyway, as well as the natural home for fish, beaver, tule elk, and antelope.[88] The complex flora along these waterways was also devastated. Land companies and settlers cut an estimated fifty thousand acres of riparian forests throughout the southern San Joaquin Valley.[89] This transformation involved not just the disappearance of trees but also the breakdown of ecologically vital floodplain communities. Riparian forests and vegetation constitute a watershed's linchpin; remove that pin and the system can collapse.[90] A disaster in ecological terms, riparian engineering adequately served agriculture's demand for a simplified, single-crop landscape.

Yet single-crop specialization—whether alfalfa, wheat, grapes, or almonds—also created unanticipated results. Crop specialization created ecological openings for undesirable species, and "pests" often thrived and multiplied in the new niche. By the mid-1880s, for instance, the tiny insect phylloxera had diligently consumed a good share of California's grapevines. The spread of intensive agriculture during the next few decades only strengthened the array of pesky insects that attacked California's new crops. Growers, university researchers, and industry responded to this threat by developing deadly pesticides, and a "chemical

shield" soon descended on the state's fields.[91] But the reclaimed and simplified landscape also opened ecological niches for larger-sized pests, and
the four-legged, long-eared variety proved the most tenacious.

Organized rabbit kills, known as rabbit drives, must rank among rural America's most peculiar institutions. In the West, and particularly in
the San Joaquin Valley, rabbit drives became a common community ritual by the late 1880s, due to the species' population growth that resulted
from irrigation and single-crop agriculture.[92] California jack rabbits *(Le-
pus californicus)* ate everything in their path, including alfalfa, wheat,
and the bark from young fruit trees. Quite simply, rabbits began to plague
the San Joaquin's reclaimed landscape and consume the profits of all agriculturalists. Though Indians had hunted rabbits for centuries, William
J. Browning takes credit for the first organized rabbit drive. In April 1880,
Miller & Lux hired Browning to kill rabbits on the Canal Farm near Los
Banos. He constructed a long moveable fence, shaped it into a large V,
and his cohorts drove rabbits into the fence. They killed only 17 rabbits
during two days' work. Browning realized that the fence was not tall
enough, and he needed far more drivers to secure a big kill. But Browning learned from the incident, and the coming years found him in business as a professional rabbit driver. His team could slaughter up to 2,500
rabbits in a single day's work.[93]

The widespread practice of rabbit drives during the 1880s and 1890s
reveals both the continuing ecological threat posed by the species and
the dedicated efforts of San Joaquin residents to eradicate that threat.
Over 155 rabbit drives took place in the San Joaquin Valley between 1888
and 1895; the body count exceeded 370,000 rabbits. Rabbit-driving clubs
formed (the Goshen Rabbit Drive Club, the Pioneer Rabbit Drive Club,
the Grand Army Rabbit Drive Club) to organize the ritual, and urban
"excursionists" received special railroad rates from San Francisco to the
site of particular drives. The San Joaquin town of Travers began cele-
brating its birthday with a rabbit drive and barbecue. Indeed, by 1890
the rabbit drive constituted a community event during which townspeople and farmers slaughtered thousands of the animals. Participants
would gather before dawn, spread out in a long line, and slowly move
across a vast field. Their forward pace accelerated as the rabbits bounded
before their advance. Men and children ran ahead, clapping their hands
and clubbing any rabbits that attempted to cut through the killing line.
The line flanked left and right around the prey, chasing them into a V-
shaped fence that channeled the rabbits into a circular pen. The real

killing began when the pen closed; men and boys clubbed away at the rabbit mass until the work was complete. Sometimes, a photographer documented the slaughter: dead rabbits in the foreground; farmers, laborers, and townspeople posed in the background. Many participants held up their trophies by the ears. A community picnic usually followed.[94] (See figure 6.)

Though brutal and grotesque, slaughtering rabbits represented a methodical and rational response to a formidable foe. Groups of farmers banded together to exterminate a threat, townspeople asserted community cohesion and pride through the ritual, and firms like Miller & Lux and the Kern County Land Company attempted to safeguard the year's cattle feed by killing the pests. On a broader level, rabbit drives comprised one element in the effort to engineer nature. Simplifying the landscape had opened ecological niches and created unforeseeable outcomes. Some wildlife (deer, antelope, and elk) almost disappeared in the reclaimed valley, while rabbits, squirrels, and insects wildly multiplied. Reclaiming the landscape from nature was an unpredictable process with many surprises.

On Buena Vista Slough itself, Miller & Lux reclaimed close to 50,000 acres of wetlands. While constructing a drainage canal in 1877, the firm's work crew discovered a vestige from the valley's past: a pair of tule elk. As noted in chapter 1, the tule elk population had reached five hundred thousand in the valley during the early nineteenth century.[95] But market hunters had decimated the elk population by 1860, and the Tulare Basin's swampland remained their final refuge. In fact, the species was considered extinct in California until the pair of elk appeared at Miller & Lux's reclamation site. In an ironic coincidence of natural despoliation and wildlife preservation, Henry Miller ordered his workers to protect the surviving elk while continuing the reclamation project that ultimately consumed the elk habitat.[96] We can only guess at Miller's motivation for preserving the tule elk, since he left no detailed records of the incident. Most likely, he viewed the tule elk as a symbol of the valley he first visited in 1854—a vast grassland filled with "wild horses and elk . . . running in every direction."[97] This landscape and its plentiful wildlife no longer existed. On a certain level, Miller recognized his firm's responsibility for the vanishing landscape, and he now hoped to safeguard some portion of it. Perhaps the protection he offered the elk represented his reparation.

If Miller & Lux's tule elk preservation and the firm's reclamation

Figure 6. Beginning in the 1880s, "rabbit drives" organized by entire communities attempted to control the agricultural damage caused by these pests. (Courtesy of J. Walter Schmitz III.)

agenda seem contradictory in nature, they sprang from the same impulse. Both actions revealed the effort to create a highly managed landscape, a productive garden where the industrial machine still allowed for some remnants of the natural past. But neither the elk nor the reclaimed landscape succumbed to complete human control. Between 1880 and 1900, Miller's elk increased (on his private reserve) to an unmanageable herd numbering 145 members. Like rabbits, they had become a liability to the firm. On November 12, 1904, Miller & Lux dispatched thirty-five vaqueros to capture the wild elk and transfer them to a holding pen in Sequoia National Park established by the United States Biological Survey. When the vaqueros approached, the herd charged and immediately scattered the experienced riders. The vaqueros roped and hog-tied only 8 tule elk that day.[98] Fighting to the end, only 1 elk submitted to this first attempt at relocation, while the rest of the herd remained free for years to come. (See figures 7 and 8.) – nature was not easy to tame

Containing the Tulare Basin's rivers and swamplands proved equally difficult. When Miller & Lux completed the Kern Valley Water Company canal during the dry year of 1877, the project diverted the waters that would have fed Buena Vista Slough. The canal's solid wood headgate and earthen levees "stood impregnable to the wildest shock," according to Pioneer.[99] So they did until the 1878 floodwater rushed down the Kern River, passed by Haggin's series of diversion canals, and met Miller & Lux's attempt to contain and channel it. The Kern River "roared and surged in tumultuous fury . . . and with appalling impetuosity and velocity [swept] everything . . . that obstructed its onward rush."[100] The middle of the canal headgate splintered into two pieces, and the deluge fractured the canal walls in four separate places. Miller & Lux's superintendent and head engineer, S. W. Wible, reported that this first diversion canal had functioned properly for only three months.[101] In the following decades, despite persistent attempts to control the Kern River and the basin's water system in general, floodwaters continued to ravage the region's lowlands. As late as 1910, the *Bakersfield Californian* complained of the "serious damage" caused by flooding "for the past three years." Echoing its own words of thirty years past, the paper stated, "The future will involve a great deal of expensive work to control the waters of Kern river so as to guard against the great danger of [the county] being overflowed."[102]

The environmental repercussions from landscape engineering interacted dynamically with the region's social tensions. Land reclamation may

Figures 7 and 8.   A small herd of elk found protection on Miller & Lux
land until 1904, when this roundup moved some of the elk to a new wildlife
preserve. Miller & Lux vaqueros hog-tied the elk and then sawed off their
antlers.

have allowed some portions of Kern County to "blossom as the rose," as the *Visalia Delta* had forecast in 1877, but changing the land did not lead to more democratic landownership patterns or the growth of stable, independent communities.[103] Rather, land reclamation only reinforced the position held by San Francisco–based corporations that sought to exploit and export the land's natural resources. During the 1880s, Miller & Lux amassed over 120,000 acres in Kern County, while the Kern County Land Company increased its holdings to 375,000 acres.[104] Miller & Lux's reclaimed region appeared uninhabited to the passerby, the flat landscape interrupted only by the presence of warehouse-size stacks of cut alfalfa. The corporation reduced the tasks of its "irrigators" to the lowest common denominators—maximum feed production and constant cattle shipments north to San Francisco. Haggin, meanwhile, diversified his activities, and according to the *Kern County Gazette*, "it looks very much as if he was fixing himself to stay here."[105] The Kern County Land Company built an immense grain warehouse and mill, a slaughterhouse, and a company store. The company assembled the county's largest herd of cattle. A good portion of Haggin's income derived from selling water to local farmers. The *Gazette* compared Haggin's "extortions" for water to the shipping rates charged by the railroad, concluding that the company's practices were "thinning out the small farmers" south of Bakersfield and dimming the town's outlook as well.[106]

After attending a meeting of local farmers, the former state senator John M. Day concluded that most of the small farmers who had previously sided with Haggin during *Lux v. Haggin* had now turned against him. The principle of water appropriation in Kern County, they realized, lent itself to corporate monopoly as easily as had the law of riparianism. Testifying in Bakersfield before the Special Committee on the Irrigation and Reclamation of Arid Lands in 1889, one farmer explained the lack of morale in Kern County's rural population: "I have 160 acres. . . . We [had] perfected our ditches and paid for our land, but we have been obliged to abandon it because of a lack of water. We are now living on rented land in Bakersfield. . . . The Kern River here is appropriated to a great extent by a large water monopoly, a water company . . . [that proposes] to build a reservoir down at the mouth of the river near Buena Vista Slough."[107] This farmer now produced alfalfa, corn, and wheat on land he rented from the Kern County Land Company. His own land sat fallow, since the waters that previously reached it were diverted to the holding reservoir outlined in the Miller-Haggin agreement. Other landowners recounted similar stories—the irrigation water they once used *just a mean landlord*

"was frequently turned out of the ditch [by Haggin] to prevent [them] from using it."[108]

Signs of community vitality did not look promising in the immediate aftermath of corporate land reclamation. Between 1880 and 1886, the population of Kern County increased only marginally in contrast to eastern Fresno and Tulare Counties.[109] Families with young children fled Kern County, and average school attendance dropped from 649 in 1880 to 246 in 1886. After touring the region surrounding Bakersfield, John M. Day reported his findings: "As near as we could tell, we rode about 20 miles over ground claimed by Messrs. Haggin and Carr. I don't remember seeing a school-house the entire way, and, in fact, very few houses of any kind."[110] Some schools, such as those in the San Emigdio District, shut down entirely.

Corporate reclamation had given the region a "perfect system of irrigation," the *Kern County Record* explained, but it was a system controlled by "non-residents," whose profits did not strengthen the community.[111] "To make good times here," the *Gazette* urged, "[we must have] men who purchase their supplies here, and whose net proceeds . . . are not sent to San Francisco, to be spent there and to swell the millions of that city, thus impoverishing the soil of Kern county." While the Kern County Land Company and Miller & Lux employed hundreds of laborers, "very few of their employees have families, and therefore the wants of families . . . are unknown."[112] Migrant day labor became a fixture on all the large ranches in Kern County. By 1890, Miller & Lux's Columbia Ranch alone employed a male workforce of over 200 hayers, irrigators, and other laborers, who earned less than one dollar per day. The monthly employee turnover rate often reached 50 percent.[113] This irrigated landscape did not offer the social rewards foreseen by William Hammond Hall in 1880. For Hall, irrigation "means not only [the] cultivation of crops, but also [the] cultivation of irrigators."[114] Corporate irrigation in Kern County cultivated a mostly dependent class of irrigators.

moving on to labor

By bringing millions of acres into production, land reclamation initiated a process that ultimately reshaped the face of the American West. Extensive and intensive agriculture thrived as irrigation expanded. The demands for farm labor also increased, bringing tens of thousands of Europeans, Asians, Mexicans, and people of African descent to the West. Reclamation inaugurated fierce competition for the region's water supply, and that competition spilled into corporate offices, government bureaucracies, and the courts. Many of these conflicts emerged in the years following *Lux* v. *Haggin*.[115] But despite the litigants' differences, *Lux* v.

Haggin revealed a desire shared by all Californians to engineer the natural landscape for resource extraction and market production. A leader in these endeavors, Miller & Lux also pioneered the introduction of other factors that soon turned the San Joaquin Valley into the world's most productive, and altered, agricultural landscape. One such factor, and one that united the history of nineteenth- and twentieth-century agribusiness, was the organization of an industrial-sized agricultural labor force. - *lead-in to next chapter*

CHAPTER 5

Laboring on the Land

Industrial change altered Americans' lives in many unanticipated ways. Joseph Warren Matthews, for instance, had to strike out on the "wage-workers' frontier" in July 1893, the same month that Frederick Jackson Turner, speaking at the Chicago World's Fair, explained the "closing" of the American frontier. The fifty-one-year-old Matthews took a temporary job at Claus Spreckels's Watsonville sugar refinery in 1893 but soon left for better pay offered on a nearby ranch. Matthews worked the next two years digging ditches and laying pipe for the Hollister Water Company. "This is my birthday," Matthews scribbled in his diary on June 6, 1896; "I am 54 years old. I worked all day filling in [the] ditch." He earned $18.70 that month from "the Water Co." Eventually laid off, Matthews sought employment wherever he could find it: quicksilver mining in California, wage labor in the Alaskan goldfields, roadwork for a Pacific Northwest lumber company, and ore smelting for the San Jose Copper Company. On March 3, 1899, Matthews hired on to one of Miller & Lux's night irrigation crews. He recorded his wages in his diary: "Accnt. for Miller & Lux, work at 75 cts per day." Now fifty-seven years old, Matthews stayed on the firm's payroll for thirty-eight days and then left for another temporary job at a nearby mine. He died six months later from a work-related injury, having spent his final years earning wages throughout the Far West.[1]

Matthews was no migrant bindle stiff. He had lived in California for forty years before embarking on his itinerant work life, and he owned a

bindle stiff: hobo - named after a bundle carried on a stick

— a mini-migrant of sorts

small farm south of the San Francisco Bay for much of that time. He was a church elder and strong temperance advocate, preaching the virtue of sobriety to friend and foe alike. Bad harvests, declining agricultural markets, and mounting debts during the 1890s financial panic forced Matthews to find employment away from home while his wife, Rebecca, tended their heavily mortgaged farm. On the road, he joined an itinerant labor force gathered from around the world, a group of "hard travelers" who sought a semblance of security in the chaos of western industrial life.[2] That Matthews spent time on a Miller & Lux irrigation crew is not surprising, given the firm's enormous labor force and constant turnover of migrant workers. But this native-born embodiment of the nineteenth-century yeoman stood in contrast to the typical Miller & Lux laborer.

As Miller & Lux developed into a large, vertically integrated enterprise between 1870 and 1900, the firm's workforce grew from 300 to over 1,200 laborers. To fill its constantly changing labor needs, the firm employed migrant, low-wage workers and divided them along racial and ethnic lines. Mexican Americans and Mexican, Italian, Portuguese, and Chinese immigrants each occupied distinct spheres of the unskilled labor force. On one level, racial and ethnic segmentation reflected the firm's attempt to organize a large and potentially unwieldy male population. But on another level, segmentation revealed a corporate ideology that assigned specific characteristics to different groups and reinforced those differences through the reproduction of the workforce over time. Like industrial employers nationwide, Miller & Lux capitalized on immigration trends and separated its workers as a way to avert strikes.[3] Segmentation met these objectives.

— not thrown together as in the mines?

— race tied to type of labor

Consistent employment remained rare for the firm's immigrant laborers. By the 1880s, Miller & Lux began grouping its dozens of ranches into larger corporate divisions in order to organize production and labor needs. The individual ranches hired workers to perform specific tasks for a few days or a few months, at the end of which time they were expected to move on. Through this process, Miller & Lux maintained a mobile, surplus labor pool that filled temporary and shifting needs. The firm increased its labor supply by creating the "Dirty Plate Route," an institutional apparatus that attracted unemployed migrants to the San Joaquin Valley and encouraged their movement from one geographic division to another. But if the prerogative to hire and fire workers resided with Miller & Lux, migrant laborers did not necessarily constitute what has been described as "an unhappy fraternity whose cohering force was a kinship of powerlessness."[4] Some of Miller & Lux's skilled and unskilled workers saw their employment in the most practical terms: the corporation provided plentiful meals and lodging, and workers left with wages in hand. Recent immigrants may have recognized their job as a first step on the wage-labor ladder, a step facilitated by gang foremen who spoke their language and secured them temporary employment. Native-born whites like Joseph Matthews often worked seasonally for Miller & Lux and then returned to their farms with much-needed cash. While Matthews used the firm in this way, Miller & Lux nonetheless represented the industrial forces that had pushed him off his farm, and he died working for one of those industries. Industrial labor did not meet his long-term hope for security.

Beyond such structural characteristics as segmentation and high turnover rates, Miller & Lux's workforce also shows that reclaiming and engineering the Far West's natural landscape was never a fait accompli. Instead, land reclamation necessitated an ever-expanding working population across a vast terrain. Accordingly, Miller & Lux's largest laboring group had little direct contact with livestock but instead found themselves employed in reclamation activities—digging ditches, building levees, running scrapers, constructing irrigation checks, and watering or draining the endless fields of alfalfa. Long hours of arduous work for low wages, often as low as $.66 a day, typified their work experience. Their labor allowed the corporation to take water from a riverbed and spread it across dry land or move mountains of cut alfalfa from one ranch to the next. Human labor, therefore, was the integral link between resource exploitation and large-scale production. Miller & Lux's power ultimately derived from the ability to tap both human and natural energy for its own ends.[5]

CREATING A SEGMENTED WORKFORCE: MEXICAN VAQUEROS

Prior to the mid-1870s, Mexican vaqueros constituted the backbone of Miller & Lux's skilled labor force.[6] Vaqueros performed the corporation's most important tasks: they conducted roundups on the open range, branded entire herds of new cattle, guided them to water and pastureland, separated "killable" cattle from those not ready for market, and drove herds across hundreds of miles to the San Francisco slaughterhouse. Such skills proved instrumental to the firm's survival. The Mexican vaqueros also possessed a detailed understanding of California's natural landscape, particularly those vaqueros who were longtime residents.

Speaking both English and Spanish, they referred to important geographic markers by the Spanish place-names, terms that signified not just a place but a historical and natural landscape.[7] This knowledge of the land informed how they performed various tasks, from finding available pasture in drought years to remembering the only location where cattle could ford a river in high water.

These skills allowed Mexican vaqueros to achieve considerable status during the firm's early years. In 1869 Miller & Lux employed fewer than twenty persons on a monthly "salary" basis, and approximately one-third of these employees had Spanish surnames and worked as vaqueros.[8] While they occupied the lower end of the pay scale, their salaries roughly paralleled those of many Anglo-surnamed employees. Concepción Políto and a man simply listed as "Miguel" occupied the bottom of the pay scale at $35 a month. Numerous vaqueros earned $40 to $50 a month, most likely depending on how long they had worked for Miller & Lux. The firm recorded these earnings as monthly salaries and not daily wages, meaning the corporation recognized them as continuing employees. The highest-paid vaquero was Tomás Díaz, who in 1869 received $80 a month. An employee of Miller & Lux since the late 1850s, Díaz received great respect from other vaqueros and ranchers for his skills and experience. Only four Anglo employees in 1869 earned higher salaries than Díaz. He remained on the firm's payroll for over twenty years, during which time Miller gave him great latitude to conduct the firm's business. Miller granted perquisites to Díaz and other skilled vaqueros that he rarely extended to most employees. In 1874, for instance, Miller instructed Lux to give vaquero David Castro $500 in wages so that Castro could "lay off for a while" in Monterey.[9] Miller met similar requests from most employees with scorn, but vaqueros were not "ordinary" workers. The following year Miller asked Lux to use "ordinary men" instead of vaqueros for unloading cattle boxcars at the Buri Buri station, since he needed all the "best vaqueros" for other duties.[10]

The vaqueros' constant movement throughout Miller & Lux's domain represented another sign of their skilled status—they went where the firm most needed their skills. But this mobility lessened during the following decade. By the late 1870s, Miller & Lux increasingly relied on the railroad for moving cattle to market, and large feedlots began to replace the open ranges of previous years. Vaqueros now worked at a particular ranch and performed the duties required by that ranch. They tended cattle within a space defined by fenced property boundaries and moved cattle to nearby railroad stations rather than distant markets. The vaqueros'

— land development required less skilled vaqueros

skills remained valuable to Miller & Lux, but their knowledge of the land declined in importance as the landscape was fenced, irrigated, and engineered. The ordering of the landscape therefore played a major role in de-skilling the vaqueros' jobs.

Changes in the Mexican population at large also altered the vaqueros' status. During the 1880s and 1890s Mexican nationals increasingly crossed the border into Texas, New Mexico, Arizona, and California, where they filled the lowest unskilled positions in the agricultural workforce.[11] The immigrant population drove down wages for all Mexicans and Mexican Americans, and violence often accompanied their attempts to gain a foothold in the borderland's rapidly developing economy. The wages Miller & Lux paid its Mexican and other Spanish-surnamed employees fell to the lowest pay rate during this period. At the San Francisco slaughterhouse in 1880, for instance, Miller & Lux employed twenty skilled workers at $45 to $130 a month. Five employees earned wages below that pay scale, including the only three Spanish-surnamed workers who tended the "live" cattle. They each brought home $30 a month.[12] In the San Joaquin Valley, Mexicans held only a small fraction of the jobs at Miller & Lux's Firebaugh Division between 1885 and 1895. Most of them appeared on the payrolls for a few months and received $1 a day or less for their labor. The one long-term Mexican employee at Firebaugh during this period, Ferdinand Salvador, worked four months in 1885, two months in 1886, nine months in 1887, all of 1888 and 1889, and then five months in 1890. During these five years Salvador's wages fluctuated between $.77 and $1.00 a day.[13]

By 1900, the firm's percentage of livestock-related jobs in California (jobs held primarily by Mexicans) had declined due to an increased reliance on Oregon-bred cattle. Whereas Mexican vaqueros had once accounted for much of the payroll at the Santa Rita ranch, they became a small minority by the turn of the century. In July 1900, the Santa Rita ranch (the largest ranch in the Los Banos Division) paid out a total of $3,570.05 in wages to its 156 employees.[14] Italian "hayers," "irrigators," and common "laborers" constituted well over half of the workforce. Santa Rita employed nine vaqueros that month, at the bottom of the pay scale ($25 a month); seven were Mexican, and two had northern European surnames. Mexicans were therefore not the only workers handling livestock, but they were hired solely for that one, low-pay position. The livestock skills that had previously earned Mexican vaqueros status in the firm now worked against them as corporate change altered tasks and production.

- Mexicans/hispanics handled livestock

In Miller & Lux's Southern Division after 1900, Mexican employees found themselves segmented by ranch location and job assignment. The Southern Division comprised ten different ranches or camps, and its payroll averaged between $7,000 and $10,000 a month.[15] In February of 1908 the Southern Division employed close to 300 workers (a seasonal low for the year), most of them recent immigrants from southern Europe.[16] Since the Southern Division primarily provided livestock feed for the northern ranches, the largest number of employees worked as irrigators and hayers. Mexican (and likely Iberian) workers held none of these jobs. Instead, they were segmented into "hog" and "cattle" crews at four different work sites, and, with two notable exceptions, they received the lowest wages. The first exception was a man named Valenzuella, whose wife worked as a ranch cook. The Southern Division's bookkeeper listed them together as "Valenzuella and wife, $50." While the other ranch cooks earned between $30 and $55 a month for their labor, the earnings of Valenzuella's wife were simply added to his salary. The few wives who cooked at Miller & Lux ranches never received their own paychecks, and the status of the few other female employees remained marginal at best.[17]

The head vaquero Rafael Cuen, who earned $60 a month, was the second exception. Unlike the vast majority of Mexican laborers, who filled temporary positions, Cuen worked almost four decades for Miller & Lux. Cuen's father had migrated from Sonora to California in 1849 to work in the mines. He soon purchased some cattle and land in Kern County, and, according to Cuen, his wealth grew considerably until the dry year of 1877 devastated his herd. The elder Cuen sold his property, and by 1880 Miller & Lux owned the land. Rafael Cuen worked briefly for Miller & Lux before the Kern County Land Company hired him away. But Miller recognized Cuen's skill with cattle, and he demanded that his Southern Division superintendent rehire Cuen as "vaquero boss." Cuen stayed with Miller & Lux for the next thirty-five years.[18] ✷

Cuen occupied a curious position as a Miller & Lux vaquero boss. While the vast majority of Mexican employees faced worsening conditions— low pay, short periods of employment, and no upward mobility—Cuen held a midlevel managerial position in a corporation run by native-born whites and northern European immigrants. His $60 monthly salary was double that of Mexican laborers, but it nonetheless fell short of the amount paid Anglo managers and skilled workers. Cuen's boss, James Ogden, earned $200 a month, and the carpenters and blacksmiths at the Southern Division received $75 a month.[19] Cuen's rise in Miller & Lux had peaked early despite his many skills. His bilingualism allowed him to mediate relations between management and Spanish-speaking workers; his responsibilities included hiring and firing employees to keep a steady labor pool moving through his department.[20] Though an unenviable task, the evidence suggests that Cuen personalized the process as much as possible. The payroll for Cuen's "Cattle Department" shows a constant repetition of family names, more than occurred at other work sites in the Southern Division. Cuen apparently honored family connections (both Anglo and Mexican) in his hiring practices; this served as both an effective labor recruitment method and a way to humanize an otherwise difficult task.[21]

Cuen's status in the corporation stood in stark contrast to that of other Mexican laborers, who by 1900 were relegated to the workforce's lowest rung. Mexican laborers worked in small crews at most Miller & Lux ranches, their movement closely supervised by Anglo (and a few Mexican) managers. These work conditions had declined during four decades of increasing corporate profits, and they became more prevalent throughout the Far West in the early twentieth century. The 1911 report of the U.S. Immigration Commission concluded that Mexican laborers received the "lowest wage[s]," were "substituted" for "members of other races for unskilled work," and could be "easily made available for work when needed" because of their "migratory" existence.[22] The United States Department of Labor soon formalized this status when it instituted the first bracero program during World War I, bringing over 50,000 Mexican nationals to California and the Southwest as migrant workers between 1917 and 1920.[23] Miller & Lux, attempting to reap some benefit from this policy, petitioned the commissioner of immigration in 1918 for special permission to import its own group of Mexican nationals.[24] Superintendent J. F. Clyne asked for a "first lot" of 500 Mexican laborers to fill the firm's labor shortage and offset wage increases. The Immigration Department denied Miller & Lux's request.[25]

THE "INDISPENSABLE" CHINESE COOKS

In contrast to the experience of Mexican vaqueros, a sizeable number of Chinese immigrants fashioned a particular domain for themselves in Miller & Lux's ranch houses during the years before and after the 1882 Chinese Exclusion Act. While Mexicans tended livestock and ethnic Europeans labored in the fields, the Chinese employees controlled the kitchens that fed the hungry workforce. They remained strictly segregated from other Miller & Lux employees, who worked and shared housing with their compatriots. Chinese cooks, by contrast, were employed individually on ranches far removed from their compatriots.[26] In this isolated and often hostile environment, Chinese cooks nonetheless developed some autonomy. The cooks controlled a defined and separate space (the kitchen) in the ranch houses, and according to many observers, they "ruled [this domain] with an iron hand."[27]

Chinese workers' segmentation into the ranch kitchens transpired during the extreme sinophobia and frequent violence of the 1870s. Denis Kearney's Workingmen's Party in San Francisco represented only the most virulent example of anti-Chinese sentiment on the Pacific Coast. In rural areas, too, "anticoolie" clubs organized against Chinese workers and their migration into the San Joaquin Valley. Large property holders, already under fire by land monopoly critics, faced additional scrutiny for using Chinese labor on construction and reclamation projects.[28] The San Joaquin and King's River Canal & Irrigation Company illustrated this process. When Miller & Lux took control of the canal company's payroll in 1873, Miller hired skilled carpenters at $100 a month and teamsters (with teams) at $80 a month. The actual excavation work, however, fell to large numbers of low-wage, unskilled laborers. To fill this demand, Miller & Lux's office administrator, John Bolton, turned to Ah Yung & Ah Yau, a San Francisco–based labor contractor. Over the next three years Chinese work gangs provided the bulk of manual labor for this largest irrigation canal in the West. Chinese gang labor proved reliable, organized, and self-sufficient. In March 1873, Ah Yung & Ah Yau supplied two large gangs listed as "Big Jim Gangs #1 & #2." Ah Yung & Ah Yau received $27 a month from Miller & Lux for each worker, and the contractor kept a portion of these wages against the workers' debts.[29] By the following summer the canal company's demand for Chinese labor increased dramatically. Seven different Chinese gangs worked on the canal in July 1873, and six additional gangs came the following month. In August, the canal company paid Ah Yung & Ah Yau over $10,000 for approximately 370 Chinese workers. This amount was more than double the combined wages paid to what the company called "white labor."[30]

Chinese laborers' top-down organization proved highly attractive to large employers like Miller & Lux. The labor contractor guaranteed Miller & Lux a specific labor supply, and the built-in structure of laborers, foremen, interpreters, and agents required little outside supervision. But this systematized labor force came with certain risks. Gang labor increased the Chinese workers' ability to organize within their own ranks. During the 1870s, for instance, Chinese workers struck for higher wages against the Central Pacific Railroad, the Pacific Mail Steamship Company, San Francisco's shoe manufacturers, and agricultural employers.[31] Henry Miller dreaded the potential for any of his workers to strike, and this fear contributed to his terminating the Chinese work gangs after the summer of 1873.[32] Miller opposed the decision of the canal company superintendent M. L. Stangroom to rehire Chinese laborers the following year, and in 1876 Miller predicted a "strike for higher wages [among the canal workers] very soon." He devised a simple plan to avert the strike: "If there is some good Italians or Portugese [sic] wanting work," Miller wrote Lux, "send them to Gilroy."[33]

The Chinese workers' ability to organize only increased the widespread racism directed toward them. Miller & Lux's corporate records document the depth of these hostilities. In correspondence, Chinese employees were given such racial monikers as "Farm Chinaman," "Camp Chinaman," and "the China Cook." The firm's payrolls exhibited similar racial thinking: one payroll recorded all "white labor" under the heading "Pay Roll of Men employed on the Works of the SJ&KRC&ICo, for the Month ending . . ." The second payroll kept track of Chinese workers, and to avoid any confusion, the word "Men" was crossed out and "Chinamen" substituted in its place.[34] Employee account books (indexed alphabetically by surname) listed all Chinese employees under the "A's"— "Ah Day," "Ah Lee," "Ah Poy," and so on.[35] Clearly, race constituted the sum of their personal identities to the corporation. Miller's personal opinion of the Chinese—"the Chinese are a necessary evil, if all of our people would work there would be no [need for] Chinamen among us"— represented equal parts racist logic and an attack on free-labor ideology.[36] Though Miller disdained Chinese workers, he could accept their presence in the ranch kitchens, a gendered space avoided by most white workers. "No man with a backbone," Miller concluded, "is willing to do a woman's work on a farm."[37]

By the early 1880s Miller & Lux hired Chinese men almost exclusively to run the kitchens at its various ranches and work camps. "I suppose we have 50 cooks [working for the firm] and there are 49 Chinamen," Miller observed in 1888.[38] Indeed, extremely long hours of hard work in a ranch kitchen rarely enticed anyone with other employment options, and the firm all but excluded single women from its masculine ranch community.[39] The Chinese ranch cooks began work well before dawn and each served three meals a day to dozens of hungry men. They spent their evening hours preparing for the next day's work and usually slept in the kitchen itself. The cooks also washed all dishes, often kept small gardens, butchered animals, ordered kitchen supplies, and tended many other tasks. Miller knew that indolent workers would never survive the job. - *a compliment to Chinese work ethic*

The cooks, such as Ah Jim (see figure 9), lived at a variety of isolated ranch locations. The different ranches in the Dos Palos Division, for instance, regularly employed between 8 and 10 cooks for almost 200 workers. For one payroll period in 1908, Ah Bow served the 12 men at the Dos Palos Farm headquarters; Ah Foo and Ah Quong cooked for 47 workers at Hog Camp; Ah Long fed the North Camp's 19 laborers; Ah Hee served 23 at Dos Palos Camp; and the Dutch Boys Camp of 35 Italian laborers employed G. Bandoni, one of Miller & Lux's few non-Chinese cooks. The remaining workers in the Dos Palos Division also ate at one of these ranches. Although Ah Bow held the least demanding position—serving the division superintendent and 11 skilled workers in the headquarters ranch house—his skills likely earned him that post. He probably spoke English fluently, cooked well, and could cope with Henry Miller's frequent visits and constant stream of instructions. In 1908, Ah Bow received $55 a month compared to the $40 a month earned by the other cooks.[40]

Between 1880 and 1910, the average salary paid to Chinese cooks rose by 25 to 30 percent. Before 1895 their wages remained fairly stagnant at $25 to $30 a month, with a few cooks earning $35 or $40 a month. Such wages, however, contributed to a high job-turnover rate, *- still a high turnover* and the majority of Chinese cooks employed between 1885 and 1895 stayed for less than six months. Gee Lee, for example, received stage fare from San Francisco to Firebaugh on October 11, 1885, worked for one month and left Miller & Lux with $25 in his pocket. He likely went in search of better pay. By contrast, Ah Lett and Ah Louis stayed for nearly five years, perhaps because they each received $35 a month.[41] By the turn of the century the wages paid to Chinese cooks had increased on average by $5 a month, and by 1910 most earned upward of $40 a month. Like Ah Bow at the Dos Palos Farm, the three top cooks in the Southern Division headquarters each earned $55 a month.[42]

These rising wages show that Chinese cooks remained in great demand throughout California, and that they could bargain effectively with their feet.[43] If Miller & Lux would not meet their individual wage demands, they sought employment elsewhere. Chinese cooks expressed their limited power in other ways as well. As will be discussed later in this chap-

Figure 9.   Miller & Lux hired Chinese workers only as ranch cooks.
This photograph, captioned "Ah Jim, 95 years old, Chinese Ranch Cook,"
appeared in H. A. Van Coenen Torchiana's 1930 novel, *California Gringos,*
based on Miller & Lux.

ter, Miller & Lux began a policy during the 1870s of feeding tramps and
wandering laborers at their ranches. The cooks immediately complained
about the increased workload. In particular, they objected to washing
the extra dishes used by the unemployed migrants, and they ultimately
refused to do so.[44] Thereafter developed the Dirty Plate Route: tramps
still received a free meal at Miller & Lux ranches, but the food arrived
on the dirty plates of employees who had finished their food. Miller
agreed with this expression of frugality by the Chinese cooks because it
reserved more of their labor for paid employees and also humbled the

hungry bindle stiffs. But the cooks' refusal to wash certain dishes was likely a protest directed more against their employer than against the wandering poor. The act expressed their way to manage an otherwise hostile work environment.

Miller & Lux's limiting of Chinese workers to a particular job (and a circumscribed space) resulted from various factors: popular antipathy to Chinese labor in rural California, the firm's fear of their organizational potential, the gendered nature of kitchen work, and the Chinese workers' ability to manage the demands of a ranch kitchen. Within this position, Chinese cooks secured some control over their employment conditions and increased their wages. But the same corporate racialism that segregated the Chinese laborer into the ranch kitchen also excluded him from all other jobs. There were no Chinese vaqueros, Chinese irrigators or hayers, and certainly no Chinese managers. For Miller & Lux, the Chinese as a race were cooks.[45] On a certain level, labor segmentation functioned by its own racist logic and perpetuated itself through years of practice. - *Chinese = cook to Miller & Lux*

"A MORE DESIRABLE LABORING POPULATION": ITALIAN IMMIGRANTS

Miller & Lux used the term "white labor" during the 1870s to designate all non-Chinese workers. This essentialist construction of race spoke more to Chinese immigrants' stigmatization than to a "white" labor identity shared by European immigrants and native-born Anglos. When Miller & Lux stopped employing Chinese laborers for positions other than ranch cook, the term "white labor" lost its resonance and subsequently disappeared from company records. Swelled by recent European immigrants, the labor force assumed new ethnic and racial dimensions in the 1880s and 1890s. While Chinese workers cooked and Mexicans tended livestock, European immigrants provided the bulk of manual labor for the firm's California properties. Italians, a group often overlooked in studies of California farm labor, increasingly filled Miller & Lux's payrolls. By 1900, they constituted the firm's largest and most segmented group of European workers.

The first significant immigration wave from Italy to the Pacific Coast coincided with the drive for Chinese exclusion. California's Italian population increased by 61 percent (4,660 to 7,537) during the 1870s, and during the following decade the number of Italian immigrants increased by 105 percent, to 15,495. The state recorded over 63,000 Italians by

1910.[46] Like the Chinese before them, many Italians worked as truck farmers in San Francisco or in mining, the fisheries, or agriculture. Italians gradually displaced Chinese laborers in each work sector. By the century's turn, Italians supplied a significant share of commercialized agriculture's labor demand, fulfilling the racist call by the *Pacific Rural Press* for "a more desirable laboring population."[47] Employers like Miller & Lux found that Italian immigrants perfectly solved their labor needs. These people migrated from the city to the country for seasonal employment, established their own job recruitment networks, and worked for wages below those paid to native-born Americans.[48] Their experience with Mediterranean crops and arid landscapes also made them highly "desirable" for California growers and ranchers.

More than any other group, Italians filled Miller & Lux's ongoing requirements for reclamation and landscape engineering. One brief example: in December 1875 heavy rains inundated the San Joaquin River and threatened to destroy the firm's new reclamation project on the Chowchilla Canal, which ran north from the San Joaquin River across Fresno County. Charles Lux dispatched the young engineer J. W. Schmitz to the thirty-mile-long canal, and Schmitz arrived just as the San Joaquin River broke through the main headgate. Schmitz reported that "Dam No. 1" was missing a forty-foot section, and "it will not take long for the whole [dam] to go." He predicted that "the water will continue to cut away the land at such a rate that before many months a great share of the San Joaquin River will be in the [reclaimed region of] Lone Willow Slough." Schmitz requested a labor force to prevent the inundation of the firm's reclaimed area, and Miller surveyed the groups available for the job. When the river subsided, Miller sent for Italian and Portuguese laborers from San Francisco.[49]

This washout on the Chowchilla Canal was not an isolated incident. On the contrary, nineteenth-century reclamation projects demanded constant upkeep in the attempt to control natural forces. Miller & Lux's Chowchilla Canal, Buena Vista Canal, and San Joaquin Canal—not to mention the entire Sacramento–San Joaquin Delta region—all experienced periodic destruction by the valley's hydrologic cycles. Such occurrences underscored the centrality of human labor to landscape engineering. As Miller & Lux expanded its reclaimed acreage and exploited the land for alfalfa and grains, the firm's dependency on immigrant labor increased accordingly. Italians filled much of this need. They worked primarily as irrigators, scrapers, diggers, and general laborers, performing the tasks that defined the reclamation process. Joseph Warren

Matthews described this labor-intensive process for an 800-acre alfalfa field in 1899:

> First the land has to be surveyed off so as to tell where to excavate the ditches and throw up the levies so as to irrigate the whole of the land. These ditches and levies are then excavated . . . by ditching machines each drawn by ten mules, then the high places are plowed and scraped off so as to level up the land inside of each check. Then follows the Stockton gang plows and each check is plowed separately to keep from tearing the levees down, then comes the seed sower which sows a light seeding of barley which is harrowed in[;] then follows the seed sower which sows the alfalfa seed on the same land to be followed by other harrows for covering it. Then follows the box hole diggers who dig holes in the canals for putting in lumber gates for damming up the water for flooding the land, then comes the carpenters box and bridge builders, then the boxes have to be filled around with dirt and puddled in with water.[50]

— labor a necessity

He estimated that 60 to 70 men and almost 250 animals worked on this one site alone. Multiply an 800-acre field by the hundreds of thousands of acres reclaimed by Miller & Lux, not to mention the millions of irrigated acres across the Far West, and one can appreciate the labor needed to reclaim the landscape.

If reclaiming the 800-acre area required such a work crew, *keeping* the land reclaimed was equally labor intensive. Earthen dams, levees, and checks experienced continual erosion from irrigation. Seepage under a levee's "toe" would force it to settle lower in the soil, while excessive flooding or heavy rains would erode the levee's "crown."[51] Consequently, earthen levees needed constant shaping and augmentation. The irrigation process itself also demanded close attention. Italian irrigators operated the check gates, dug out obstacles to ensure proper water flow, repaired levees and checks, and leveled the ground to prevent waterlogging in depressed places. As the firm's irrigation systems expanded, Miller & Lux's crews worked day and night to maximize water use. "Irrigated all night," Matthews scribbled in his diary after one shift. "In looking around at night one can see the gleam of [workers'] lanterns in every direction."[52]

Beyond irrigation work, Italians also served as mowers, hayers, pitchers, and stackers and performed other tasks related to the large-scale production of cattle feed. After horse-drawn mowers cut the grass, work teams immediately pitched the hay into "shocks" (or piles) to reduce exposure to sunlight. Teamsters then collected and delivered the shocks to central hay-stacking sites. Horse-powered derricks, attached by cable to three-pronged Jackson Forks, lifted the hay high in the air.[53] The resulting rectilinear haystacks often exceeded fifty feet in height. These towering monuments to irrigation covered Miller & Lux properties; on a yearly basis, the corporation cut and piled hay by the tens of thousands of tons. At any given time, Miller & Lux reported (for tax assessments) between $30,000 and $50,000 worth of hay stockpiled in reserve at their California ranches alone. The actual value of the firm's stockpiled feed far exceeded this amount.[54]

Italian hayers and irrigators earned on average $1 a day. This pay rate fluctuated with the labor supply, and it also varied by season. The bottom end of the pay scale fell to $.77 (and sometimes $.66) a day during the winter months, when farm labor was most plentiful. The hot summer months, by contrast, required that Miller & Lux pay at least $1 a day to fill its payrolls. Like other immigrant laborers, Italians came and left Miller & Lux's employ on a regular basis. For example, Ansana Cigarelli began working for the firm in 1885, and he worked until mid-1886, earning $1 a day, averaging twenty-four days a month. Cigarelli returned in 1887 and soon thereafter began receiving a $30-a-month salary. For Italian workers, a monthly salary designated a crew boss position. Cigarelli's salary increased to $35 a month in 1890, and it increased again in 1893 to $40 a month.[55] Apparently, Cigarelli had proven his worth. He spoke English to Anglo managers and Italian to his workers. But language skills guaranteed upward mobility to only a few of Miller & Lux's immigrant workers. Other Italians learned English in order to leave Miller & Lux. Dominick Petrucelli worked as a hayer for four years until he "could talk good enough to get another job," and he found work with the Southern Pacific.[56] Ansana Cigarelli's position also required that he maintain a steady work crew. Family connections served him well in this regard: the Firebaugh payrolls recorded five other Cigarellis during Ansana's tenure as foreman, and the surnames Cognotti, Toscano, Marino, and Mandoli each appear three to five times on his work crew.[57] The wages remained low for all these Italian workers, as Miller & Lux paid well below the rates offered in canneries, mines, and fisheries. But for newly arrived male workers who hoped for landowner-ship and valued the companionship of their countrymen, Miller & Lux was a place to start. They worked for a few months at various ranches and then sought higher wages elsewhere.

California's Italian population increased by 179 percent (to 63,601) during the first decade of the twentieth century, while the number of Italians living in the San Joaquin Valley more than tripled.[58] Simultaneously, Miller & Lux's payrolls topped 1,200 workers in 1900, and the annual expenditure for labor neared $1 million by the decade's end.[59] The work-force in Merced and Fresno Counties, containing over half of the firm's laborers, became increasingly Italian. For example, the Dos Palos Division employed 187 workers in July of 1901, and 100 of them (53 percent) were Italian. By 1908, 155 of the 195 Dos Palos workers (or 79 percent) were Italian. A few of them worked alongside native-born whites (like Joseph Matthews) or immigrants from Germany, Ireland, and Portugal. But the vast majority of Italians in the Dos Palos Division were segmented into four particular work sites—Parson Place, North Camp, Dutch Boys Camp, and Hog Camp.[60] Like their compatriots on other Miller & Lux ranches, they produced cattle feed and tended the ever-expanding irrigation systems.

The persistent segmentation of Italian workers between 1880 and 1910 illustrates Miller & Lux's desire for an orderly, self-replacing workforce that responded to immediate labor needs. Italians immigrated to California in large numbers at the exact moment when Chinese workers faced exclusion from the primary sectors of the workforce. Italian immigrants were disproportionately single, male, and unskilled, making them ideal recruits for Miller & Lux. When they found better jobs, other Italian immigrants filled their places. Segmentation also capitalized on the internal dynamics of the Italian laboring population. Italians formed their own employment networks based on family, regional place of origin, and frequent migrations from city to country for employment options.[61] Miller & Lux fostered such migrations by providing only temporary employment. For recent immigrants, segmentation created a familiar work environment that compensated to some degree for the low wages and inconsistency of work. Finally, the increase of Italian immigrants at the turn of the century coincided with the firm's demand for additional reclamation workers—jobs already designated for Italians. — *jack of all trades*

As revealed by the experiences of Mexicans, Chinese, and Italians, dividing the workforce was not simply about segregating social groups. Segmentation treated groups as independent components of a larger production process: it rationalized wage differentials, divided skilled from unskilled labor, and structured work crews. As a group, Chinese workers increased their wages moderately without increasing their representation in the workforce. Mexicans, on the other hand, experienced declining wages and shorter periods of employment. Italians increased rapidly their representation in the labor force without appreciable gains in their work conditions. None of these groups, however, advanced into the upper ranks of management. *↳ how each group progressed*

Yet many native-born Americans and northern European immigrants also did not attain management positions with the firm. Even German immigrants, a group Miller & Lux favored for its top ranks, often found their upward mobility halted for personal reasons or simply because of the oversupply of qualified employees. Many sought better work elsewhere, while some Germans continued as common laborers despite their growing resentment against the firm. Such was August Koenig's case. Koenig, a German immigrant, began working for Miller & Lux in the mid-1880s, and his name frequently appeared in the firm's account books between 1885 and 1900. He earned $1 a day before quitting in September 1886, worked four months in 1887, six months in 1888, and then the first four months of 1890. Koenig worked at the Davis Ranch in the Firebaugh Division and usually took one-third of his monthly wages in merchandise at Miller & Lux's company store in Firebaugh.[62] Later circumstances suggest that whiskey was his preferred merchandise.

On Sunday, April 27, 1890, Koenig returned to the Davis Ranch from a day spent drinking in Firebaugh. According to the *Fresno Evening Expositor,* he arrived "worse for liquor, and invited the boys with whom he worked to join him in emptying a gallon demijohn [of whiskey]." Koenig became a "raving maniac" and soon "swore vengeance against everyone on the ranch."[63] Grabbing his pistol, Koenig went in search of Henry Miller and ranch superintendent E. L. Davis. Another laborer disarmed him, but Koenig soon reappeared, this time brandishing a shotgun. "You have taken my pistol," Koenig exclaimed, "but I'll kill Miller or Davis before night! I'll kill both of them!" When he could find neither Miller nor Davis, Koenig turned his anger on the next symbol of Miller & Lux management, ranch foreman Henry Berger. Koenig raised and fired his shotgun, "and Berger dropped dead with a charge of buckshot in his breast."[64] The *Expositor* relished the events that followed. Koenig "struck out across [a] field" and wandered until nightfall, when a well-armed posse found him hiding in a patch of high grass. There, western-style justice took its course. Koenig apparently threatened his pursuers, but before Koenig could act they shot him in the head. Constable J. J. Mullery took the wounded man back to Fresno, and by the following day, Koenig lay dying in the county jail. "If Henry Miller had been on the Davis ranch yesterday," concluded the *Expositor,* "he would in all probability have been dead today."[65]

The industrial West had no lack of murder and violence. From the labor wars in the Coeur d'Alene mining region to the pitched battle in the

San Joaquin's Mussel Slough area between Southern Pacific henchmen and disgruntled settlers, violence permeated the West's incorporation.[66] While Koenig's action was certainly not the first such violent outbreak on a Miller & Lux ranch, it did contain particular significance. Koenig reportedly "swore vengeance against everyone" around him, but he directed his anger against only the firm's managerial class. When he could not find Henry Miller or E. L. Davis, Koenig killed the management's next available representative, the unfortunate Henry Berger. The *Expositor* had described Koenig as simply "a German laborer" whose drunkenness led to the violent act. But Koenig was also a longtime employee. He had worked periodically for Miller & Lux for over five years, yet he still earned only $1 a day. Like the vast majority of the firm's day laborers, he had failed to enter the managerial ranks. Koenig probably appreciated the parallels between Miller and himself—the two German immigrants bore a striking resemblance and shared common hopes for success in the United States.[67] But while Miller had prospered, Koenig remained just one of a thousand other immigrant laborers who never attained wealth. Henry Berger's murder, the *Expositor* announced, was "the Wicked Work of August Koenig."[68] A more complete explanation was that Henry Berger had stood in the place of Koenig's true target, Henry Miller. _ lone wolf labor uprising

ON BINDLE STIFFS AND BUTCHERTOWN

From the San Joaquin's irrigated fields to the fetid Butchertown killing floors, Miller & Lux workers performed the many tasks that turned hinterland resources into slabs of cut meat for the city's hungry consumers. Human labor therefore mediated the connection between city markets and hinterland resources. This production system drew upon all of the firm's accumulated assets and interests. Land and water rights secured unencumbered access to resources; landscape engineering maximized cattle and feed production; vertical and horizontal integration brought disparate corporate functions into a dynamic whole; and increasing consumer demand drove the firm's expansion from San Francisco across the San Joaquin Valley and soon into Oregon and Nevada (see chapter 6). While the components of Miller & Lux's system may have differed from those employed by the nation's most celebrated industries, it nonetheless shared many characteristics with other modern enterprises. Minimizing labor costs and stabilizing the workforce represented a key com-

monality. Miller & Lux controlled labor expenses in the countryside by
tapping into a constant flow of migrant workers, and the firm encouraged this flow through the Dirty Plate Route.

Bindle stiffs, tramps, hobos, hard travelers, migrant laborers—the terms
all signified the wandering unemployed that inhabited the nation's rural
areas during the late nineteenth century.[69] Red Lizard, a rail-riding hand-
out-seeking rover, embodied one sort. He crisscrossed the West and frequently hit the Dirty Plate Route with fellow travelers such as Spoonbill,
Seldom-Seen Murphy, Gunnysack Swede, Holy Joe, and D.C. Slim. Red
Lizard enjoyed the route and characterized it as a luxury that "had no
equal in life's poker game for a man without a pair."[70] A man like Joseph
Warren Matthews represented a different traveling type in the San
Joaquin Valley. Matthews, the farmer-turned-migrant-laborer, received a
few free meals on the route until he found a Miller & Lux ranch that
needed his labor. He worked six weeks on a night irrigation crew, sent
home his wages, and then struck out in search of better employment.[71]

Miller & Lux developed the Dirty Plate Route in response to people
like Red Lizard and Matthews. By the mid-1870s, wandering laborers
and tramps filled California's interior valleys, and according to the *San
Francisco Bulletin,* "the evil [they represent] is assuming large proportions."[72] Many rovers deliberately searched for work. The worst elements sabotaged railroad lines, begged meals, burned barns, and created a "serious nuisance" to citizens and property alike. Few residents
attempted to distinguish the "careless rover" from the worker actually
desiring employment, a problem only exacerbated by the large number
of migrant harvesters and threshers seasonally employed on large-scale
Central Valley wheat operations.[73] Miller & Lux, like other ranchers,
viewed the wandering unemployed as a grave threat to its property. They
could drive off cattle, pull down fences, or leave cattle gates open. Miller
particularly feared the intentional or unintentional burning of haystacks,
an act that would only increase in regularity if he did not generate good-
will among the migrants. Feeding tramps at the firm's ranches seemed
an acceptable expense for insuring the protection of both cattle and
haystacks.

By the 1890s, Miller & Lux often fed up to 800 migrants a day at two
dozen different ranch houses. Some bindle stiffs took the "grand whirl"
throughout Miller & Lux's "entire reservation," receiving their free meal
at one ranch before ambling off to the next one. Others limited themselves to an "inside whirl" or "southern whirl," thereby accepting the
firm's generosity in just one part of the San Joaquin Valley.[74] The meals

varied little: plentiful beef, boiled potatoes, and sometimes fruit or vegetables from the ranch garden. The dining procedure varied even less. The tramps waited for Miller & Lux workers to eat and vacate their seats—leaving the dirty plates behind—at which time first-come, first-served ruled the dining hall. The Chinese cooks managed this procedure, and by one account, "the China cook gets after [the tramps] if they attempt to crowd in among the work hands."[75] After meals, the employees returned to work or the bunkhouses while the unemployed moved on to their roadside "roosts" or the ranch barn. Those actually seeking work could gather leads at the ranch house from the foreman or fellow rovers. The true tramp rarely signed on for consistent work, but he did occasionally labor long enough to "choke off a piece of booze money." Everyone in the valley understood the Dirty Plate Route's preventive function, as set in verse by one frequent traveler:

Here's to Uncle Hank, who lets us satisfy
The belly chiefly, not the eye.
Keeping the barking stomach wisely quiet,
Less with a neat than a needful diet
For he, from sad experience knows,
The hungrier man gets, the more desperate he grows.[76]

The Dirty Plate Route's second, and possibly more important, rationale was aimed at the firm's own employees. Miller & Lux maintained three objectives in relation to its unskilled laborers: to keep wages as low as possible, to limit overall labor costs by hiring workers according to daily demands, and to prevent all possible strikes for higher wages. These objectives demanded an ever-present reserve pool of laborers that could fill shortages caused by employees walking off the job. The firm's geography worked against this goal, especially in the San Joaquin Valley, where vast distances separated the properties, and labor shortages could arise on short notice. The Dirty Plate Route resolved these risks by guaranteeing an unemployed army streaming across Miller & Lux lands. For every dozen bindle stiffs like Red Lizard who entertained few thoughts of working an irrigation shift, there were a few laborers like Joseph Matthews whom the firm could count on for temporary work. In the end, the migrants' constant presence—whether they intended to work or not—served Miller & Lux's goal by reminding employees of their replaceable status and insecure existence.

Feeding tramps and migrant workers was nothing new in rural America. The Dirty Plate Route simply institutionalized and capitalized on what many rural Americans had practiced for over a century. That Miller

& Lux formalized this vestigial practice is hardly surprising, given both the threat vagrants posed to property and the opportunity wandering laborers offered the firm for controlling labor costs. In this light, the Dirty Plate Route represented a highly rational response to existing social and economic conditions. It kept wages in check and permitted Miller & Lux to maintain a large portion of its workforce as day-to-day laborers. Furthermore, it allowed the firm to avoid the periodic labor shortages experienced by many California growers at the turn of the century.[77] If Miller & Lux's labor system, as one former superintendent wrote, "was vicious and bred industrial oppression on a large scale, with the accompanying resentment and hatred," such hostilities only sporadically and incidentally impacted the firm's hinterland production.[78] The Dirty Plate Route proved itself effective in this regard.

At the opposite end of Miller & Lux's production chain—San Francisco's Butchertown—lay the more familiar urban industrial landscape. Located on a wharf over San Francisco's southern tidelands at Islais Creek, the slaughterhouse plants sat above the discarded offal from millions of butchered animals. From this mass of death and decay, according to one city health inspector, rose "the most revolting and noisome of effluvia."[79] Despite its questionable health conditions, Butchertown thrived as the largest meatpacking district west of Chicago's Union Stockyards. Cattle and other livestock arrived in Butchertown from all over the Far West. Some meatpacking firms, such as Miller & Lux, operated their own integrated systems of cattle production, disassembly, and marketing. Other meatpackers, such as Henry Levy Wholesale Butchers, Roth & Blum, and Brandenstein Brothers, purchased livestock from middlemen or direct from California ranchers. The city's retail butchers, meanwhile, took pride in their business relationships with the local packinghouses, certain that they marketed the best meats nationwide. San Francisco consumers also placed confidence in Butchertown's products, even if they avoided Butchertown itself like the plague. By 1900, San Francisco had sustained an independent meatpacking sector for fifty years.[80] That regional independence would soon change.

Though a landscape of death for cattle and other livestock, Butchertown was also a landscape of labor. Miller & Lux's Butchertown workforce remained fairly small until the mid-1880s. Only 20 employees labored in the cattle yard or on the killing floors in June 1880. Mexican Americans filled most of the unskilled jobs tending livestock and earned $30 a month, while native-born whites and northern European immigrants earned between $45 and $150 a month inside the slaughterhouse.

Almost half of the payroll went to 6 skilled workers (earning between $100 to $150 a month) who constituted the "butcher aristocracy": the "floorsman" removed the steer's hide, the "cattle splitter" cut the carcass in half, while the "backers" and "rumpers" cleaved the halves into manageable pieces. The second-tier skilled workers received appreciably lower wages than the aristocracy, from "George" the "hog man" at $50 a month, up to W. Sweeny, who earned $85 a month for "snatching" guts and "pulling" internal organs.[81] In contrast to the San Joaquin Valley wage scale, Miller & Lux paid good monthly salaries to maintain a stable slaughterhouse labor force, where personnel changes could upset the killing floor's dismembering rhythm. By means of comparison, these 1880 wages roughly paralleled other San Francisco employers' pay scales for both unskilled and skilled workers, and likely exceeded the slaughterhouse wages in Chicago's Union Stockyards.[82]

From a monthly payroll of $1,445 in 1880, Miller & Lux's slaughterhouse payroll quadrupled by 1900 and peaked at $16,684 a month during the following decade. The firm now supplied a much larger San Francisco Bay Area market, and the firm's annual kill increased from 83,332 animals (cattle, sheep, and hogs) in 1881 to 988,357 animals in 1912.[83] Equally important, slaughterhouse workers now performed a multitude of in-house tasks previously handled by outside shops, from sausage making and lard production to fertilizer preparation and hide curing. Significant wage differentials accompanied the workforce expansion: the 5 foremen and top superintendent took home monthly salaries averaging $160, while the semiskilled and unskilled workers received *weekly* salaries ranging from $7 to $35. Calculated at a monthly rate, their average salary was $64, actually *less* than the average wage paid in 1880. Miller & Lux's weekly employees experienced frequent layoffs, evidenced by the firm's refusal to pay them a monthly salary. Nationwide packinghouse trends reflected Butchertown's worsening labor conditions. The Chicago stockyard's workforce increased by 800 percent between 1870 and 1890, but the percentage of skilled "regular" employees sharply declined while the number of unskilled temporary workers rapidly increased.[84] In both Chicago and San Francisco, economies of scale and task coordination allowed the firms to develop greater labor controls. Packinghouses in both cities also vigilantly opposed organized labor's attempt to reverse this trend.

Miller & Lux experienced few challenges from organized labor in the hinterlands. A steady turnover of immigrant workers, the firm's segmentation practice, and the flow of unemployed migrants directed by the

- labor unity a problem in Butchertown (handwritten margin note)

Dirty Plate Route all diminished rural workers' ability to undertake group action against their employer. San Francisco was a different story. Between 1880 and 1920, organized labor turned San Francisco into a union stronghold through a succession of centralized labor federations: the Trades Assembly, the Knights of Labor, the San Francisco Labor Council, and, perhaps the nation's most successful federation, the Building Trades Council.[85] Workers in manufacturing, construction, the shipyards, breweries, restaurants, and a dozen other trades made appreciable gains in wages and work conditions as San Francisco employers reluctantly recognized their workers' combined strength. The city's fledgling retail Butchers' Union, however, met constant opposition from Miller & Lux and other meatpackers who formed the Wholesale Butchers' Association. During a peak of citywide union activity in 1901, Miller & Lux and other packers refused to supply meat to retail markets that displayed union house cards in their windows, forcing the Butchers' Union to back down on this organizational tactic. In Butchertown itself, Miller & Lux consistently fired suspected union members, and in 1911 the firm locked out employees who sought an eight-hour workday to replace Miller & Lux's standard twelve-hour day.[86] The packinghouses kept Butchertown union-free, but this tactic would soon alienate the city's butchers who had new supply avenues.

A Butchertown devoid of organized butchers; rural workers searching the countryside for a traditional rural order; livestock fattened on hinterland resources only to be disassembled from tail to tongue; and urban consumers who appreciated their Sunday roast far removed from Butchertown or Buena Vista Slough's irrigated fields—modern industrial enterprise fostered deep tensions throughout society while it simultaneously obscured the connections between production and consumption.[87] Not coincidentally, those who labored in the fields or slaughterhouses held the best view on those linkages. Joseph Matthews painstakingly described the reclamation process for an 800-acre field that would soon produce alfalfa for dairy cows; two weeks later he detailed the inner workings of the company's large creamery. Ted White witnessed Butchertown's gruesome activity for years: "dead dropping" the steers on the killing floor and "hearing the whine and the pain" of endless livestock as they were slaughtered for the city's consumers. "It gets through to you," concluded White, who spent his later years as a union organizer.[88] As workers deeply enmeshed in certain tasks, Matthews and White understood not only the relationship between labor and capital but also the connections between hinterland production and city markets.

good section on the experience/understanding of workers (handwritten margin note)

PROFITS AND PROBLEMS:
THE COMPANY AND ITS WORKFORCE

By 1900 Miller & Lux had become the nation's largest integrated cattle and meatpacking enterprise. Chicago's "Big Five" meatpackers processed far more livestock than Miller & Lux, and the Texas-based XIT ranch likely ranged more cattle. But Miller & Lux's scale and scope, with its dozen subsidiaries, set the corporation apart from all competitors. Beyond its enormous assets in property and water, the firm's 1905 inventory counted 122,165 head of cattle, 98,910 sheep, 16,159 hogs, and 5,361 horses in California, Nevada, and Oregon. The estimated value of livestock came to $3,793,403.36, a figure not including the small amount ($30,683.36) of stock already disassembled in San Francisco and Oakland. Corporate sales that year had been exceptional. "Dressed meats" alone brought in $2,483,167.44, up from $2,002,457.55 in 1899. Grain and wool sales in 1905 accounted for almost $200,000, and the value of meat by-products alone was double that amount.[89] In the year before the great earthquake leveled San Francisco and fire incinerated the city—including Miller & Lux's headquarters and slaughterhouse— the future appeared promising. That outlook would soon change.

Various factors contributed to Miller & Lux's financial power. One primary source was the corporation's organization of a vast labor force that could engineer the natural landscape for mass production. The firm segmented its laborers by ethnicity as a means to organize and control a potentially unwieldy work environment. Miller & Lux's daily wage schedule, hiring and firing practices, and Dirty Plate Route created a "floating army" of unemployed workers to fill immediate labor needs. In contrast to the northern European managers, the Mexican, Chinese, and southern European workers found little security or opportunity for advancement with the firm. Indeed, California's 1914 *Report on Unemployment* discovered that the most chronic unemployment were rates among "ranch workers," "teamsters," and "common laborers"—all specialties at Miller & Lux operations.[90] This mass of jobless and migrant workers represented both a product and key ingredient of Miller & Lux's system.

Miller & Lux workers literally built the enterprise during the late nineteenth century. By the early twentieth century, however, the expanded workforce posed a serious financial dilemma to the firm. In order to gross $2.5 million in 1905, Miller & Lux spent nearly $700,000 on wages. This figure did not include the labor costs from its major subsidiaries or the housing and "subsistence" expenses.[91] Total labor expenditures rose close to $1 million. Furthermore, the firm needed to expand its work-force to counter such environmental problems as overgrazed rangeland and soil exhaustion. Miller & Lux faced a rapidly changing business, so-cial, and natural environment, with many problems on the horizon. These problems fell to Henry Miller and his top managers.

CHAPTER 6

Confronting New Environments at the Century's Turn

Charles Lux led an extremely busy and public life in San Francisco. His daily routine began with an early visit to Butchertown, where he greeted most employees by name and inspected the morning kill. Afternoons found Lux conducting meetings and directing managers at the firm's Kearny Street headquarters. Many days he traveled to Sacramento to lobby the state's politicians and bureaucrats on issues vital to Miller & Lux's success. Merchants in San Francisco's bustling business district knew Lux as a man who had risen gracefully from their ranks to become one of the city's leading industrialists. The business elite, meanwhile, received Lux as the genial half of a powerful partnership that owned more property than most of the city's firms combined. His reputation among members of both groups only grew following the momentous 1886 *Lux v. Haggin* decision. But Charles Lux had little time to enjoy that victory— he died eleven months after the state supreme court delivered its verdict.

The *San Francisco Call* reported that his health "had been failing all the winter," and the sixty-four-year-old Lux finally succumbed to pneumonia on March 15, 1887. Newspapers from San Francisco to Bakersfield eulogized him as a German immigrant, a pioneer Californian, a "butcher boy" turned "empire builder," and, finally, the victorious litigant in *Lux v. Haggin*. The *Call* also recounted his long and profitable partnership with Henry Miller, "which lasted until death dissolved it . . . and during which not one shadow ever darkened the brightness of their friendship." This characterization likely exaggerated their closeness. Miller's name, for instance, remained notably absent from the list of friends who carried Lux's casket from his Nob Hill mansion. Instead, Miller marked his passing by ordering all flags at Butchertown lowered to half-mast. This fitting gesture from one butcher to another was probably lost on Lux's family, friends, and associates—people who steered clear of the noxious slaughterhouse district.[1]

Lux's last will and testament, published a week later in San Francisco newspapers, revealed two important personal items. First, city residents would remember Lux as a generous benefactor. Guided by his wife's interest in charitable causes, Lux bequeathed close to one hundred thousand dollars to private societies, hospitals, and asylums. Miranda Wilmarth Lux particularly supported groups assisting women and children, and their combined estate eventually endowed San Francisco's Lux School of Industrial Training for young women.[2] But the will also revealed the presence of many "expectant heirs"—relatives who expected Henry Miller to abide by an 1884 partnership agreement to liquidate the firm's assets within seven years of either partner's death.[3] Lux and Miller had each signed the agreement to guarantee their respective families' shares of the firm's assets. Miller, however, did not intend to fulfill the liquidation promise, though in the coming years he would move toward a financial settlement with Lux's heirs that allowed him complete control of the enterprise.[4]

Lux died during a decade of tremendous growth for the firm and a decade of critical developments in corporate America. Like many corporations nationwide, Miller & Lux continued to consolidate assets and expand outward. The company acquired vast properties in eastern Oregon and northern Nevada to complement its California holdings, thereby extending its reach throughout the Far West. Miller & Lux's cattle herds soon ranged on 200,000 acres in this northern hinterland. Southern Pacific boxcars delivered the livestock to company feedlots in the San Joaquin Valley, where they feasted on baled hay and alfalfa before shipment to Butchertown (and other Miller & Lux slaughterhouses in Oakland and Los Banos). The firm's expansion required a larger managerial class similar to those assembled by corporations across the nation.[5] Trained managers proliferated throughout the company during the 1880s and 1890s. They coordinated the burgeoning workforce and struggled to integrate a dozen subsidiaries into a dynamic whole. Miller & Lux also encountered political reformers and novel regulatory practices, while business competitors threatened the firm in the city and countryside alike. Henry Miller met these challenges with new business alliances, capital investment, and a constant stream of litigation.[6]

Miller & Lux ranked among the country's largest corporations at the century's turn, but both national market integration and specific regional industries tested the firm's power.[7] Between 1880 and 1920, Pacific Coast agribusiness flourished due to improved transportation networks, irrigation, marketing cooperatives, migrant farm labor, and above all, intensive specialty crops.[8] These factors, some of which Miller & Lux had successfully exploited during the previous decades, adversely affected the company's production and marketing after 1900. Meanwhile, the national market trends that sent oranges and peaches to the East also brought products and large corporations to the Pacific Slope. This exchange was neither new nor exceptional to the American West, but it now threatened regional firms like Miller & Lux in important ways. As business transformations reverberated throughout the corporation, shifts in the political arena turned previous allies into hostile adversaries. Finally, the natural landscape that Miller & Lux had engineered for decades exhibited severe and costly problems. The firm confronted a significantly transformed society, polity, economy, and landscape in the early twentieth century—most signs indicated big trouble ahead.

— summary of what's to come

ORGANIZING A NEW HINTERLAND: THE PACIFIC LIVE STOCK COMPANY

These concerns remained in the future as Miller & Lux developed a new resource hinterland northeast of California during the 1880s and 1890s. Large-scale enterprises throughout the Far West had commenced a particularly expansionary phase: they sought out new territory, consolidated natural resources, and crossed extractive sectors to integrate production. On the Pacific Coast, Claus Spreckels extended his California Sugar Refinery Company from San Francisco to Hawaii by merging sugarcane production, landownership, shipping lines, and marketing under one management. In Montana, the Helena & Livingston Mining and Reduction Company and the Anaconda Copper Mining Company grew in scale and scope by absorbing competitors and exploiting new resource frontiers. From Phelps Dodge's activity in the Arizona mining sector to Weyerhaeuser's massive consolidation of Pacific Northwest timberlands, corporate expansion reached a furious pace by 1900.[9] This industrial development, of course, paralleled the strategic mergers, acquisitions, and improved technologies of large-scale eastern firms. By 1900, imperious and increasingly efficient enterprises dominated the nation's industrial landscape.

Miller & Lux's expansion outside California (and takeover of rival companies) fit within these business trends. Five hundred miles from San Francisco markets, the eastern Oregon and northern Nevada hinterlands offered inexpensive rangeland and a new geography for corporate growth. Here was Johann von Thunen's "central place theory" transposed to the Far West's industrial landscape: an area of livestock country beyond California's costly agricultural zones that surrounded the central market city. Though von Thunen had not anticipated such factors as railroad transport or industries' spread into the hinterlands, his functional approach to land use geography nonetheless explains a good part of Miller & Lux's expansion.[10] Environmental problems in California explain the other part. In 1878, splenic fever (or "Texas" fever) broke out among the firm's southern herd in Kern County, and the cattle driven north that season infected Miller & Lux's northern herd.[11] The fever dropped cattle by the thousands, forcing the firm to isolate the infected livestock in large corrals. Miller & Lux slaughtered the survivors and quietly marketed the beef. According to one butcher, "No evil effects resulted" from consuming the meat, but Miller & Lux carefully avoided selling the cuts next to the hide, which "seemed to be of an unnatural color."[12] Miller followed the same procedure when splenic fever broke out the following summer, but he also began searching for rangeland in a cooler climate unaffected by the "big melt" (or enlarged spleen).[13]

Miller & Lux had purchased cattle from Nevada and eastern Oregon since the early 1870s, but buying out-of-state cattle came with certain risks. Miller liked to inspect cattle prior to purchase, necessitating a long trip. Livestock transport posed another dilemma. From the eastern Oregon and northern Nevada range, cattle had to be driven south to Winnemucca, Nevada, loaded onto boxcars, and shipped to California. Due to rough handling, cattle often arrived in poor condition. "Shrinkage," or the loss of weight during shipment, also took its toll. Cattle "fat on the ranch" were not necessarily fat at the slaughterhouse, Miller reminded Lux prior to a large purchase of Nevada cattle in 1876.[14] Miller preferred to buy imported cattle, alive and undamaged, on arrival in California— a procedure that rarely pleased the Oregon or Nevada suppliers. The other option—raising cattle out of state through a new subsidiary—appeared increasingly practical following the splenic fever outbreak.

Miller & Lux's expansion into Nevada and Oregon repeated the strat-

• taking advantage of poor enviro conditions to gain cheap land

egy previously used in the San Joaquin Valley: initial investments coincided with environmental crises in the region, allowing the firm to consolidate massive land and water rights. Yet unlike the previous move into
the San Joaquin, large ranching enterprises already dominated the
Nevada and Oregon range.[15] The most prominent companies—Todhunter & Devine, Overfelt & Company, and French & Glenn—claimed
Oregon's fertile bottomlands in Harney, Grant, and Malheur Counties,
as well as Nevada's Quinn River basin. Miller evaluated these ranch operations and judged them vulnerable to climatic risks. Severe weather conditions from 1879 to 1881 proved him correct. Two deep-freeze winters
forced both Todhunter & Devine and Overfelt & Company to dump their
herds on California markets. Miller & Lux purchased these cattle and
began buying rangeland through the Oregon middlemen N. A. H. Mason, F. A. Hyde, and John Wheeler. Mason extended generous loans to
financially strapped ranchers, while Hyde and Wheeler filed "dummy"
claims to public land in Nevada and Oregon. (Hyde was later convicted
in federal court for his fraudulent land claims.)[16]

Miller & Lux initiated its major consolidations in 1885. The firm acquired all the rich riparian land owned by Overfelt & Company, including
the isolated headwater streams of the Silvies and Malheur Rivers in the
Blue Mountains. Miller & Lux next incorporated its Nevada and Oregon holdings as the Pacific Live Stock Company in 1887. Miller, always
anticipating the next drought, instructed his ranch foremen to stockpile
hay before winter and construct large feedlots surrounded by barbed
wire.[17] Almost on order, little rain or snow fell for the next two years.
The Pacific Live Stock Company's cattle endured the drought owing to
its stockpiled feed, but Todhunter & Devine went bankrupt. Miller &
Lux purchased their property for $1 million and folded it into the Pacific
Live Stock Company.[18] By the end of the decade, Miller & Lux had created the largest ranching enterprise in Oregon and Nevada, bringing new
hinterland resources under its control.

The Pacific Live Stock Company acted on many fronts to protect and
extend its property rights during the 1890s.[19] It organized the Harney
County Stockgrowers' Association to halt cattle rustling and evicted settlers from company-owned swampland following a favorable decision
from the secretary of the interior in 1891.[20] Attempting to control transportation routes and the pace of rural development, the Stockgrowers'
Association opposed the construction of local market roads and railroad
connections strongly supported by settlers.[21] Whenever possible, the
Pacific Live Stock Company filed on public lands most desired by new-

+ Lux died in March 1887

comers. In 1899, the company superintendent, John Gilcrest, informed Miller that settlers would soon "swarm" the land adjacent to their new irrigation ditch if Miller & Lux did not buy the land first. Gilcrest sent Miller a list of those lands to be purchased.[22] Despite his experience with local discontent in the San Joaquin Valley, Miller seemed surprised by the depth of public opposition to his company in Oregon. At one point he asked his Oregon foreman, F. M. Payne, "Do the people feel that we want more than our rightful share of the government domain?"[23] Possibly not wanting to offend Miller, Payne ignored the question in his reply.

Miller & Lux took some steps to improve the Pacific Live Stock Company's reception. It constructed a new building for the Harney County seat, drilled drinking wells for local businesses, and overlooked the occasional grabbing of cattle from its herds.[24] But the Pacific Live Stock Company's most important tool for curbing discontent was its employment practices. Miller & Lux asked Gilcrest, who was a widely respected local rancher, to superintend the new subsidiary, and Gilcrest in turn demanded the right to hire as many local residents as he deemed necessary. In 1888, the Pacific Live Stock Company paid a total of $36,610 in salaries. Gilcrest doubled the labor expenditures during the following year and increased the payroll to $128,720 in 1890. By 1891 the payroll topped $208,000.[25] Despite Miller's attempt to contain labor expenses, the Pacific Live Stock Company quickly became the area's largest employer—a fact that went a long way toward tempering community dislike for the company.[26]

In sharp contrast to Miller & Lux's ethnically diverse ranch workforce in California, the Pacific Live Stock Company hired native-born whites, most of whom were midwestern migrants to the region. Only a few Chinese cooks and Mexican vaqueros appeared on the company's payrolls. Miller specifically advised the foremen against hiring Paiute Indians from the nearby Malheur River Reservation, since tensions ran high between eastern Oregon settlers and Indians.[27] Miller occasionally dispatched individual workers from California, such as José Antonio Eigilo, who was sent to fill a vaquero position in 1887. But Miller realized that importing laborers to Oregon and Nevada would only jeopardize the company's position in the region, while employing locals would soften the firm's ill repute as a community outsider.[28] For some young residents, advancement in the Pacific Live Stock Company's ranks soon became a sign of status and financial stability.[29]

By the mid-1890s, the Pacific Live Stock Company produced the bulk of young livestock for Miller & Lux. The company delivered its cattle to a main transportation hub in Winnemucca, Nevada, where discreet payoffs to the local Southern Pacific shipping agent ensured their timely arrival at the firm's California properties.[30] Once in California, Miller & Lux employees took charge of the livestock and transferred them to the range, feedlots, or slaughterhouse. This production system offered Miller & Lux promising results: the new rangeland produced healthy cattle, extended the firm's reach in the Far West, and freed up California properties for other uses. The new hinterland also buffered the firm against environmental risks. Drought in California would no longer threaten Miller & Lux to the same extent as in years past, and heavy grazing pressure could be spread across a much larger domain. The firm's expansion into the region therefore represented a highly rational response to existing business and environmental conditions.

Miller & Lux's growth had a very different meaning for eastern Oregon's rural communities. The farmers, ranchers, and timber workers of the settler community that Miller & Lux confronted there had developed their own market connections, and they planned to expand them outward. The towns of Bend and Harney City, in particular, hoped to link the region with markets throughout the Far West. The Pacific Live Stock Company, with its primary interest in producing cattle for San Francisco markets, threatened these plans. Opposition to the company arose from these tensions. The *East Oregon Herald,* for instance, claimed that Miller & Lux monopolized 14,439,300 acres in the Far West—a highly exaggerated figure, but one that showed the deep distrust of the company. "God speed the time," the *Herald* announced, "when the reign of said cattlemen in this valley will be brought to an end."[31] Settlers protested the Pacific Live Stock Company's swampland grabs and water rights acquisitions, while some locals turned to sabotage and theft. In 1891, the Pacific Live Stock Company lost three hundred tons of baled hay to arson. Three years later Miller received reports that a "gang" of disgruntled neighbors was conducting a lucrative butchering business based on cattle rustled from the company.[32]

Few residents cheered Miller & Lux's arrival in the region. Indeed, the region's first *Illustrated History,* published in 1902, deplored Miller & Lux's "empire-like" advance and attacked it for "opposing . . . anything having a tendency to promote settlement."[33] These critics were correct: Miller & Lux desired open cattle range, not an independent farming community that would ultimately challenge the stock raisers'

Not popular in Oregon

economic and political power. Here, the firm hoped to replicate the conditions found in the San Joaquin Valley during the 1860s—unregulated range and uncontested water rights. The plan succeeded for a few short years, but events in California soon shifted the firm's attention away from this new hinterland.

THE "VISIBLE HAND" OF MANAGEMENT: NORTHERN EUROPEANS

Henry Miller gained complete control of the multimillion-dollar corporation in the years following his partner's death. Miller initiated a long settlement process with Lux's heirs, and his private landholding company (the Las Animas & San Joaquin Land Company) acquired the vast majority of the new Miller & Lux, Inc. By 1899, he owned over 99 percent of Miller & Lux, Inc.[34] Miller gave no thought to relinquishing control to a board of directors. Instead, he continued making the daily decisions that guided the business. He plotted water-rights litigation with attorneys, organized San Francisco's meatpackers against outside competitors, and expanded the sale of wool, grains, and meat by-products to national markets. Unable to cede too much authority to his managers, Miller sent daily instructions to superintendents, foremen, and even the ranch cooks. Miller would continue as the company's owner and president until 1914 (two years prior to his death), when his son-in-law and company vice president, J. Leroy Nickel, took over the corporate reins. By remaining a family-run proprietary enterprise—instead of an investor-dominated firm with managerial coordination—Miller & Lux missed a crucial phase of American corporate development that might have offered promising directions for business growth.[35]

Despite Henry Miller's propensity for micromanaging an integrated empire, the corporation did develop what one historian has called the "new sub-species of economic man," the salaried, midlevel manager.[36] Between 1880 and 1910, the firm's managerial class expanded in proportion to the overall workforce. Managers oversaw the work conducted on every ranch and throughout the various departments, from the Silvies River Ranch in eastern Oregon to the wool-pulling and shipping departments in Butchertown. Managers coordinated the transportation of cattle, supervised the construction of irrigation systems, kept detailed account books, operated the company stores and banks, and held a range of other responsibilities. In contrast to the formally trained business managers employed by many corporations, Miller & Lux preferred the homespun variety. The corporation's mid- and upper-level managers, with a few notable exceptions, had worked their way up the firm's ranks by impressing Miller with their experience, discipline, and loyalty. Like many vaqueros, cooks, and field-workers, they either proved their value to the firm or faced quick dismissal. Miller & Lux's managers also illustrated the strict ethnic division between management and labor: they were almost exclusively native-born whites or northern European immigrants.

The top-level managers under Miller's control directed the main corporate departments, such as the San Francisco business office, the Butchertown plant, and the "Engineering Department." They also superintended the ranch divisions and managed the subsidiary companies. Their salaries varied widely (from $100 to $500 a month) depending on their position and amount of time employed by Miller & Lux. This salary range reflected Miller's sense of job performance, and he kept careful mental notes on each manager's progress and rewarded him appropriately. In 1889, for instance, Miller increased the salary of S. W. Wible (superintendent of the Southern Division) from $100 to $150 a month, but Miller made that raise retroactive for the entire previous year, netting Wible a $600 bonus. Clearly impressed with Wible's work, Miller soon promoted him to superintend the Los Banos Division, where he earned $200 a month.[37] Like many top managers, Wible stayed with the firm for over two decades.

John Walter Schmitz stayed even longer. A twenty-five-year-old German immigrant, Schmitz hired on as a fence builder in 1871. He quickly distinguished himself and became a foreman on the San Joaquin Canal before serving as a general "engineer" on Miller & Lux's various reclamation projects. In 1878, Lux sent the young German to reconstruct the storm-damaged Chowchilla Canal; impressed with his work, Miller & Lux put Schmitz in charge of the nearby Poso Farm, with a salary of $150 a month.[38] Schmitz was promoted to divisional superintendent during the 1890s, and by the end of the decade he earned $300 a month and managed over 200 employees.[39] As a superintendent, Schmitz received daily letters from Miller on all aspects of his duties, from the proper shape of haystacks to the necessity of maximizing laborers' work time. "When the men work on the [irrigation] ditch a distance from the [ranch] house," Miller advised him on one occasion, "they ought to have a camp and [chuck] wagon. In that way they can work a greater number of hours, and will spare the trouble of going forward and backward."[40] Schmitz rose to a top managerial position precisely because he could implement Miller's difficult demands. But as happened with the other managers, Schmitz's own ideas on business development were rarely solicited.

Miller & Lux also appropriated top managers from rival companies. To head up the Pacific Live Stock Company, Miller persuaded John Gilcrest to leave the rival firm French & Glenn with the enticement of a $5,000 a year salary. Miller grabbed another manager, Dan Leonard, from the Kern County Land Company and moved him into the Dos Palos Farm manager's office. Leonard proved to understand numbers better than cattle, so Miller & Lux transferred him to the company-owned Dos Palos Bank.[41] Dan Wallis had worked for numerous land-based enterprises before coming to Miller & Lux, where he put his experience to work in the Los Banos Division. Gilcrest, Leonard, and Wallis were all native-born Americans, and each stayed in the firm's employ for over two decades. But Miller & Lux also filled its managerial ranks with northern European immigrants, such as Gustav Reichstetter, a German transplant who had previously managed a San Francisco bank, and the Dutch-born H. A. Van Coenen Torchiana, who oversaw a smaller ranch prior to coming to work for Miller & Lux.

Torchiana superintended the Los Banos Division between 1895 and 1901. Thirty years later he published *California Gringos,* an account of his years with the fictitious ranching enterprise Carpenter & Singer. Torchiana knew Miller & Lux's history and its managerial system from personal experience, and he structured the novel around various events from the company's past. James Haggin appears as Colonel William Davidson, a "Teutonic-bred land owner" from Kentucky who held "high industrial ideals" and "furnished the true leaven that that rough-and-ready society so badly needed."[42] August Koenig's 1890 killing of Henry Berger forms the novel's climax—but in Torchiana's version the German immigrant Koenig becomes a half-crazed worker named Swede Olsen, and Berger is a "cultivated" if "slightly pickled" Englishman. Olsen is brought to justice by a knife-wielding Mexican vaquero named Martinez Toralles, who lands himself in San Quentin Prison for attacking Olsen.[43] The Dutch superintendent Hendrik Van Doorne (Torchiana) assumes guardianship of Toralles's son at the novel's end, a thinly veiled testament to conquest and cultural supremacy. Racial stereotypes fill *California Gringos,* from the "hot-tempered Latins" to the "combative" German partner Herman Carpenter (Henry Miller). Nonetheless, Torchiana's novel does accurately depict the racial structure of Miller & Lux's managerial class. The bosses, office managers, and superintendents were all native-born whites or northern Europeans—in Torchiana's words, members of a "stronger race" that heroically "invaded the lost Mexican provinces."[44]

Torchiana left Miller & Lux after six years of employment. He objected to Miller's autocratic management, which closely resembled Herman Carpenter's style as a "corporation head of the old school."[45] Few of the firm's top managers would have contested this portrayal of Miller, who demanded strict and unquestioning obedience. With little opportunity to influence Miller's decision-making process, managers often commiserated among themselves. Writing to the Nevada manager Thomas Rutledge in 1901, C. J. Columbet commented, "He [Miller] is certainly trying on some occasions, giving an order one minute and countermanding it the next, but you and I have both been with him long enough to understand that he must have some good reason when he makes these sudden changes. However, Tom, he pays the bills, and we have to follow orders."[46] Simply following Miller's "orders" prevented the top management from exploring other business directions, such as different options for land use. Instructions descended through the command chain, and new ideas rarely filtered up to the "solitary" Henry Miller.[47] — *one-way leadership style*

The man who would be Miller's immediate successor, J. Leroy Nickel, had managerial problems of his own. This Yale-educated lawyer married Miller's daughter Nellie in 1884, and he worked in the firm's legal department before assuming the vice presidency in 1897. Despite sour relations between Miller and his son-in-law, Nickel's duties steadily increased after 1900. He served as the company's vice president from 1897 to 1914 and president from 1914 to 1925. By his own admission, Nickel mainly oversaw the firm's litigation and "matters of [a] purely business nature," leaving the cattle-ranching details to foremen and superintendents.[48] But he occasionally sought outside advice, such as a 1913 study by the University of California agricultural specialist R. L. Adams. When Adams's report revealed a steady increase in Miller & Lux ranch expenditures between 1912 and 1913, Nickel ordered "considerable reductions" in the labor force and engineering projects throughout the San Joaquin Valley.[49] Managers complied with the cutbacks, but they questioned whether efficiency and profits could be achieved by curtailing improvements. The ongoing engineering projects were costly but an essential part of the corporation's production process. Nickel's sparse knowledge about this end of the business generated friction with many ranch superintendents, and his consultations with outside experts further separated him from the older managers.[50] — *more trouble when son-in-law took over*

Greater avenues of communication did exist between top- and midlevel managers. As Miller & Lux increased production and expanded its labor force in the 1880s and 1890s, the number of middle managers rose rapidly. By 1900, the firm employed over 100 ranch foremen, bookkeepers, cattle and irrigation bosses, and office workers, who earned between $40 and $75 a month. The ranch foremen and crew bosses generally came up from the labor force, while the bookkeepers and office workers were hired from outside the corporation. In 1874, for example, the San Francisco office manager John Bolton sent a family friend to fill a clerical position at Canal Farm near Los Banos. J. H. Ham Jr. arrived at Canal Farm in early November with a letter outlining his duties and a $50 per month salary.[51] Ham kept the books at Canal Farm for the next year, recording the daily wages for canal laborers and reporting on the "renters" who worked parcels of Miller & Lux's land.[52] By summer, young Ham clearly considered himself part of the management system. "Our renters," he wrote Bolton in one letter, "are all hard at work harvesting and we are ditto trying to secure what is due us. A number of the Renters [sic] owe money outside and great care has to be taken that the[ir] grain is not attached [to their debts]. . . . I am in hopes that we will be able to come out even with most of the renters but it is hard to tell at this time [because] the harvest bills are so high."[53] By passing this type of information up the management ranks, Ham functioned as an intermediary between the local situation and the firm's San Francisco headquarters.

But like many young men hired by Miller & Lux in San Francisco and sent to the San Joaquin Valley, Ham could not adjust to ranch life. Summers were dusty and hot, the work tedious, and he was ill most of the time. In September, he watched a fatal accident involving a "young Italian" who was "dragged [by a mule] three-fourth of a mile and was horribly mutilated. . . . His body from his thigh bones up I do not think had a whole bone left."[54] Such industrial accidents occurred regularly on Miller & Lux ranches, and Ham wanted no part of them. He left the corporation two months later and received a letter of reference from John Bolton. Ham carefully avoided Henry Miller during his departure, since he knew Miller deeply resented salaried employees who left the firm.[55]

The midlevel managers who worked in the fields tended to stay much longer than Ham. Conrad Rodemer had emigrated from Germany to New York City five years before Henry Miller, and had traveled to California in the 1860s. He went to work for Miller & Lux as a laborer in 1869, and by the late 1870s Rodemer had taken charge of the firm's dairy near Los Banos. His son, Carl, also found work with Miller & Lux. Carl

Rodemer started out as a laborer, and by the late 1880s he was promoted to foreman at "Camp 13" along the San Joaquin Canal. Among other duties, Rodemer helped choose the firm's sharecrop farmers, or, as Miller put it, "who is worthy of being furnished the coming season."[56] Rodemer ended his career as foreman of Miller & Lux's Centinella Ranch, and he retired to farm on the 120-acre Widman Ranch near Los Banos, also owned by Miller & Lux.[57]

In contrast to the transience that Miller & Lux fostered in the unskilled workforce, the firm developed various incentives for long-term employment among its managers. Monthly salaries that increased over time constituted one primary incentive. Managers enjoyed job mobility throughout the firm's departments and ranch divisions, and in many cases they earned promotions up the corporate ladder. Some, such as J. W. Schmitz and Carl Rodemer, eventually retired on Miller & Lux land. Managers also received the firm's version of expense accounts. When traveling through the San Joaquin Valley, they carried wooden Miller & Lux "meal tokens" that proved "Good for 1 Meal" at most boardinghouses.[58] Perhaps the strongest incentive for managerial stability was familial: the corporation allowed the managers' families to live with them at the ranch house. Carl Rodemer's wife and children, for instance, accompanied him from one location to the next throughout his years with Miller & Lux. Aside from a "washerwoman's" occasional appearance, the manager's wife was usually the only woman seen on a company ranch.[59]

In sum, Miller & Lux built and nurtured a large managerial class during the late nineteenth century. Managers were almost exclusively native-born whites and northern European immigrants, a group whose cohesion was in part based on their ethnic difference from the unskilled workforce. As in the case of employment practices across industrializing America, race and ethnicity played a central role in determining which workers would fill the managerial ranks. But unlike many successful firms, Miller & Lux did not develop a system that encouraged managers' input for long-range company planning. Experienced bosses, particularly division superintendents in the San Joaquin Valley, might have advised significant changes to the firm's land use and crop development had they been allowed to do so. They might have steered the company in a direction different from the one Miller maintained at the turn of the century. But with Miller's attention increasingly focused on San Francisco's meatpacking industry, new uses for hinterland property would have to wait.

- another form of the segmented work force - Manager = white/American/Euro-

BIG TROUBLE IN "THE JUNGLE":
THE CHICAGO TRUST AND THE 1906 EARTHQUAKE

Miller vigilantly guarded San Francisco's meat trade because he knew the firm's power derived from this source of income. Meatpacking profits allowed the firm to purchase and develop its hinterland resources, and these properties in turn supplied the city business with marketable products. Miller & Lux thrived so long as operations in the city and country complemented one another, but events around 1900 tested this interdependent system. Industrial enterprises throughout the Far West encountered similar challenges. New industries like petrochemicals thrived due to abundant resource fields and boom markets, while other regional industries succumbed to consolidation by national corporations (such as the Amalgamated Copper Company's takeover of the Anaconda Copper Mining Company).[60] A few firms transformed themselves into multinational conglomerates; others disintegrated in the new market environment. Miller & Lux's trouble in San Francisco therefore illuminates not just one company's bottom-line crisis, but the outcome of overlapping trends on the local, state, and national levels.

After controlling San Francisco's meat markets for almost fifty years, Miller & Lux drew competition from the unlikely location of Baden—Lux's country estate immediately south of the city.[61] The firm's early success owed much to Baden. The former Rancho Buri Buri, Baden during the 1860s and 1870s served as the final feeding stop for Miller & Lux cattle en route to San Francisco. When improved railroad transport outmoded cattle drives up the peninsula, Baden's location declined in importance to the firm. Miranda Lux put the 1,700-acre family estate on the market following her husband's death, and Miller apparently made no attempt to buy the property. Gustavus Swift, representing the Chicago-based American Cattle Trust, came West in 1887 to examine Baden, and three years later Swift's agent, Peter Iler, purchased the property and the surrounding 3,400 acres.[62] Ironically, the nation's most powerful business conglomerate used Baden as its beachhead to invade the West Coast and Miller & Lux's market.

The arrival of the American Cattle Trust (including the meatpackers Swift, Armour, Cudahy, Wilson, and Morris) in San Francisco certainly challenged Miller & Lux's market control, but these new and aggressive competitors did not simply topple Miller & Lux through economies of scale. Instead, they relied on greater capitalization, Progressive-era regulation, and national production networks to consolidate power in the region.[63] The Cattle Trust moved quickly to exert its power. It formed the South San Francisco Land & Improvement Company in 1891 and established the Western Meat Company for meatpacking. The Cattle Trust shipped in refrigerated meat from Chicago, underbid San Francisco meatpackers on California cattle, and constructed a $2.5-million packing plant at Baden that put Miller & Lux's Butchertown facilities to shame. With de-skilled workers operating labor-saving machinery, the Western Meat Company produced dressed beef and meat by-products at a lower cost than San Francisco packinghouses.[64] As part of a rising conglomerate that soon held the controlling interests in 564 domestic and foreign companies, the Western Meat Company could operate at a loss if necessary and thereby squash competition.[65] (See figure 10.) Chicago, the "gateway city" to the American West, had finally extended its reach to the Pacific Coast, sparking a new phase of industrial competition in the Far West.

Anticipating economic disaster, Miller & Lux organized the Butchers' Board of Trade of San Francisco and Alameda Counties (BBT) in 1893. (See figure 11.) Though controlled by the city's top meatpackers, the BBT emphasized that "the battle [we] are now waging against the money-grabbing octopus at Baden affects every class of people in the city and through the State." San Francisco's meatpackers and butchers initiated a boycott and a remarkable propaganda campaign against Baden's products. In particular, the BBT characterized Baden's method of refrigerating freshly cut carcasses "as being highly dangerous to the public health."[66] According to the BBT, the Western Meat Company slaughtered cattle in a "feverish state" and then washed (or "embalmed") its meat before refrigeration. "As a safeguard against tuberculosis and other dangers which lurk in embalmed, refrigerated and canned meats," the BBT warned, San Francisco residents should "have no dealings with Baden butchers."[67] The BBT contrasted this supposedly unhealthy meat with its own time-tested procedure and product: "It [is] possible [in San Francisco] as in few other places in the world . . . to let the beef hang in the open air after it [has] been cleaned and the hide removed. . . . This process impart[s] a bright red color to the exposed surfaces of the meat and the fat [keeps] a yellowish tinge."[68] Most San Francisco residents had little cause to question such reasoning, since they had consumed unrefrigerated beef for decades. But these consumers were also loyal to their neighborhood butchers, who in turn remained loyal to the hometown

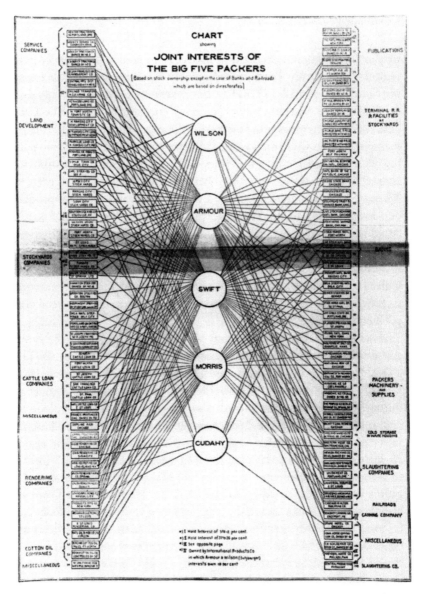

Figure 10.   The multinational interests of Chicago's "Big Five" meatpacking firms were depicted in this diagram for the U.S. Federal Trade Commission's 1919 *Report on the Meatpacking Industry*.

Figure 11.   "A Strong Combination, 1896." The leaders of the San Francisco Butchers' Board of Trade included Henry Miller, bottom row, left. (Courtesy of the Bancroft Library, University of California at Berkeley.)

meatpackers. Such loyalties—in combination with the supposed threat posed by "embalmed" beef—made the boycott of the Western Meat Company highly effective. (See figures 12 and 13.)

Henry Miller's response to Chicago's market incursion was both contradictory and sagacious. Miller had the most to lose in the meat war, and he attempted to protect his markets by organizing Butchertown's various packing plants against Baden. But Miller also recognized the Cattle Trust's tremendous power and capital resources, so he hedged his bets. In 1891 Miller invested forty thousand dollars in the South San Francisco Land & Improvement Company and was elected to the company's

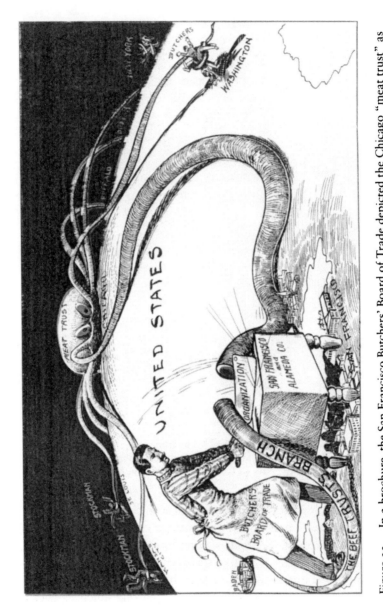

Figure 12. In a brochure, the San Francisco Butchers' Board of Trade depicted the Chicago "meat trust" as a deadly octopus attempting to strangle local butchers and packers. Few Californians would have missed the allusion to the Southern Pacific Railroad's monopolistic power. (Courtesy of the Bancroft Library, University of California at Berkeley.)

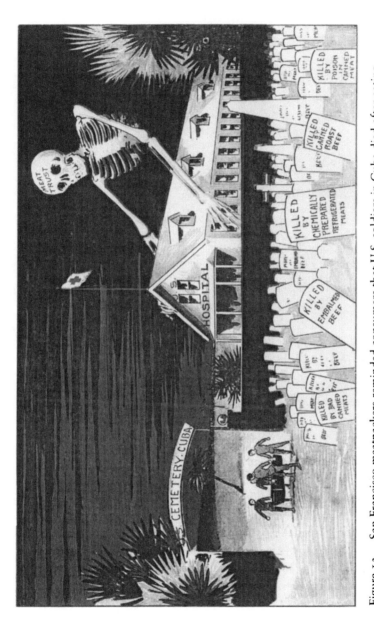

Figure 13. San Francisco meatpackers reminded consumers that U.S. soldiers in Cuba died after eating Chicago's refrigerated and "embalmed" products. (Courtesy of the Bancroft Library, University of California at Berkeley.)

Figure 14. The 1906 earthquake demolished much of Butchertown, which
was erected on pilings above the San Francisco Bay tidelands. (Courtesy of the
California Historical Society, FN-31301.)

first board of directors. Miller therefore positioned himself to understand
the competition.[69] When the BBT's boycott hit full force in 1894, Miller
served as an intermediary between the city's meatpackers and the Western Meat Company.[70] His interests, of course, remained with San Francisco and the BBT, but he likely anticipated a future agreement between
his corporation and the Chicago firms to share San Francisco's beef trade
(similar to his recent agreement with James Haggin over water rights after the *Lux* v. *Haggin* decision). In the best scenario, Miller & Lux could
take over Baden, with its modern packing plant, and increase the firm's
share of San Francisco markets.[71]

Miller had clearly overestimated his bargaining power with the

Chicago meatpackers. During the mid-1890s, the Western Meat Company slashed prices in its six San Francisco butcher shops and opened a large wholesale store. It increased trade with Chinese merchants (who were barred from the BBT) and opened a massive smokehouse at the corner of Sixth and Townsend Streets in San Francisco.[72] In 1898, Western Meat underbid Miller & Lux for the contract to supply San Quentin Prison with meat, a contract Miller & Lux had held since the 1870s. The following year Western Meat secured a contract to supply ten to twenty thousand pounds of beef daily to the U.S. military in the Philippines.[73] By 1900 the Cattle Trust had revealed the trump card it had used in other large regional markets—the ability to operate temporarily at a loss while making gradual inroads on its competitors' profits. - ✗

Nonetheless, the BBT boycott remained strong until an earthquake with a magnitude greater than 7.7 crashed through San Francisco on the morning of April 8, 1906, and fire consumed most of its buildings. Miller & Lux's Kearny Street offices burned during the firestorm's first hours—the office managers David Brown and C. Z. Merritt had only enough time to fill the steel safe with some business records before retreating with what they could carry.[74] Most of Butchertown, including Miller & Lux's slaughterhouse, burned to the ground. Those facilities constructed over the tidelands toppled off their pilings (see figure 14). The Western Meat plant south of the city remained standing, and the company received a government contract to supply the city's homeless residents with meat. Miller & Lux and other San Francisco meatpackers quickly rebuilt Butchertown with refrigerated facilities, all but conceding that their earlier campaign against the Western Meat Company's methods had been a farce. - *Environmental disaster changes / speeds change*

REGULATION AND THE MARKET FOR "INEDIBLE TALLOW"

While the 1906 earthquake and fire leveled Butchertown, events in the political arena that year also rippled through the city's meatpacking industry. Chief among them was the publication of Upton Sinclair's muckraking novel *The Jungle*. Sinclair had hoped to raise public consciousness about slaughterhouse labor conditions in Chicago's Union Stockyards. Sinclair missed his target: "I aimed at the public's heart and by accident I hit it in the stomach," he later admitted.[75] As stomachs turned across the nation in response to Sinclair's vivid description of meatpacking procedures, President Theodore Roosevelt signed the Meat Inspection Act and the Pure Food and Drug Law. Building upon earlier measures (primarily the Export Meat Inspection Acts of 1890 and 1891), these laws greatly expanded the parameters of federal regulation for meat labeling, sanitation, and interstate commerce.[76]

Federal regulation of the meat industry did not impact all interests equally.[77] The American Cattle Trust, and by extension the Baden interests, accepted those regulatory measures that promised to drive smaller, less modernized meat processors out of business. Chicago meatpacker J. Ogden Armour's response to the meat inspection laws, serialized in the *Saturday Evening Post,* emphasized the positive role played by "large packing houses" in eliminating "the dangers [that] may arise from consumption of unwholesome meats." "Big plants" had little to fear from regulation, Armour wrote, as "it is good business for the packer to be careful."[78] Miller & Lux had much more to fear. Suddenly, government agents appeared and began inspecting its packing plants, relabeling export products, and curtailing the hours of operation. Inspectors began to examine livestock before slaughter, and meat by-products, such as compound lard, came under particular scrutiny.

During the late nineteenth century Miller & Lux could market just about anything as lard. After 1906, government inspectors graded lard for its purity and decided what could pass as an "edible" product for export. They demanded that lard production take place only during the daytime inspection hours, a stipulation that infuriated Miller & Lux's slaughterhouse superintendent, Charles Stewart. He informed J. Leroy Nickel that scraping lard off the boiling tanks had to continue around the clock for maximum production, and he demanded that Nickel challenge this regulatory policy. "Have our Senator take [this issue] up with [the chief meat inspector] Webster," Stewart instructed Nickel.[79] U.S. senators likely had more pressing matters than discussing lard with a meat inspector, but Stewart's complaint nonetheless shows how national regulations exasperated local managers and tested many firms' ability to survive in the new business environment.

The interstate commerce regulations contained in the 1906 Meat Inspection Act demanded strict labeling of products shipped across state borders.[80] Miller & Lux, attempting to expand its canned by-product exports in the early twentieth century, refused government inspection of some products as too costly. Without inspection, Miller & Lux had to relabel its canned tallow destined for national markets. To a New York distributor, Miller & Lux wrote, "We expressed you today a 3# tin of our Prime A. Tallow which we call in California 'Edible Tallow' but not being Government Inspected, we will have to ship same as 'Inedible Tallow.'"[81] Such tallow sold well in California—Miller & Lux produced thirty barrels weekly and had orders filled for the next three months. But shipping this product outside California as "inedible" proved problematic, and Miller & Lux's exports sharply declined. The Western Meat Company's processing plants, equipped with the latest machinery, had few problems with inspection, and their products sold throughout the Far West.[82] Interstate commerce regulations effectively cleared the way for market consolidation by the Cattle Trust.[83]

Between 1906 and 1913 Miller & Lux gradually lost market share to the Western Meat Company. The Baden interests developed South San Francisco as a new industrial suburb and dispatched agents throughout the Far West to purchase the region's supply of livestock.[84] Miller & Lux, meanwhile, began importing livestock (mainly hogs) from Chicago as livestock production costs rose on its California ranches. Livestock fattened on labor-intensive irrigated alfalfa cost more than cattle and hogs produced on midwestern feedlots. Such "eastern meats" comprised over half of the firm's $5.2 million in total sales in 1913. Charles Stewart, the superintendent of Miller & Lux's abattoir, noted the result: "In 1912, eastern meats were 21% of our total business. . . . In 1913, eastern meats were 57% of total business. . . . From this synopsis it is very evident that handling eastern meat pays; not only in increased business and profits, but in decreased expenses. It will be nothing less than a business crime to discontinue [the practice]."[85] Competition from Baden had forced Miller & Lux to rely on imported meat—a startling adjustment from which the firm would never recover. As a sign of its declining profitability, Miller & Lux's slaughterhouse foreman killed off thirty-two jobs in late 1913.[86]

In losing control of the region's meatpacking trade, Miller & Lux lost its share of the fastest-rising portion of the nation's gross national product for consumer durable goods. Between 1865 and 1920, livestock production decreased as a percentage of the gross national product, while meatpacking's share expanded to 10.9 percent of total output.[87] Cutting and packaging meat was big business across the nation, and the Chicago-based oligopoly now controlled the industry from the Atlantic to the Pacific Coast. However, the Cattle Trust's penetration of western markets had developed gradually and did not necessarily spell the end for Miller & Lux. The firm still possessed a veritable empire of land and resources in the countryside. Its water rights alone could serve as the foundation for a transformed, intensive agriculture enterprise. Miller & Lux had capitalized on rural growth, political shifts, and environmental circumstances in the past. The early twentieth century tested the firm's viability in each of these areas.

CHANGES ON THE LAND:
CROPS AND GOVERNMENT "CRUSADES"

As new competitors and market regulations undermined Miller & Lux's business in the city, similar forces altered the firm's position in the hinterlands. Like many nineteenth-century western enterprises, Miller & Lux had consolidated power through steady expansion and the integration of various subsidiaries into a remarkably complex system. The whole operation represented something more than the sum of its parts—increasing profits in meatpacking, for certain, but also the power to influence local economies and developmental patterns. Despite its diverse economic interests in the countryside, the system was still centered on the single commodity chain of beef. From the 1890s onward, however, specialty crop agriculture emerged as the leading industry throughout rural California. Capitalized growers tested new crops and business arrangements in their efforts to cultivate the engineered landscape. The dilemma for Miller & Lux was not simply cattle versus crops. Rather, the problem arose in attempting to sustain a bulky, vertically integrated enterprise in a new era of intensive agriculture based on more dynamic production and marketing systems.

California growers succeeded or failed on their ability to utilize the latest information on markets, farm technology, labor, and the agricultural landscape. High production costs (for irrigation, labor, and land) forced them to develop crop systems responsive to business trends and technological innovation. Large and small growers learned to specialize in fruits and vegetables suited to the state's many subregions. They deployed modern farm equipment and chemical insecticides field-tested by the University of California's experimental stations, and they developed crop-specific labor systems for the region's diverse working populations.[88] Growers formed cooperatives to process and market their produce or sold directly to large packing corporations that canned, dried, and shipped the goods. Refrigerated boxcars delivered the products nationwide as advertising campaigns trumpeted the special attributes of California's crops.[89] Each component of the industry combined to maximize production, increase consumer demand, and function efficiently. The results varied by region, season, grower, and crop, but statewide farm values and output increased at an astonishing pace, and California growers led the nation in the production of numerous crops.[90] – *a change from cattle ranches*

In contrast to the advances made by specialty crop agriculture, Miller & Lux's continuing focus on cattle appeared increasingly obsolete. Its herd of 100,000 cattle required all the feed Miller & Lux could produce and purchase, which in turn relied on costly labor, irrigation works, railroad transport, and litigation. The firm competed against intensive agriculture in each of these areas. Some of its land (and fixed capital) remained highly productive, but decades of grazing and overirrigation had exhausted much of the firm's San Joaquin land. The effort to complement ranching with company-town development (Los Banos, Firebaugh, and Gustine) generated little income. In fact, Henry Miller had to write off more than three hundred thousand dollars in debts owed to the corporation by Los Banos–area farmers and residents during the 1890s depression, and payroll cutbacks in 1913 caused panic in the company towns.[91] To avoid a run on its Firebaugh and Los Banos banks, according to one manager, the firm had to discount "the story that Miller & Lux are in hard financial straits."[92] It was a story difficult to counter. Having lost control of the city's meat markets, Miller & Lux's interests in the hinterlands dragged like a dead weight. The strategy that had worked so well in the developing economy of the 1870s and 1880s—corporate expansion and integration—impeded Miller & Lux's adjustment to a different economy in the early twentieth century.

In part, Miller & Lux's inability to capitalize on California's emerging agribusiness exposed the lack of management foresight. In the past, Henry Miller and Charles Lux had made innovative decisions that revealed tactical, long-term planning. The corporation had built an impressive network of public and private agents, seized the most extensive water resources in the West, developed an aggressive litigation strategy, and created numerous subsidiary operations. But throughout, the dynamic aspects of Miller & Lux centered on land and resource consolidations for the cattle business. When agricultural land values and taxes rose after 1900, the firm's cattle fattened on labor-intensive irrigated feed proved disastrously uneconomical.[93] Miller & Lux had made *some* concessions to arable agriculture. It shifted most cattle production to Oregon and Nevada during the 1880s in order to free up grazing land in California for irrigated fields. Most of this irrigated land produced alfalfa and hay for the feedlots, but the firm (and its renters) also harvested grain for mar-

ket. In 1905, the firm had $85,222.55 in grains stored at its Los Banos
warehouse and on various ranches. Miller & Lux had planted small or-
chards at Bloomfield Farm and the Peach Tree Ranch.[94] Water sales to
San Joaquin farmers also increased in the early twentieth century.

These concessions to arable agriculture revealed an awareness of rural trends, but the corporation showed no commitment to capitalize on
agribusiness' booming markets. Miller & Lux certainly possessed the resources (capital, land, water, and labor) to plant trees, lay vines, and grow
produce on a large scale. Indeed, gradually altering land use would have
posed few insurmountable barriers to the company. Miller & Lux's city
managers could look across San Francisco Bay to Oakland, where the
California Fruit Canners Association (soon to be CalPak and later Del
Monte) reaped large profits exporting fruit, and dozens of other companies were revolutionizing the food-processing industry.[95] Henry Miller,
however, did not reward visionary managers who may have suggested
significant changes, nor did J. Leroy Nickel when he took charge. On
the contrary, Nickel's business decisions struck many ranch managers as
haphazard and uninformed. In July 1915, for instance, he curtailed the
firm's longtime practice of feeding tramps and unemployed workers in
the valley. The resulting arson showed exactly why Miller had established
the Dirty Plate Route decades earlier: towering haystacks burned across
Miller & Lux ranches following Nickel's order.[96]

While the increasing power and profitability of specialty crop agriculture revealed Miller & Lux's missed opportunity, this rural transformation did not transpire in an economic vacuum. Miller & Lux's business in the countryside—like its urban affairs—had always depended on
political institutions and public agents responsive to its needs. From
friendly land officers to favorable court decisions, the nineteenth-century
state proved amenable to Miller & Lux's developmental goals. After
1900, Progressive-era reform altered almost every aspect of the firm's
operations: its access to the public domain, use of water resources, livestock shipping practices, and meatpacking procedures. Taken as a whole,
reform and regulation hit Miller & Lux hard in both the city and the
hinterlands.

Though hardly anticorporate, Progressive reformers did hope to mod-
ify the rules by which big business played and to weed out the most egre-
gious forms of public-private collusion.[97] In San Francisco, Mayor Eugene Schmitz, the union boss Abraham Ruef, and the Southern Pacific's
chief counsel, William F. Herrin, each faced criminal prosecution for illegal business dealings between 1905 and 1910. Miller & Lux was in-

dicted alongside the SP in the fall of 1908 for receiving railroad rebates. The grand jury's target was clearly the SP and not Miller & Lux; indeed, a serious investigation into Miller & Lux's dealings with the railroad company could have revealed rebates dating back to the 1870s. Miller & Lux avoided prosecution by turning over evidence and pleading special circumstances.[98] The trial, however, indicated that the public and private networks by which Miller & Lux gained advantage in the past had now changed.

The same year, Miller & Lux's primary Oregon land agent, F. A. Hyde, was convicted of "conspiracy to defraud the government out of valuable lands in the far west."[99] Miller & Lux again evaded indictment in this case, but in *United States v. Pacific Livestock Company* the firm did face prosecution in Oregon for fencing 20,000 acres of the public domain.[100] Britton & Gray, the company's longtime legal counsel in Washington, D.C., suggested a quick removal of the illegal fences. The company superintendent John Gilcrest complied with the request, but he continued to fume against "the crusade by the Department of the Interior against fences enclosing public land."[101] Miller & Lux's unfettered use of public lands vanished with the Progressive conservation movement's drive to regulate access to the public domain.[102] For instance, Miller & Lux lost its grazing permits to the Sierra National Forest in 1908 owing to a U.S. Forest Service policy of encouraging use by "small landowners." In a last-ditch effort to retain his firm's grazing rights, Miller attempted to trade his herd of wild tule elk for special grazing privileges. The Forest Service supervisor Charles Shinn, a rising conservationist and strong advocate of "modern intensive horticulture," shunned the offer. Shinn suggested that Miller direct his complaints to the Department of the Interior.[103] This new bureaucratic maze likely infuriated the eighty-one-year-old Miller.

As rangeland regulations restricted Miller & Lux's public land use, competition from irrigators and municipalities forced the company to defend its long-held water rights. In a series of lengthy and costly court cases, rival water users employed ideas of efficiency and conservation against Miller & Lux's wasteful irrigation methods. Challengers like the Madera Canal Company and the Fresno Flume and Irrigation Company—both of which sold water to specialty crop growers—argued for "conservation, storage, and the economical use of streams."[104] Progressive conservationists like the San Joaquin newspaper editor Chester Rowell attacked Miller & Lux as a "water octopus" in dire need of reform.[105] Though hardly a new charge against the firm, it did represent a broader institutional environment that viewed water conservation as a key ingredient of modern agribusiness throughout the Far West.

In 1911 California's progressive Republican governor Hiram Johnson teamed up with the state legislature to establish the California Water Conservation Commission. The commission's 1912 *Report* singled out a Los Banos–area riparian landowner who "flood[ed] his almost limitless cattle pastures with unnecessarily enormous quantities of water, and d[id] not permit even the excess to be used on the irrigable lands of others, where it would be of great value to those others and therefore to the state."[106] The commission's water bill, which passed the California assembly in 1913 despite Miller & Lux's intense opposition, threatened to force riparian irrigators to prove the "beneficial use" (as opposed to "reasonable use") of their water claims. The corporation's practice of flooding uncultivated San Joaquin lands—to promote grasses and flush the land of salinity—was clearly not a "beneficial use" of water.[107] Unlike the regulatory reforms that changed Miller & Lux's slaughtering and meatpacking practices, water reform was high on rhetoric and short on enforcement. But the growing support for government intervention into water affairs nonetheless suggested Miller & Lux's declining power in a valley it had once dominated.

The Progressive-era reforms and regulations that altered Miller & Lux's business activity neither arose from a single source nor cohered into a uniform movement. Regulation of meatpacking, for instance, was national in scope and fairly prompt in its results. In contrast, water reform represented an attempt to rectify regional and largely irreconcilable conflicts over resource allocation. The ascendant interests in both cases—namely the national meatpackers and California growers—tapped into Progressive-era ideas and increased their economic power. Miller & Lux, on the other hand, faced constant pressure to change its business practices even as its profits waned. From management's perspective, government agents, prosecutors, and competitors besieged the firm from all directions. In 1903, Miller & Lux still retained great influence in California politics. That year the firm successfully lobbied California's Governor George C. Pardee (against intense pressure by the Los Angeles railway magnate Henry E. Huntington, the Pacific Light & Power Company, and the timber baron William G. Kerckhoff) for the appointment of its attorney, Paul Bennett, to fill the vacant judge's seat in the superior court in Kern County.[108] A decade later, with the firm under attack by growers, reformers, and other powerful interests, Miller & Lux had lost any semblance of such political power.

NATURE'S REVENGE:
PROBLEMS ON THE ENGINEERED LANDSCAPE

As the social environment of markets and state institutions moved beyond Miller & Lux's control, so changed the natural landscape upon _*the*_
which the firm was built. The region's nineteenth-century engineers had *terra*
not created the perfectly balanced landscape of contained waterways, ir- *forming*
rigated fields, and farming communities they had once imagined. Instead, *wasn't*
they had crafted a productive landscape dependent on costly inputs and *perfect*
deeply fractured by social and ecological tensions. Wealth and power continued to derive from the ability to manipulate both environmental and
social resources. The reliance on migrant farm labor only increased in
the early twentieth century. Repeated outbreaks of violence and protest—
highlighted by organizational drives by the Industrial Workers of the
World throughout rural California—showed the deep social cleavages
that crossed ethnic, class, and community lines.[109] Miller & Lux largely
escaped organized labor actions, owing in part to the continuation of
the Dirty Plate Route, until 1915. But serious environmental problems
revealed the limits of both social and ecological exploitation.

Water and rangeland problems constituted two principal concerns.
Range conditions deteriorated significantly throughout the Far West during the first two decades of the twentieth century. Forced by federal regulations after 1908 to end its extensive use of public lands, Miller & Lux
stocked its Oregon, Nevada, and California properties far beyond carrying capacity. A 1916 U.S. Department of Agriculture study reported
drastic rangeland degradation across most of the West. In California and
Oregon, the carrying capacity of public and private rangeland had
dropped an astonishing 30 percent since 1906.[110] A drought between
1911 and 1913 certainly contributed to this decadal decline, but the fact
remained that ranchers everywhere faced a hard choice between de-
creasing their livestock or ruining their grassland. Miller & Lux ranch
managers struggled to keep their cattle and sheep from further damag-
ing the exhausted range. Attempting to gain control of the situation, J.
Leroy Nickel asked his Nevada superintendent for "any recommenda-
tions [on range resources] that would afford us any relief."[111] With no
recommendation forthcoming, Miller & Lux had to produce more baled
hay and alfalfa to feed its cattle. Of course, irrigated feed depended on
fertile land and water.

Miller & Lux still controlled the most extensive private water delivery system in the Far West. From Bakersfield to Los Banos on the San

Joaquin Valley's Westside, the firm's canals and ditches could spread a solid sheet of water across more than a thousand square miles. Such regularity on the land, however, concealed mounting problems above and beneath the soil surface. Groundwater pumping by irrigators increased exponentially as their pumps penetrated deeper into the earth. Farmers' artesian wells stopped flowing in the Tulare Basin by 1900; steam- and gas-powered pumps next assumed the task of mining the subsoil water supply.[112] The cost of deep wells and modern pumps prohibited smaller landowners from reaching the water, but Miller & Lux, the Kern County Land Company, and other big operations continued pumping the aquifer at a rapid pace. Groundwater pumping in the basin expanded thirtyfold after 1905, and this depletion led to land subsidence in many places— that land actually sank in upon itself.[113] Stuck between a declining groundwater supply and rising soil salinity levels, Miller & Lux scaled back its Tulare Basin operations in 1913. After decades of intense landscape exploitation, nature showed its limits.

While desperate for groundwater in the southern San Joaquin Valley, Miller & Lux's northern properties were literally drowning. Decades of flood irrigation (from the San Joaquin River) in western Fresno and Merced Counties had brought the water table to the land's surface. Salinity accompanied the rising water; and to rid the soil of salt, Miller & Lux flushed the land with still more water.[114] Declining yields of alfalfa and grasses resulted, since the salts poisoned the plants' roots. The firm's problem with waterlogged land became painfully evident in the second decade of the twentieth century and early 1920s when the California Water Conservation Commission began collecting data on groundwater levels. "We have to admit that the water table is entirely too high," the ranch superintendent J. F. Clyne warned J. Leroy Nickel, "and that it would be a serious disadvantage to have the actual height made a matter of state record." With the company's efforts to sell off land foremost in mind, Clyne suggested noncompliance with the Water Conservation Commission until Miller & Lux could control its "drainage" problem. "Water measurements taken now," he wrote, "would create a false impression, which would work a serious injury to us in the sale of our lands."[115] Evidently, the market for waterlogged land was slow.

High salinity levels wrought havoc on the land's productivity. Indeed, both Clyne and the superintendent James Ogden considered large portions of the firm's land "worthless" for grazing or crop production.[116] The irrigation practices that led to exhausted soils and concentrated salinity also held broader ecological repercussions. Since the 1880s, Miller

& Lux had flushed its irrigation runoff into swampy sink areas directly
north of Los Banos. In heavily reclaimed areas—which included much
of Miller & Lux's San Joaquin lands—the alkaline runoff also contained
high levels of selenium, a toxic soil compound brought to the surface by
dredging and scraping the landscape. Miller & Lux's ranch managers
had always prohibited livestock from grazing these polluted sinks, but
wildlife (particularly birds on the Pacific flyway) continued to inhabit the
areas as a safe refuge. The largest sink (known as Kesterson) became increasingly polluted in the early twentieth century, and decades later numerous wildlife species exhibited extreme deformities caused by the toxic
brew of selenium and salinity.[117] An obvious environmental disaster, the
Kesterson sinks also highlighted the fact that one of the landscape's
defining features, dynamic wetlands, had not existed in the valley since
the 1870s.

Water was everywhere in the valley; it filled the canals, ditches, irrigated fields, and reservoirs, as well as the highly controlled rivers. Water continued to make life and all forms of production possible. But the
natural waterscape of lakes, marshes, and sloughs that shaped and reshaped the valley over the centuries had almost vanished. The waterscape,
once a tool and symbol of nature's complexity and power, now symbolized the social and economic demands for regularity and productivity. Some old-timers recognized and regretted this marked change. Asked
during the 1930s to consider the most important transformation in the
San Joaquin Valley since his arrival in 1864, one of Miller & Lux's longtime vaqueros, José Messa, replied, "The disappearance of the water."[118]
Messa had witnessed industry's impact on the landscape, and he knew
that seemingly simple changes could signify far larger social and ecological circumstances.

Messa's response would have puzzled Henry Miller. He had spent
much of his career watering dry land, reclaiming swampland, and battling in court for his company's right to the valley's water supply. Miller
had prized water above all other resources and he strove to maximize its
presence in the valley, or at least its presence on his land. "Use every bit
of water you can possibly get," he commanded one superintendent in
1905: "If the [irrigation] checks are too large cut them in two. It looks
now as if we will have another fight against starvation, and our only resource is the water. If [our water] will not fail us we can pull through.
Therefore you want to see so no water runs to waste."[119] Clearly, Miller
considered it a waste to not exploit all available water resources. Most
westerners agreed with him—to waste water was not to overuse it but

rather to use too little. This philosophy had guided Miller & Lux and all western land-based enterprises since the 1870s.

Henry Miller did not live to see the marvels of the twentieth century's engineered waterscape—the massive dams that regulated almost every river, the turbine pumps that sent water south over the Tehachapi Mountains into Los Angeles, and the Central Valley's concrete channels clearly visible from outer space. Nor, after his death in 1916, did Miller & Lux maintain any semblance of the power it once held. Many factors contributed to the firm's decline: fierce competition in San Francisco by the world's largest meatpacking corporations, changing land use practices in the hinterlands, political reforms that favored other interests, and a corporate structure resistant to adaptation. But nature also played a crucial role. The environmental advantages gained through resource consolidation and landscape engineering relied on balancing the costs of ecological and social exploitation. Those material and ecological costs eventually became too high. The firm gradually collapsed upon exhausted soils, crumbling waterworks, and simplified ecosystems—products of the drive to engineer the landscape during the late nineteenth century.

CONCLUSION

Unreconstructed Cowboys
in an Industrial Nation

During the final years of his life Henry Miller clung to the business that defined his existence. Though stooped and arthritic, the eighty-three-year-old rancher inspected his San Joaquin properties one last time in 1910, leaving each manager with an earful of detailed instructions. He thereafter lived in the San Francisco home of his daughter Nellie and son-in-law J. Leroy Nickel. Six decades had passed since Miller first arrived in San Francisco. While other migrants had rushed off to the Sierra goldfields, Miller had stayed in the city and established a profitable butchering trade. In San Francisco he had joined forces with Charles Lux, and gradually they had built a business enterprise with properties sprawling across the Far West. San Francisco's investment capital, markets, and hungry consumers had driven the firm's expansion and success. Miller knew the city well, but he had never much liked urban life and therefore had spent most of his working days in the San Joaquin Valley. Lux's death had forced Miller to work more frequently at the firm's San Francisco offices, and his own declining health kept him in the city after 1910. Miller spent his mornings dictating increasingly obscure letters to distant ranch managers. A chauffeur-driven buggy took him through Golden Gate Park in the afternoons.[1] He longed for the valley's open space and the smell of livestock.

In 1915, the year before Miller died, San Francisco commemorated its preeminent role in the Pacific Basin by hosting the Panama Pacific International Exposition. The city had much to celebrate. San Franciscans had rebuilt their homes and livelihoods from the devastation caused by the 1906 earthquake, and the "Pacific Coast Metropolis" appeared to be once again on the rise. While some city businesses would never regain their former power, others (such as A. P. Giannini's Bank of Italy, soon to be the Bank of America) seized the opportunity to reestablish San Francisco's regional position. In the midst of this important transition, the Panama Pacific International Exposition honored San Francisco's historic legacy as it marked the completion of the Panama Canal.[2] During the exposition's ten-month residence, 19 million people viewed the scientific, agricultural, and international exhibits. Civic boosters, meanwhile, proudly (if shortsightedly) predicted their city's cultural and industrial leadership for the twentieth century. Henry Miller visited the fairgrounds every week, despite his poor health. With wonders to see from around the globe, Miller—the unreconstructed rancher and butcher—attended only the livestock displays.[3] Miller stuck with what he knew to the end.

When Miller died on October 14, 1916, his firm had entered a steady decline from which it would not recover. The Chicago meatpacking syndicate continued to consolidate its market share in western cities, and Miller & Lux made no attempt to play catch-up with agricultural changes in the hinterlands. The company's finances were in disarray. Miller & Lux had borrowed $5 million in 1910 to meet a final settlement with Charles Lux's heirs, and by 1920 this and other debts amounted to $15 million (including state and federal taxes on Henry Miller's estate).[4] The corporation began selling its assets following World War I—by one estimate the company's land was valued at $40 million and water rights at $13,742,000.[5] But farm sales lagged during the postwar agricultural depression, and decades of intense grazing pressure and overirrigation had seriously degraded the "small farms and plantations" Miller & Lux attempted to sell. The firm continued to produce livestock during the 1920s. But in 1930 a subsidiary of Swift & Company purchased the corporation's breeding herd, including the "HH" cattle brand.[6] The "HH" brand had once symbolized the firm's great power in the Far West; Miller would have abhorred its sale to the Chicago-based meatpackers.

The family's bitter legal battles over the estate might have also disappointed Miller, but he surely could have appreciated his heirs' courtroom tenacity. Between 1920 and 1960, Miller's heirs liquidated most of the empire and fought over the proceeds.[7] They marketed land to growers and multinational corporations alike and sold some of the inherited water rights back to the government, from which those rights had originated.[8] A few of Miller's heirs remained prominent players in California agribusiness and water politics. The Bowles Farming Company, managed by Miller's descendent Philip Bowles, today grows cotton and alfalfa on the old Delta Ranch near Los Banos. George Nickel Jr., Miller's great-grandson, produces tomatoes, cotton, and other crops on the nearby San Juan Ranch where Miller & Lux ran cattle 140 years ago.[9] Nickel's splendid home sits on the north bank of the Kern River, where he can observe the water flow that his great-grandfather and James Haggin fought over during the early 1880s. Nickel still holds some of the water rights secured in *Lux* v. *Haggin.*

Like these water rights, the industrial agriculture that today dominates the San Joaquin Valley can trace its lineage back to Miller & Lux and other landed companies that emerged in the late nineteenth century. Furthermore, Miller & Lux symbolized a crucial component of a broader industrial society that transformed the region and the nation during the late nineteenth century. The Far West's industrial economy sprang initially from the phenomenal Sierra gold strikes and the vast terrain seized during the Mexican-American War. The subsequent rush on land and resources constituted a pivotal phase in U.S. expansion and the growth of extractive industry. The region's capitalist enterprises thereafter developed clear emphases: innovative and multilayered approaches to resource extraction and processing, vast land acquisitions to consolidate assets and overcome environmental risks, and rural itinerant labor forces to engineer the physical landscape. Large-scale industrial enterprises fanned out across the West and plundered its public domain and natural resources—Miller & Lux, Anaconda Copper, Phelps Dodge, the Southern Pacific Railroad, the California Sugar Refinery Company, and the Kern County Land Company illustrate this process. While these developmental characteristics were not exceptional to western industry, they nonetheless textured a national transformation with regional significance and revealed how environmental factors interacted with economic and social ones to shape U.S. industrial enterprise.

The Far West and its large-scale enterprises, however, are rarely viewed as an integral part of this transformation.[10] Instead, eastern firms define the process of business modernization and economic consolidation that altered the nation during the late nineteenth century. From Andrew Carnegie's steel conglomerate to the Chicago meatpacking companies, the growth of modern industry represented the nation in the midst of dynamic change. While companies merged, integrated production, and built marketing systems to feed consumer demands, small proprietors faced increased competition and workers searched for security in new organizational forms. Despite the restricted geography and contested meanings of this narrative, it still signifies a crucial transition in American political, economic, and social history. By recognizing that far western firms like Miller & Lux operated at the heart of this activity, we can understand industrialism as a historical process that enveloped an entire nation *and* contained important regional contingencies.

Miller & Lux's decline after 1900 marked the downfall of one of the largest and most innovative industrial enterprises in the Far West, but it also symbolized broader changes to the region and nation. New corporate powers and agricultural modernization outmoded Miller & Lux's system of production—a system rutted too deeply in nineteenth-century practices. The firm's command over natural resources and its ability to control environmental variables collapsed as its influence waned in the public arena. From a regional business perspective, large investments in irrigated cattle feed that demanded a vast labor force had become highly irrational. But rather than breaking from the past, these circumstances emerged after 1900 from historical and geographic factors that had been successfully exploited by Miller & Lux and other western firms since the 1850s.

Responding to the environment's natural extremes and complexities, Miller & Lux had monopolized natural resources and mobilized capital and labor to engineer the landscape. The firm's increasing power resided in its ability to transform the land and link those changes to a larger system of production. Ordering the landscape, however, required ever-expanding financial inputs and divisions of labor to counter natural change. In the long run, these investments did not produce a reliable resource base or an efficient business system. With overgrazed and salinized soils, Miller & Lux's system ceased to function rationally as changing demands for land and water revalued those resources.

Miller & Lux's extensive property rights and its use of government institutions also came under scrutiny at the turn of the century. During the 1850s and 1860s, the firm established its power by accumulating private holdings and exploiting capitalist property relations in the Far West. Mexican rancheros, for instance, did not lose their land because they failed to press their private claims; they lost land because American economic and legal institutions privileged ascendant interests like Miller & Lux. The corporation had built a network of agents to utilize and shape these institutions, and in some areas, such as water litigation, Miller & Lux enjoyed continuing success well into the twentieth century.[11] But the strategy of property consolidation through which Miller & Lux rose to prominence ultimately hampered its ability to manipulate markets and government agencies after 1900. The firm faced mounting pressure to change—from rival landowners, industrial enterprises, and political reformers—as its reputation declined in those agencies adjudicating business and property relations. The region's twentieth-century power brokers correctly viewed Miller & Lux as an anachronism on the land.

The erosion of Miller & Lux's regional business system also stemmed from factors initiated in the 1850s. Like other San Francisco–based enterprises, Miller & Lux brought industry to the hinterlands and marketed hinterland resources in the city. The corporation's expansion down the San Francisco peninsula, across the San Joaquin Valley, and into Oregon and Nevada vividly illustrated the city's imperial expansion in the Far West. But the spatial relations of power that initially favored Miller & Lux and the city as a whole changed by the turn of the century. New industries and firms challenged the older regional enterprises like Miller & Lux, while other West Coast cities and new industrial suburbs contested San Francisco's power. The arrival of Chicago's multinational meatpacking firms, which broke Miller & Lux's grip on regional markets, exemplified this trend. In the context of maturing national and global markets, San Francisco and the Far West were irrevocably swayed by larger capitalist forces that had previously spurred the region's phenomenal growth.

The land-based enterprises that succeeded Miller & Lux in the San Joaquin Valley inherited a radically altered landscape that they would engineer still further. The native grasses, largely replaced by imported species during the nineteenth century, remained only in isolated pockets in the valley's foothills. Naturally changing waterways gave way to earthen canals, followed by concrete aqueducts, mobile irrigation systems, and computer-controlled river currents. Migrant laborers once enlisted to produce cattle, feed, and grains soon harvested the world's richest fruit, vegetable, and cotton crops. In the southern San Joaquin, thousands of oil derricks joined the earlier artesian wells that mined the underground water supply. The drive to transform the landscape and extract its natural wealth proceeded with unabated determination during the twentieth century, continuing the region's deep social divisions and disregard for ecological constraints. Wealth and power remained with those who could engineer the landscape and temporarily elude the environmental and social consequences.

Notes

INTRODUCTION

1. Carleton Watkins's work has inspired a growing body of literature. Historical studies include Richard Steven Street, "A Kern County Diary: The Forgotten Photographs of Carleton E. Watkins, 1881–1888," *California History* 61 (winter 1983): 242–63; Mary Warner Marien, "Imaging the Corporate Sublime," in *Carleton Watkins: Selected Text and Bibliography,* ed. Mary Rule (Boston: G. K. Hall and Company, 1993), 1–34; and Peter E. Palmquist, *Carleton E. Watkins: Photographer of the American West* (Albuquerque: University of New Mexico Press, 1983).

2. Watkins's relationships with James Haggin, the Southern Pacific Railroad founder Collis P. Huntington, and other western industrialists is described in Street, "A Kern County Diary," 242–54; and Marien, "Imaging the Corporate Sublime," 9–10.

3. Marien, "Imaging the Corporate Sublime," 3–4.

4. On S. W. Wible and Rafael Cuen, see *Memorial and Biographical History of the Counties of Fresno, Tulare, and Kern, California* (Chicago: Lewis Publishing, 1890), 505–7; Rafael Cuen oral history, 4 March 1944, typescript, box 4 (1), Frank Latta Collection, Huntington Library, San Marino, California.

5. Leo Marx, *The Machine in the Garden: Technology and the Pastoral Ideal in America* (New York: Oxford University Press, 1964). Studies of late-nineteenth-century western industry include William G. Robbins, *Colony and Empire: The Capitalist Transformation of the American West* (Lawrence: University Press of Kansas, 1994); Earl Pomeroy, *The Pacific Slope: A History of California, Oregon, Washington, Idaho, Utah, and Nevada* (New York: Alfred A. Knopf, 1966); Carey McWilliams, *Factories in the Field: The Story of Migratory Farm Labor in California* (Boston: Little, Brown, and Company, 1939); Carlos Arnaldo Schwantes, *Hard Traveling: A Portrait of Work Life in the New Northwest* (Lincoln: Uni-

versity of Nebraska Press, 1994); David M. Emmons, *The Butte Irish: Class and Ethnicity in an American Mining Town, 1875–1925* (Urbana: University of Illinois Press, 1989); Mansel G. Blackford, *The Politics of Business in California, 1890–1920* (Columbus: Ohio State University Press, 1977); and Terry L. Anderson and Peter J. Hill, eds., *The Political Economy of the American West* (Lanham, Md.: Rowman and Littlefield, 1994). For a survey of this literature and a conceptualization of western industrialism, see David Igler, "The Industrial Far West: Region and Nation in the Late Nineteenth Century," *Pacific Historical Review* 69 (May 2000): 159–92.

6. The personal papers of Henry Miller and Charles Lux, and the business records of Miller & Lux, are contained in three separate collections. Miller's letters for the years 1869–77 can be found in the Henry Miller Papers, Bancroft Library, University of California at Berkeley. The Miller & Lux Collection at the Bancroft Library contains over seven hundred cartons of business correspondence, records, legal files, court cases, and maps. The bulk of this collection covers the years after 1906 (when the San Francisco earthquake and fire destroyed Miller & Lux's main office). For letters and business records prior to 1906, see the Latta Collection. The historian Frank Latta collected these records on various Miller & Lux ranches during the 1930s and 1940s. For a comprehensive and compelling study of Miller & Lux's water litigation, see M. Catherine Miller, *Flooding the Courtrooms: Law and Water in the Far West* (Lincoln: University of Nebraska Press, 1993). The first historical treatment of Miller & Lux as an agricultural (and proto-industrial) enterprise was McWilliams, *Factories in the Field*, 29–39.

7. For biographical information on Henry Miller and Charles Lux, see their autobiographical statements in the Bancroft Library taken for H. H. Bancroft's *Chronicles of the Builders of the Commonwealth* (San Francisco: History Company, 1891–92). Miller & Lux's chief counsel after 1907, Edward F. Treadwell, wrote a glowing biography of Miller, titled *The Cattle King: A Dramatized Biography* (New York: Macmillan, 1931). William D. Lawrence's "Henry Miller and the San Joaquin Valley" (M.A. thesis, University of California at Berkeley, 1933) provides some additional information on landownership but largely follows Treadwell's biography. For a small collection of biographical material on Charles Lux, see the Lux Family Papers, California Historical Society, San Francisco.

8. Thomas R. Navin, "The 500 Largest American Industrials in 1917," *Business History Review* 44 (autumn 1970): 360–86. The most influential study of U.S. industrial enterprise is Alfred D. Chandler, *The Visible Hand: The Managerial Revolution in American Business* (Cambridge: Harvard University Press, 1977). Recent assessments and revisions of Chandler include Philip Scranton, *Endless Novelty: Specialty Production and American Industrialization, 1865–1925* (Princeton: Princeton University Press, 1997); Martin J. Sklar, *The Corporate Reconstruction of American Capitalism, 1890–1916* (Cambridge: Cambridge University Press, 1988); Naomi R. Lamoreaux and Daniel M. G. Raff, eds., *Coordination and Information: Historical Perspectives on the Organization of Enterprise* (Chicago: University of Chicago Press, 1994); Richard R. John, "Elaborations, Revisions, Dissents: Alfred D. Chandler, Jr.'s *The Visible Hand*

after Twenty Years," *Business History Review* 71 (summer 1997): 151–200; and Michael Storper and Richard Walker, *The Capitalist Imperative: Territory, Technology, and Industrial Growth* (Cambridge: Blackwell Publishers, 1989). For broader studies on the origin and impact of industrialization, see Thomas Cochran, *Frontiers of Change: Early Industrialism in America* (New York: Oxford University Press, 1981); Christopher Clark, *The Roots of Rural Capitalism: Western Massachusetts, 1780–1860* (Ithaca: Cornell University Press, 1990); Hal S. Barron, *Mixed Harvest: The Second Great Transformation in the Rural North, 1870–1930* (Chapel Hill: University of North Carolina Press, 1997); Alan Trachtenberg, *The Incorporation of America: Culture and Society in the Gilded Age* (New York: Hill and Wang, 1982); and Robert H. Wiebe, *The Search for Order, 1877–1920* (New York: Hill and Wang, 1967). On industrialization in the South, see Douglas Flamming, *Creating the Modern South: Millhands and Managers in Dalton, Georgia, 1884–1984* (Chapel Hill: University of North Carolina Press, 1992); and James C. Cobb, *Industrialization and Southern Society, 1877–1984* (Lexington: University of Kentucky Press, 1984).

9. For nineteenth-century assessments of the West's extreme natural conditions, see John Wesley Powell, *Report on the Lands of the Arid Region of the United States* (1878; reprint, Cambridge: Harvard University Press, 1963); and William Hammond Hall, *Report of the State Engineer to the Legislature of the State of California—Session of 1880* (Sacramento: State Office of Printing, 1880). On the dialectic of flood and drought in California, see Robert Kelley, *Battling the Inland Sea: American Political Culture, Public Policy, and the Sacramento Valley, 1850–1986* (Berkeley and Los Angeles: University of California Press, 1989); and Mike Davis, "Los Angeles after the Storm: The Dialectic of Ordinary Disaster," *Antipode* 27 (July 1995): 221–41.

10. Paul Wallace Gates, *Land and Law in California: Essays on Land Policies* (Ames: Iowa State University Press, 1991); Ellen Liebman, *California Farmland: A History of Large Agricultural Land holdings* (Totowa, N.J.: Rowman and Allanheld, 1983); John Osborn, *Railroads and Clearcuts* (Spokane: Inland Empire Public Lands Council, 1995); Joseph E. King, *A Mine to Make a Mine: Financing the Colorado Mining Industry, 1859–1902* (College Station: Texas A and M University Press, 1977).

11. William Cronon, *Nature's Metropolis: Chicago and the Great West* (New York: W. W. Norton and Company, 1991). A sampling of the city-systems approach includes: Allan Pred, *Urban Growth and City-Systems in the United States, 1840–1860* (Cambridge: Harvard University Press, 1980); Michael P. Conzen, "The Maturing Urban System in the United States," *Annals of the Association of American Geographers* 67 (March 1977): 88–108; Carl Abbott, "Regional City and Network City: Portland and Seattle in the Twentieth Century," *Western Historical Quarterly* 23 (August 1992): 293–322; Eugene Moehring, "The Comstock Urban Network," *Pacific Historical Review* 66 (August 1997): 337–62.

12. Richard White, *The Organic Machine: The Remaking of the Columbia River* (New York: Hill and Wang, 1995).

13. The most concise synthesis of industrialization as an eastern, manufacturing-based phenomena is Walter Licht, *Industrializing America: The Nineteenth Century* (Baltimore: Johns Hopkins University Press, 1995).

14. William G. Robbins, *Hard Times in Paradise: Coos Bay, Oregon, 1850–1986* (Seattle: University of Washington Press, 1988); Thomas R. Cox, *Mills and Markets: A History of the Pacific Coast Lumber Industry to 1900* (Seattle: University of Washington Press, 1974); Nancy Langston, *Forest Dreams, Forest Nightmares: The Paradox of Old Growth in the Inland West* (Seattle: University of Washington Press, 1995); Michael P. Malone, *The Battle for Butte: Mining and Politics on the Northern Frontier, 1864–1906* (Helena: Montana Historical Society Press, 1981); Richard Peterson, *The Bonanza Kings: The Social Origins and Business Behavior of Western Mining Entrepreneurs, 1870–1900* (Lincoln: University of Nebraska Press, 1977); King, *A Mine to Make a Mine;* William Deverell, *Railroad Crossing: Californians and the Railroad, 1850–1910* (Berkeley and Los Angeles: University of California Press, 1994); John Opie, *The Law of the Land: Two Hundred Years of American Farmland Policy* (Lincoln: University of Nebraska Press, 1987), 70–92; Osborn, *Railroads and Clearcuts,* 1–15.

15. On the importance of industrial capital to agricultural enterprise, see Charles Post, "The American Road to Capitalism," *New Left Review* 133 (1982): 30–51; and Brian Page and Richard Walker, "From Settlement to Fordism: The Agro-Industrial Revolution in the American Midwest," *Economic Geography* 67 (October 1991): 281–315. On corruption in the California State Land Office, see Gerald D. Nash, "The California State Land Office, 1858–1898," *Huntington Library Quarterly* 27 (August 1964): 347–56; Nash, *State Government and Economic Development: A History of Administrative Policies in California, 1849–1933* (Berkeley: Institute of Government Studies, 1964).

16. The best account of Haggin's lobbying and land consolidations is Margaret Aseman Cooper Zonlight, *Land, Water, and Settlement in Kern County, California, 1850–1890* (New York: Arno Press, 1979).

17. William Issel and Robert W. Cherny, *San Francisco, 1865–1932: Politics, Power, and Urban Development* (Berkeley and Los Angeles: University of California Press, 1982); Gunther Barth, *Instant Cities: Urbanization and the Rise of San Francisco and Denver* (New York: Oxford University Press, 1975); Richard Walker, "Industry Builds the City: The Suburbanization of Manufacturing in the San Francisco Bay Area, 1850–1945," *Journal of Historical Geography* (forthcoming); Gray Brechin, *Imperial San Francisco: Urban Power, Earthly Ruin* (Berkeley and Los Angeles: University of California Press, 1999); Roger W. Lotchin, *San Francisco, 1846–1856: From Hamlet to City* (New York: Oxford University Press, 1974).

18. Chandler, *The Visible Hand,* 1–12.

19. The classic statement of this thesis is Bernard DeVoto, "The West: A Plundered Province," *Harper's Magazine* 169 (August 1934): 355–64.

20. William G. Robbins, "The 'Plundered Province' Thesis and the Recent Historiography of the American West," *Pacific Historical Review* 55 (November 1986): 577–97; and Igler, "The Industrial Far West."

21. The environmental context of business activity has been largely ignored by economic and environmental historians. Recent efforts to fill this gap include Steven Stoll, *The Fruits of Natural Advantage: Making the Industrial Countryside in California* (Berkeley and Los Angeles: University of California Press,

1998); Theodore Steinberg, *Nature Incorporated: Industrialization and the Waters of New England* (Cambridge: Cambridge University Press, 1991); and Susan Archer Mann, *Agrarian Capitalism in Theory and Practice* (Chapel Hill: University of North Carolina Press, 1990).

22. Robert Glass Cleland, *The Cattle on a Thousand Hills: Southern California, 1850–80* (San Marino: Huntington Library, 1941).

23. On Miller & Lux and other land monopolists in this period, see Henry George, *Our Land and Land Policy* (San Francisco: White and Bauer, 1871); California State Board of Agriculture, *Biennial Report of the State Board of Agriculture for the Years 1870 and 1871* (Sacramento, 1872); and California Constitutional Convention, *Debates and Proceedings of the Constitutional Convention of the State of California Convened at the City of Sacramento, Saturday 28, 1878* (Sacramento, 1880); Donald Pisani, "Land Monopoly in Nineteenth-Century California," *Agricultural History* 65 (fall 1991): 15–35; Gerald D. Nash, "Problems and Projects in the History of Nineteenth-Century Land Policy," *Arizona and the West* 2 (winter 1960): 327–40.

24. On this theme in environmental history, see William Cronon, "Modes of Prophecy and Production: Placing Nature in History," *Journal of American History* 76 (March 1990): 1122–31; Barbara Leibhardt, "Interpretation and Causal Analysis: Theories in Environmental History," *Environmental Review* 12 (spring 1988): 23–36; Richard White, "Historiographical Essay, American Environmental History: The Development of a New Historical Field," *Pacific Historical Review* 54 (August 1985): 297–335.

25. A depiction of nature as disorderly does not necessarily discount certain balances of ecological systems within natural communities. Rather, forces of natural chaos and order interact dynamically over time and space, culminating in complex, historical patterns of natural change. A construction of nature as disorderly does not, contrary to the concerns of some environmental historians, legitimize human control or despoliation of the natural environment. Instead, it embraces the caution expressed by Donald Worster—"What, after all, does the phrase 'environmental damage' mean in a world of so much natural chaos?"— by separating nature's autonomous and unpredictable action from human attempts to control and simplify natural landscapes. In a disorderly nature, "environmental damage" includes (but is not limited to) actions that limit nature's capacity for change. See Donald Worster, "Ecologies of Order and Chaos," *Environmental History Review* 14 (spring-summer 1990): 16. For dynamic models of nature, see Neil Evernden, *The Social Creation of Nature* (Baltimore: Johns Hopkins University Press, 1992); M. Mitchell Waldrop, *Complexity: The Emerging Science at the Edge of Order and Chaos* (New York: Simon and Schuster, 1992); Daniel B. Botkin, *Discordant Harmonies: A New Ecology for the Twenty-first Century* (New York: Oxford University Press, 1990); and William Cronon, "The Trouble with Wilderness; or, Getting Back to the Wrong Nature," in *Uncommon Ground: Toward Reinventing Nature*, ed. William Cronon (New York: W. W. Norton and Company, 1995), 69–90.

26. Annette Kolodny, *The Land before Her: Fantasy and Experience of the American Frontier, 1630–1860* (Chapel Hill: University of North Carolina Press, 1984); Carolyn Merchant, "Reinventing Eden: Western Culture as a Recovery

Narrative," in *Uncommon Ground: Toward Reinventing Nature*, ed. William Cronon (New York: W. W. Norton and Company, 1995), 69–90; Henry Nash Smith, *Virgin Land: The American West as Symbol and Myth* (Cambridge: Harvard University Press, 1950), 123–263.

27. Numerous studies of water in the American West have addressed this point; see Donald Worster, *Rivers of Empire: Water, Aridity, and the Growth of the American West* (New York: Pantheon Books, 1985); Donald Pisani, *From the Family Farm to Agribusiness: The Irrigation Crusade in California and the West, 1850–1931* (Berkeley and Los Angeles: University of California Press, 1984); Norris Hundley, *The Great Thirst: Californians and Water, 1770s–1990s* (Berkeley and Los Angeles: University of California Press, 1992); and Kelley, *Battling the Inland Sea*.

28. Socrates Hyacinth [Stephen Powers], "Wayside Views of California," *Overland Monthly* 2 (1869): 229.

29. Theodore Steinberg, *Slide Mountain: Or the Folly of Owning Nature* (Berkeley and Los Angeles: University of California Press, 1995); and Richard White, *Land Use, Environment, and Social Change: The Shaping of Island County, Washington* (1980; reprint, Seattle: University of Washington Press, 1992), xv.

30. Worster, *Rivers of Empire*, 7.

31. Ibid.

32. John Walton argues that "waterworks" do not "determine" history in the arid American West but rather "the reverse is closer to the truth. History, the record of human agency and institutional development, explains what is significant about water—its varied uses, its appropriations, and the struggle over its benefits." John Walton, *Western Times and Water Wars: State, Culture, and Rebellion in California* (Berkeley and Los Angeles: University of California Press, 1992), 5. Both Catherine Miller's *Flooding the Courtrooms* and Donald Pisani's *To Reclaim a Divided West: Water, Law, and Public Policy, 1848–1902* (Albuquerque: University of New Mexico Press, 1992) find Worster's analysis overly deterministic. Pisani argues that *Rivers of Empire* "reduces complicated history to little more than a morality play" by disregarding "the context of reclamation: local political and economic conditions, the legal structure, the depression of 1893, the Populist movement, and many other forces that impeded planning and coordinated action" (332). Similarly, Miller points out that "the move to centralize control came not from those who had water, but from those who lacked it" (182). While Miller's point is certainly instructive, it should not obscure the fact that the water rights of corporate interests were clearly protected during bureaucratic centralization during the twentieth century.

33. On the commodification of particular resources, see Arthur F. McEvoy, *The Fisherman's Problem: Ecology and Law in the California Fisheries, 1850–1980* (New York: Cambridge University Press, 1986); Duane A. Smith, *Mining America: The Industry and the Environment, 1800–1915* (Lawrence: University Press of Kansas, 1987). For a good overview, see Richard White, *It's Your Misfortune and None of My Own: A History of the American West* (Norman: University of Oklahoma Press, 1991), 212–97.

34. Morton Horwitz, *The Transformation of American Law, 1770–1860*

(Cambridge: Harvard University Press, 1977), 31; Harry N. Scheiber and Charles W. McCurdy, "Eminent-Domain Law and Western Agriculture, 1849–1900," *Agricultural History* 49 (January 1975): 112–30; M. C. Miller, *Flooding the Courtrooms;* and Carol M. Rose, *Property and Persuasion: Essays on the History, Theory, and Rhetoric of Ownership* (Boulder: Westview Press, 1994).

35. Rose, *Property and Persuasion,* 27–30. Stephen Aron's study of Kentucky illustrates this dynamic on the early-nineteenth-century frontier. See Aron, *How the West Was Lost: The Transformation of Kentucky from Daniel Boone to Henry Clay* (Baltimore: Johns Hopkins University Press, 1996).

36. Cronon, *Nature's Metropolis,* 340. Cronon uses "first nature" to designate the "original, prehuman nature," and "second nature" to describe "the artificial nature that people erect atop first nature." He admits that these terms are problematic, particularly "when we recognize that the nature we inhabit is never just first or second nature, but rather a complex mingling of the two" (xvii). For a critique of Cronon's use of "nature," see Carolyn Merchant, "William Cronon's *Nature's Metropolis,*" *Antipode* 26 (April 1994): 135–40.

37. See Peter R. Decker, *Fortunes and Failures: White Collar Mobility in Nineteenth-Century San Francisco* (Cambridge: Harvard University Press, 1978).

38. H. A. Van Coenen Torchiana, *California Gringos* (San Francisco: Paul Elder and Company, 1930); Mary Austin, *Earth Horizon* (New York: Literary Guild, 1932), 207.

39. Little information exists on Charles Lux's life prior to 1850. The best sources are his autobiographical statement for H. H. Bancroft's *Chronicles of the Builders;* and the Lux Family Papers.

40. Henry Miller, "Dictation of Henry Miller, Esq.," 4, Bancroft Library, University of California at Berkeley.

41. Wolfgang Kollman and Peter Marschalck, "German Emigration to the United States," *Perspectives in American History* 7 (1973): 528.

42. See Panikos Panayi, *German Immigrants in Britain during the Nineteenth Century, 1815–1914* (Oxford: Berg Publishers, 1995), 35–87; Kathleen Neils Conzen, "Germans," *Harvard Encyclopedia of American Ethnic Groups* (Cambridge: Harvard University Press, 1980) 405–25; and Conzen, *Immigrant Milwaukee, 1836–1860: Accommodation and Community in a Frontier City* (Cambridge: Harvard University Press, 1976), 22–43.

43. H. Miller, "Dictation," 3.

44. Ibid.

45. During the mid–nineteenth century, England served increasingly as a "staging post" between Europe and North America for German immigrants, and the city of Liverpool in particular contained a large group of German butchers from Kreiser's Wurttemberg province. See Panayi, *German Immigrants in Britain,* 62, 106.

46. H. Miller, "Dictation," 7.

47. Treadwell, *The Cattle King,* 26.

48. In 1850, Mexicans comprised the largest group of foreign-born residents (6,454), followed by English (3,050), German (2,926), Irish (2,452), and French (1,546). See Doris Marion Wright, "The Making of Cosmopolitan California:

An Analysis of Immigration, 1848–1870," *California Historical Society Quarterly* 20 (March 1941): 340.

49. "Papers Delivered to F. A. & M. D. Hyde this date, 25 September 1888," box ML 7 (1), Latta Collection; and Charles Lux, "Dictation of Charles Lux, Esq.," 1, Bancroft Library, University of California at Berkeley.

50. German San Franciscans, in particular, formed partnerships as clockmakers, bakers, and butchers. Issel and Cherny, *San Francisco, 1865–1932*, 57–8.

51. Miranda Sheldon came from a wealthy Rhode Island family. She was born in 1825, and she married Jesse Potter in 1846. Potter left for California in 1850 or 1851, while Miranda Sheldon Potter and their one son, Jesse Sheldon Potter, followed in 1854. Miranda's husband was killed in a boating accident the following year. After her marriage to Lux, she devoted much of her time to philanthropic and reform causes, and her estate later established the Lux School of Industrial Training for young women in San Francisco. See box ML 7 (1), Latta Collection; Lux Family Papers.

52. George Frink to Charles Lux, 2 December 1875, box 22, Latta Collection.

53. H. Miller, "Dictation," 15–16; Treadwell, *The Cattle King*, 149.

CHAPTER 1. THE SAN JOAQUIN VALLEY

1. H. Miller, "Dictation," 13–14.

2. Ibid., 13.

3. For three recent studies that explore the intersection between memory and history, see Richard White, *Remembering Ahanagran: Storytelling in a Family's Past* (New York: Hill and Wang, 1998); Simon Schama, *Landscape and Memory* (New York: Random House, 1996); Michael G. Kammen, *Mystic Chords of Memory: The Transformation of Tradition in American Culture* (New York: Random House, 1993).

4. Edward Bosqui, *Memoirs* (San Francisco: n.p., 1904), 62; Jessie Benton Fremont, "My Grizzly Bear," in *No Rooms of Their Own: Women Writers of Early California*, ed. Ida Rae Egli (Berkeley: Heyday Books, 1992), 157. Generations of Yokuts had witnessed the San Joaquin Valley floor covered in water repeatedly during flood times, and they correctly associated those floods with its original condition. One creation story begins: "In old times water covered all this earth. We can see by the gulches how water was here at the spot where we are sitting." A. H. Gayton and Stanley Newman, "Yokut and Western Mono Myths," *Anthropological Records* 5 (October 1940): 28.

5. Dale R. McCullough, *The Tule Elk: Its History, Behavior, and Ecology* (Berkeley and Los Angeles: University of California Press, 1971), 21–26.

6. Robbins, *Colony and Empire*; Pomeroy, *The Pacific Slope*; Rodman Paul, *The Far West and the Great Plains in Transition, 1859–1900* (New York: Harper and Row, 1988); Worster, *Rivers of Empire*.

7. On the tension between human engineering and natural change, see Steinberg, *Slide Mountain*; McEvoy, *The Fisherman's Problem*; Langston, *Forest Dreams, Forest Nightmares*; David Igler, "When Is a River Not a River?: Reclaiming Nature's Disorder in *Lux v. Haggin*," *Environmental History* 1 (April 1996): 52–69.

8. Walter Prescott Webb, "The American West, Perpetual Mirage," *Harper's Magazine* 214 (May 1957): 26.

9. On Mediterranean landscape ecology, see W. James Clawson, *Landscape Ecology: Study of Mediterranean Grazed Ecosystems* (Nice, France: Proceedings of the Man and Biosphere Symposium, 1989); Francesco di Castri, David Goodall, and Raymond Specht, eds., *Mediterranean Type Shrublands* (New York: Elsevier Scientific Publications, 1981). Mike Davis offers a provocative discussion of California's Mediterranean ecology in "Los Angeles after the Storm," 221–41.

10. For discussions of landscape complexity, see Dean Urban, Robert V. O'Neill, and Herman H. Shugart Jr., "Landscape Ecology," *Bioscience* 37 (February 1987): 119–27; James Bartolome, "Ecological History of the California Mediterranean-Type Landscape," in *Landscape Ecology: Study of Mediterranean Grazed Ecosystems* (Nice, France: Proceedings of the Man and the Biosphere Symposium, 1989): 2–15; Mark A. Blumler, "Invasion and Transformation of California's Valley Grassland, a Mediterranean Analogue Ecosystem," in *Ecological Relations in Historical Times: Human Impact and Adaptation,* ed. Robin A. Butlin and Neil Roberts (Oxford: Blackwell Press, 1995), 308–32.

11. William H. Brewer, *Up and Down California in 1860–64: The Journal of William H. Brewer* (Berkeley and Los Angeles: University of California Press, 1966), 202–3. Brewer's journal is compiled from a series of letters written during his tenure on the California Survey, which was directed by Josiah Dwight Whitney.

12. Ibid., 242–44. Despite the severity of flooding in the Central Valley during 1861–62, this season constituted only a medium-strength El Niño/Southern Oscillation (ENSO), showing that ENSO patterns have different levels of impact globally. Oregon's Willamette Valley also experienced severe flooding during 1861–62. Robert Bunting, *The Pacific Raincoast: Environment and Culture in an American Eden, 1778–1900* (Lawrence: University Press of Kansas, 1997), 74–5. For a historical approach to El Niño, see William H. Quinn, "A Study of Southern Oscillation–related climatic activity for A.D. 622–1900 Incorporating Nive River Flood Data," and Daniel R. Cayan and Robert H. Webb, "El Niño/Southern Oscillation and Streamflow in the Western United States," in *El Niño: Historical and Paleoclimatic Aspects of the Southern Oscillation,* ed. Henry F. Diaz and Vera Markgraf (New York: Cambridge University Press, 1992), 29–68, 119–50.

13. J. M. Guinn, "Exceptional Years," *History Society of Southern California* (1890): 33–39; Thomas E. Bishofberger, "Early Flood Control in the California Central Valley," *Journal of the West* 14 (July 1975): 85–94; Kelley, *Battling the Inland Sea.*

14. Bishofberger, "Early Flood Control," 88.

15. *California Farmer,* 20 December 1861.

16. For estimates of the Sacramento and San Joaquin Rivers' flood capacities, see Charles M. Weber, *An Approach to a California Public Works Plan* (Stockton: Weber Foundation, 1960), 211–12.

17. *California Farmer,* 20 December 1861, and 24 January 1862.

18. C. Weber, *An Approach to a California Public Works Plan,* 212.

19. *California Farmer,* 24 January 1862.

20. Gerald Haslam, Robert Dawson, and Stephen Johnson, *The Great Central Valley: California's Heartland* (Berkeley and Los Angeles: University of California Press, 1993), 157.

21. Frank F. Latta, "William J. Browning," typescript oral history, 11–12, Latta Collection.

22. For the first government study, see B. S. Alexander, *Report of the Board of Commissioners on the Irrigation of the San Joaquin, Tulare, and Sacramento Valleys of the State of California* (Washington, D.C.: Government Printing Office, 1874). Kelley's *Battling the Inland Sea* provides the best account of subsequent flood control measures.

23. *Stockton Independent*, 27 February 1864.

24. *Sacramento Daily Union*, 3 March 1864.

25. Brewer, *Up and Down California*, 379, 508.

26. *Sacramento Daily Union*, 24 March 1864, and 7 April 1864; and the *San Francisco Evening Bulletin*, 5 April 1864.

27. *San Jose Mercury*, reprinted in the *Sacramento Daily Union*, 9 September 1864.

28. *California Farmer*, 1 April 1864. (Emphasis in original.)

29. Charles R. Johnson to Abel Stearns, 17 November and 18 December 1863, and 11 January and 14 March 1864, box 37, Abel Stearns Collection, Huntington Library, San Marino, California.

30. Cleland, *The Cattle on a Thousand Hills*, 131, 184–207.

31. *Los Angeles Southern News*, 22 January 1864.

32. Latta, "William J. Browning," 13.

33. Nineteenth-century irrigation studies include Alexander, *Report*; W. H. Hall, *Report of the State Engineer*; E. W. Hilgard et al., *Report on the Climatic and Agricultural Features and Agricultural Practices and Needs of the Arid Regions of the Pacific Coast* (Washington, D.C.: Government Printing Office, 1882).

34. Mike Davis, *Ecology of Fear: Los Angeles and the Imagination of Disaster* (New York: Metropolitan Books, 1998), 16–20.

35. Allan Schoenherr, *A Natural History of California* (Berkeley and Los Angeles: University of California Press, 1992), 58–62, 518–20; Robert M. Norris and Robert W. Webb, *Geology of California* (New York: John Wiley and Sons, 1990), 425–27; Bartolome, "Ecological History of the California Mediterranean-Type Landscape," 2–15; John McPhee, *Assembling California* (New York: Farrar, Straus, and Giroux, 1994).

36. In the north, the Sacramento Valley received water and silt runoff from five major rivers—the Sacramento, Feather, Yuba, Bear, and American Rivers. The San Joaquin Valley received its runoff from five smaller rivers in the south— the Calaveras, Stanislaus, Tuolumne, Merced, and San Joaquin Rivers. Both the Sacramento and the San Joaquin Rivers converged in the Delta, a vast marshy region of islands and sloughs. At the southern end of the San Joaquin Valley lay the Tulare Lake Basin, separated from the San Joaquin Valley by the slight rise of the King's River alluvial fan. Here, the King's, Kaweah, Tule, White, and Kern Rivers drained into Tulare, Kern, and Buena Vista Lakes. Jeffrey F. Mount, *California Rivers and Streams: The Conflict between Fluvial Process and Land Use* (Berkeley and Los Angeles: University of California Press, 1995).

37. William Preston, *Vanishing Landscapes: Land and Life in the Tulare Lake Basin* (Berkeley and Los Angeles: University of California Press, 1981). On species invasion, resource depletion, and population dynamics on a hemispheric scale, see Alfred W. Crosby, *Ecological Imperialism: The Biological Expansion of Europe, 900–1900* (Cambridge: Cambridge University Press, 1986); Carolyn Merchant, *Ecological Revolutions: Nature, Gender, and Science in New England* (Chapel Hill: University of North Carolina Press, 1989).

38. Edwin F. Katibah, "A Brief History of Riparian Forests in the Central Valley of California" (paper presented at the California Riparian Systems Conference, University of California at Davis, 17–19 September 1981); Anne Sands, *Riparian Forests in California,* Special Publication no. 15 (Davis, Calif.: Davis Institute of Ecology, 1977); Kenneth Thompson, "Riparian Forests of the Sacramento Valley, California," *Annals of the Association of American Geographers* 51 (September 1961): 294–314.

39. Mary Lee Spence, *The Expeditions of John Charles Fremont,* vol. 3 (Chicago: University of Illinois Press, 1970), 512–16.

40. Katibah, "A Brief History of Riparian Forests," 23.

41. Juan José Warner, "Reminiscences of Early Life in California," Hubert Howe Bancroft Collection, Bancroft Library, University of California at Berkeley.

42. Robert F. Heizer and M. A. Whipple, *The California Indians* (Berkeley and Los Angeles: University of California Press, 1975), 90–91; Robert F. Heizer and Albert B. Elsasser, *The Natural World of California Indians* (Berkeley and Los Angeles: University of California Press, 1980); M. Kat Anderson, Michael G. Barbour, and Valerie Whitworth, "A World of Balance and Plenty: Land, Plants, Animals, and Humans in a Pre-European California," *California History* 76 (summer-fall 1997): 12–47; Henry T. Lewis, *Patterns of Indian Burning in California: Ecology and Ethnohistory,* Anthropological Paper no. 1 (Ramona, Calif.: Ballena Press, 1973).

43. H. T. Lewis, *Patterns of Indian Burning in California,* 58.

44. William Preston, "Serpent in the Garden: Environmental Change in Colonial California," *California History* 76 (summer-fall 1997): 260–98.

45. The geographer Kenneth Thompson concludes that these forests were "modified with a rapidity and completeness matched in few parts of the United States." Thompson, "Riparian Forests of the Sacramento Valley," 294.

46. Andrew Rolle, "Turbulent Waters: Navigation and California's Southern Central Valley," *California History* 75 (summer 1996): 128–37; Katibah, "A Brief History of Riparian Forests," 27. By 1870, the California State Agricultural Society urged caution against continuing forest destruction: "The rapid disappearance of the forest trees, especially in localities bordering upon our rivers and sloughs, has for several years excited the attention of all who claim a home in California and feel an interest in the future welfare of our State." "Statement of Mr. E. T. Aiken, of Sacramento County," *Transactions of the California State Agricultural Society during the Years 1870 and 1871* (Sacramento: State Printing Office, 1872), 133.

47. John Muir, *The Mountains of California* (New York: Century, 1894), 235.

48. Marjorie Holland et al., eds., *Ecotones: The Role of Landscape Boundaries in the Management and Restoration of Changing Environments* (New York:

Chapman and Hall, 1991); William Cronon, *Changes in the Land: Indians, Colonists, and the Ecology of New England* (New York: Hill and Wang, 1983) 51, 108.

49. Perennial bunchgrasses, such as purple needlegrass, squirrel-tail grass *(Sitanion)*, and wheat grasses *(Agrophyron)* grew upright in "bunches" and regenerated each year from the same roots. In the driest areas of the valley, native annual grasses such as fescue *(Vulpia microstachys and V. actogflora)* dominated. These annual grasses grew anew each year from seeds that were spread naturally or by humans and domesticated livestock. The San Joaquin's marshes were dominated by cattail *(Typha latifolia)*, spike rush (*Eliocharis* spp.), and sedges (*Carex* spp.), while the high-alkaline areas were dominated by saltgrass *(Distichlis spicata)*. H. F. Heady, J. W. Bartolome, M. D. Pitt, G. D. Savelle, and M. C. Stroud, "California Prairie," in *Natural Grasslands: Introduction and Western Hemisphere*, ed. Robert T. Coupland (New York: Elsevier Press, 1991), 315; Blumler, "Invasion and Transformation in California's Grasslands"; Raymond Dasmann, *California's Changing Environment* (San Francisco: Boyd and Fraser Publishing, 1981), 23.

50. Evidence of the spread of European grasses by explorers prior to Spanish settlement is presented in George W. Hendry and Margaret P. Kelley, "The Plant Content of Adobe Bricks," *California Historical Society Quarterly* 4 (1925): 361–73.

51. Heady et al., "California Prairie," 316.

52. Edwin Bryant, *What I Saw in California* (1848; reprint, Santa Ana, Calif.: Fine Arts Press, 1936), 280, 430.

53. Spence, *The Expeditions of John Charles Fremont*, 514.

54. The California "prairie," or pristine grasslands, was estimated by L. T. Burcham to cover 22.3 million acres. However, he estimated that the total "grazeable" area of the state covered 52.7 million acres, almost half of California's total area. See Burcham, *California Range Land*, publication no. 7 (Davis: University of California at Davis, Center for Archaeological Research, 1981), 102.

55. James E. Perkins, "Sheep Husbandry in California," *Transactions of the California State Agricultural Society* (1863): 134–45.

56. Heady, "Valley Grassland," 497.

57. Mark Blumler, "Some Myths about California Grasslands," *Fremontia* 20 (April 1992): 25.

58. Heady et al., "California Prairie," 318.

59. Brewer, *Up and Down California*, 185. His reference is to Major Thomas Russell, who Brewer says "had been with the Mormons" before taking a farm west of Sacramento. (Emphasis in original.)

60. Bosqui, *Memoirs*, 16.

61. William Preston, "Serpent in Eden: Dispersal of Foreign Diseases into Pre-Mission California," *Journal of California and Great Basin Anthropology* 18 (1996): 2–37; Jon M. Erlandson and Kevin Bartoy, "Protohistoric California: Paradise or Pandemic?" *Proceedings of the Society for California Archeology* 9 (1996): 304–9.

62. McCullough, *The Tule Elk*, 21.

63. Alice B. Maloney, *Fur Brigade to the Bonaventura: John Work's California Expedition, 1832–33* (San Francisco: California Historical Society, 1945), 31.

64. Indian raiding parties were quite successful at driving off livestock from the Spanish coastal settlements. The livestock population multiplied rapidly in the interior valleys, partly replacing Indian reliance on wild game. George H. Phillips, *Indians and Intruders in Central California, 1769–1849* (Norman: University of Oklahoma Press, 1993).

65. Joaquin Pina, "Diario de la espedicion al Valle de San Jose al mando del Alferez de caballeria C. Mariano Guadalupe Vallejo," in "Expeditions to the Interior of California, Central Valley, 1820–1840," ed. S. F. Cook, *Anthropological Records* 20 (February 1962): 177.

66. The severe impact of imported disease on tule elk during drought years is well documented. See Peter J. P. Gogan and Reginald H. Barrett, "Comparative Dynamics of Introduced Tule Elk Populations," *Journal of Wildlife Management* 51 (1987): 20–27.

67. Tule elk are slightly smaller than the Roosevelt elk *(Cervus elaphus roosevelti)* that inhabited the coastal regions of the Pacific Northwest or the Rocky Mountain elk *(C. e. nelsoni),* from which both subspecies evolved. The California elk population varied in size and location according to climatic conditions, range resources, and natural predators, but a rough estimate is that there were five hundred thousand prior to Spanish settlement. See McCullough, *The Tule Elk,* 25–26.

68. C. L. Camp, *James Clyman, American Frontiersman, 1792–1881* (San Francisco: California Historical Society, 1928), 174.

69. Bryant, *What I Saw in California,* 282.

70. R. A. Thompson, *Historical and Descriptive Sketch of Sonoma County, California* (Philadelphia: L. H. Everts and Company, 1877), 54.

71. Barton Warren Evermann, "An Attempt to Save California Elk," *California Fish and Game* 1 (1915): 89.

CHAPTER 2. LAYING THE FOUNDATION

1. "Deed Charles D. Carter to Charles Lux, Outside Water Lot Property," 23 September 1853, and "Ysidro Sanchez and Wife to Lux & Edmondson, Deed, December 19, 1853," Lux Family Papers; *Alta California,* 23 June 1852.

2. On San Francisco's early financial and social elite, see Gunther Barth, "Metropolism and Urban Elites in the Far West," in *The Age of Industrialism in America: Essays in Social Structure and Cultural Values,* ed. Frederic Cople Jaher (New York: Free Press, 1968), 158–87; Lotchin, *San Francisco;* Issel and Cherny, *San Francisco, 1865–1932,* 23–52; Brechin, *Imperial San Francisco;* Walker, "Industry Builds the City."

3. San Francisco's favorable geography in relation to its immediate hinterland certainly lends itself to central place theory. But the deliberate actions of individuals (both in San Francisco and around the globe) and the resulting historical contingencies suggest the limitations of one geographic-historical model. Cronon, *Nature's Metropolis;* Robbins, *Colony and Empire;* M. P. Conzen, "The

Maturing Urban System in the United States," 88–108; Allan Pred, *City-Systems in Advanced Economies* (New York: John Wiley, 1977).

4. Leonard Pitt, *The Decline of the Californios: A Social History of the Spanish-Speaking Californians, 1846–1890* (Berkeley and Los Angeles: University of California Press, 1966), 98–103; Albert Camarillo, *Chicanos in a Changing Society: From Mexican Pueblos to American Barrios in Santa Barbara and Southern California, 1848–1930* (Cambridge: Harvard University Press, 1979), 34–37; Paul Wallace Gates, "The California Land Act of 1851," in *Land and Law in California: Essays on Land Policies* (Ames: Iowa State University Press, 1991), 24–63.

5. *Daily Journal of Commerce*, 1 March 1850.

6. Barth, *Instant Cities*; Decker, *Fortunes and Failures*.

7. H. Miller, "Dictation," 11. Miller's thirty-page autobiographical statement was taken by Edwin W. Fowler in preparation for Hubert H. Bancroft's *Chronicles of the Builders of the Commonwealth*. Fowler interviewed Miller on two separate occasions: the first prior to Charles Lux's death in 1887, the second after Lux had died.

8. H. Miller, "Dictation," 13.

9. U.S. Department of State, *Cattle and Dairy Farming: Reports from the Consuls of the United States on Cattle and Dairy Farming and the Markets for Cattle, Beef, and Dairy Products in the Several Districts* (Washington, D.C.: Government Printing Office, 1887), 391–406, 450–74, 691, 743.

10. H. Miller, "Dictation," 14.

11. Camarillo, *Chicanos in a Changing Society*, 26–27.

12. On Lux and Edmundson's purchase of the Buri Buri and Lux's subsequent buyout, see "Papers Delivered to F. A. & M. D. Hyde this date, 25 September 1888," Latta Collection; Frank M. Stanger, "A California Rancho under Three Flags," *California Historical Society Quarterly* 17 (September 1938): 255.

13. H. Miller, "Dictation," 15.

14. Miranda Wilmarth Sheldon had previously been married to Jesse Potter, who died in 1854. Her family traced its lineage back to Roger Williams of Rhode Island. See "Sheldon Family Tree," Lux Family Papers.

15. "Family of Henry Miller," compiled by Patricia Snar, Gilroy Historical Museum; H. Miller, "Dictation," 15.

16. H. Miller, "Dictation," 15.

17. The letters between the two partners, particularly from the late 1860s and early 1870s, are dominated by the details of cattle purchases and land acquisition. A daily accounting of Miller & Lux's cattle purchases and meat sales for the years 1869–79 can be found in "Journal A," vol. 192, Miller & Lux Collection.

18. Patricia Nelson Limerick, *The Legacy of Conquest: The Unbroken Past of the American West* (New York: W. W. Norton, 1987), 55–77. The best collection of work on land policy is Paul Wallace Gates, *Landlords and Tenants on the Prairie Frontier: Studies in American Land Policy* (Ithaca: Cornell University Press, 1973). For a concise summary of Gates's work and his detractors, see Jon Gjerde, " 'Roots of Maladjustment' in the Land: Paul Wallace Gates," *Reviews in American History* 19 (March 1991): 142–53.

19. For a collection of Parrott's letters, business records, and biography, see Barbara Donohoe Jostes, *John Parrott, Consul, 1811–1884: Selected Papers of a Western Pioneer* (San Francisco: Lawton and Alfred Kennedy, 1972). See also letters in the Abel Stearns and Samuel Barlow Collections at the Huntington Library, San Marino, California; and the Thomas O. Larkin Papers at the Bancroft Library, University of California at Berkeley.

20. John Coffin Jones to Thomas O. Larkin, 14 October 1845, Larkin Papers. Jones also noted, "[Parrott] is a person not the most desirable to have in one's family. His moral principles are not the most refinde [*sic*]." Jones to Larkin, 3 September 1845, Larkin Papers.

21. Jostes, *John Parrott*, 108–10.

22. Parrott announced the establishment of Parrott & Company in September 1855, with his associate Walter B. Comstock. A copy of the printed announcement can be found in Parrott to Abel Stearns, September 1855, Stearns Collection.

23. On real estate law in early California, see Gordon Morris Bakken, *Practicing Law in Frontier California* (Lincoln: University of Nebraska Press, 1991), 72–82.

24. Paul Wallace Gates, "California's Embattled Settlers," in *Land and Law in California: Essays on Land Policy* (Ames: Iowa State University Press, 1991), 156–84.

25. Barlow had invested in the San Francisco branch of the Page & Bacon Bank, which began to fail in 1855. Parrott, whose Granite Building housed Page & Bacon, sent Barlow regular reports on the bank's declining fortunes. John Parrott to Samuel L. M. Barlow, 20 September, 19 November, and 5 December 1855, Barlow Collection. On Barlow's law practice and real estate investments, see Albert V. House, "The Samuel Latham Mitchell Barlow Papers in the Huntington Library," *Huntington Library Quarterly* 28 (August 1965): 341–52.

26. Parrott to Barlow, 2 April 1858, Barlow Collection.

27. Parrott to Barlow, 19 February 1861, Barlow Collection.

28. For Haight's correspondences with various clients, see the Henry Haight Papers, box 1–4, Huntington Library, San Marino, California.

29. Haight to Fletcher Matthews Haight, 17 July 1850, Haight Papers.

30. Haight to George Bissell, 3 May 1861, Haight Papers. Haight transferred his allegiance from the Democratic Party to the Republicans in the mid-1850s, but he returned to the Democrats at the close of the Civil War. This letter confirms his ambivalence to party politics and democracy in general; he writes, "I acknowledge no allegiance to any party whenever a good opportunity occurs for changing our form of government into something stronger than democracy."

31. Bakken, *Practicing Law in Frontier California*, 103.

32. "Squatters" was a somewhat pejorative term used to describe settlers who claimed unsurveyed property by right of use and improvement. The difference between a "settler" and a "squatter" usually had more to do with an observer's perspective on this activity than with any clear legal distinction. See Gates, *Land and Law in California*, 156–84.

33. The Sherman O. Houghton Papers at the Huntington Library, San Marino, California, contain records of his military service, law practice, busi-

ness dealings, and unsuccessful petitioning for a seat on the district court. Also see Oscar T. Shuck, *History of the Bench and Bar of California* (Los Angeles: Commercial Printing House, 1901), 531–33.

34. In *Scott v. Ward* (1859), Houghton argued against the rights of married persons to hold community property in land, a key feature of Mexican land grant policy established by the colonization laws of 1824. In *Donner v. Palmer* (1860), he argued that publicly entered documents relating to land grants held legal standing over the original documents held by Californio landowners. These cases involved American contestants, but the verdicts also affected Mexican landowners attempting to prove title in court. See Shuck, *History of the Bench and Bar,* 532.

35. *Alta California,* 1 July 1871.

36. Shuck, *History of the Bench and Bar,* 417–21.

37. *Colton v. Stanford* (1885), Houghton Papers.

38. Ira Cross, *Financing an Empire: History of Banking in California* (Chicago: S. J. Clarke Publishing, 1927); George D. Lyman, *Ralston's Ring: California Plunders the Comstock Lode* (New York: Scribner's, 1937); David Lavender, *Nothing Seemed Impossible: William C. Ralston and Early San Francisco* (Palo Alto: American West Publishing, 1975); Issel and Cherny, *San Francisco, 1865–1932,* 23–52.

39. Parrott purchased portions of Rancho Llano Seco in Butte County and Las Pulgas in San Mateo County, Mills bought a large part of Buri Buri, and Latham also developed real estate holdings in San Mateo County. Latham ultimately lost his California fortune in the late 1870s through bad land deals, but shortly thereafter he went east and became president of the New York Mining and Stock Exchange. For Latham's correspondence, see the Milton Slocum Latham Papers, Huntington Library, San Marino, California. His obituary provides a concise summary of his business dealings. *San Francisco Chronicle,* 6 March 1882.

40. In addition to his original interests in Rancho Los Alamitos, Stearns acquired large portions of La Laguna from Balestro Lugo, Las Bolsas from Justo Morrillo, La Bolsa Chica from Joaquin and Catarina Ruiz, Temescal from the Serrano family, Los Coyotes from Pio Pico, Santiago de Santa Ana from the Yorba heirs, and Jurupa from his indebted father-in-law, Juan Bandini. Cleland, *The Cattle on a Thousand Hills,* 194–97.

41. Among their correspondences, see Parrott to Abel Stearns, 17 June 1861, and 11 August, 22 August, and 22 October 1864, Stearns Collection.

42. Parrott to Stearns, 11 August 1864.

43. Parrott to Stearns, 22 August 1864.

44. This group included Alfred Robinson, Sam Brannan, Edward F. Northam, Charles B. Polhemus, and Edward Martin. Stearns retained a one-eighth interest in the holdings. Cleland, *The Cattle on a Thousand Hills,* 203.

45. Camarillo, *Chicanos in a Changing Society,* 6–52; Lisbeth Hass, *Conquests and Historical Identities in California, 1769–1936* (Berkeley and Los Angeles: University of California Press, 1995), 45–77.

46. The regional landownership patterns are revealing. According to Albert Camarillo, Santa Barbara and southern California rancheros were able to profit

from the cattle trade and protect their acreage until the late 1850s. But even during this time, "many rancheros were faced with rising expenditures and dwindling income, legal fees, and the increasing number of Anglo squatters on rancho land." In both Santa Barbara and the Los Angeles area, the property remaining in the rancheros' possession was devastated by drought and floods during the 1860s. Camarillo, *Chicanos in a Changing Society*, 27, 33.

47. On the romanticization of rancho California by historians and novelists, see Josiah Royce, *California: From the Conquest in 1846 to the Second Vigilance Committee in San Francisco* (1891; reprint, New York: Alfred A. Knopf, 1948), 25–26; John Hittell, *History of California* (San Francisco: n.p., 1897); Myrtle Garrison, *Romance and History of California Ranchos* (San Francisco: Harr Wagner Publishing, 1935); Cleland, *The Cattle on a Thousand Hills*, 29–31; Helen Hunt Jackson, *Ramona* (New York: Roberts Brothers, 1884), Frank Norris, *The Octopus* (New York: Doubleday Page and Company, 1901); Charles D. Stuart, *Casa Grande, a California Pastoral* (New York: Henry Holt and Company, 1906); Maria Amparo Ruiz Burton, *The Squatter and the Don* (San Francisco: S. Carson and Company, 1885). On trade and property ownership in Mexican California, see David Hornbeck, "Land Tenure and Rancho Expansion in Alta California, 1784–1846," *Journal of Historical Geography* 4 (fall 1978): 371–90; Karen Bradley Clay, "Trade without Law: Private-Order Institutions in Mexican California," *Journal of Law, Economics, and Organization* 13 (April 1997): 202–32; Clay, "Economic Institutions in Theory and History," (Ph.D. diss., Stanford University, 1994), ch. 3.

48. W. W. Robinson, *Land in California: The Story of Mission Lands, Ranchos, Squatters, Mining Claims, Railroad Grants, Land Script, Homesteads* (Berkeley and Los Angeles: University of California Press, 1948), 106; David Hornbeck, "The Patenting of California's Private Land Claims, 1851–1885," *Geographical Review* 69 (October 1979): 435. According to Paul Wallace Gates, "It is asserted that in this long and involved process many claimants lost their possessions to lawyers, speculators, settlers. No one has offered anything but scattered and questionable facts to support this indictment." Gates, "The Adjudication of Spanish-Mexican Land Claims," *Land and Law in California: Essays on Land Policy* (Ames: Iowa State University Press, 1991), 12. Rather than an attack on the Californios' property, Gates concludes, the Land Law of 1851 reveals "the careful protection Anglo-Saxon-American law has given private property." Gates's own data makes these assertions highly problematic. He reveals that 133 claims were granted to "non-Mexicans" and 213 claims originally granted to Californios were conveyed to non-Mexicans. Gates, "The California Land Act of 1851," 35, 59.

49. In New Mexico, the slowness of adjudication allowed for speculation by both Mexicans and Anglos (the "Santa Fe Ring" being the most infamous group of speculators) into the 1890s. Approximately one-third of New Mexico's land grant claims were eventually confirmed, but landownership by Mexicans declined sharply during this process. According to Armando Alonzo's recent study, *tejanos* in the Lower Valley of Texas continued to hold small tracts of land into the early twentieth century, though these unirrigated tracts were "less conducive to successful commercial ranching." Armando C. Alonzo, *Tejano Legacy:*

Rancheros and Settlers in South Texas, 1734–1900 (Albuquerque: University of New Mexico Press, 1998), 265–66; Malcolm Ebright, *Land Grants and Lawsuits in Northern New Mexico* (Albuquerque: University of New Mexico Press, 1994).

50. Treadwell, *The Cattle King,* 57.

51. *Expediente* for Rancho Buri Buri; cited in Stanger, "A California Rancho under Three Flags," 249.

52. An *expediente* normally included a number of pertinent documents: a *(diseño)* sketch of the property, a *(informe)* report of the local official, the decree of concession, the petition to the governor by the applicant, a certificate from the governor, a *(borrador)* copy of the title. Henry Putney Beers, *Spanish and Mexican Records of the American Southwest* (Tucson: University of Arizona Press, 1979), 249–50.

53. Stanger, "A California Rancho under Three Flags," 249.

54. Map (n.d.) in docket 104, Buri Buri, Records of the General Land Office, Bancroft Library, University of California at Berkeley (microfilm); "Will of Jose Sanchez," 8 October 1842, reprinted in the *San Mateo Times,* 10 July 1937.

55. Stanger, "A California Rancho under Three Flags," 257.

56. José de la Cruz Sánchez, in need of capital to pay taxes and legal fees as the official claimant for the Buri Buri, borrowed $1,820 in 1854. One year of accumulated interest (at 5 percent a month) raised his debt to $3,263, and other loans taken by Sánchez brought his total indebtedness to $6,620. Sánchez's share of the Buri Buri was foreclosed in 1856, and two years later the banker D. O. Mills purchased the property for $20,000. See "Papers Delivered to F. A. & M. D. Hyde this date, 25 September 1888," Latta Collection; *Ansel I. Easton and D. Ogden Mills* v. *Charles Lux et al.,* case no. 349 (1867), San Mateo County District Court.

57. The 1858 survey and 1864 plat map are contained in docket 104, Buri Buri, Records of the General Land Office.

58. "To the Committees on Public Lands in the Senate and House of Representatives of the United States," 13 June 1862, in docket 104, Buri Buri, Records of the General Land Office.

59. R. S. Thornton to U. S. Grant, 5 September 1872, in docket 104, Buri Buri, Records of the General Land Office.

60. Francisco Sánchez, one of José Sánchez's five sons, sold his one-tenth interest in Buri Buri in 1856. He had been granted the neighboring Rancho San Pedro in 1839 for his service as alcalde of Yerba Buena.

61. Francisco Sánchez to Hon. Thomas C. Hendricks (commissioner of the General Land Office), 18 November 1858, in docket 104, Buri Buri, Records of the General Land Office.

62. Affidavit of Henry Haight, 3 August 1859, *United States* v. *Sanchez,* in docket 104, Buri Buri, Records of the General Land Office.

63. "Papers Delivered to F. A. & M. D. Hyde this date, 25 September 1888," Latta Collection.

64. Miller to Lux, 15 January 1869, 9 January 1873, and 1 July 1877, Miller Papers.

65. While the vast majority of Miller & Lux land was purchased by the cor-

poration and held as company property, a small percentage was owned separately by Lux or Miller. This pattern of landholding changed after Lux's death in 1887. The two partners also kept some company funds in separate bank accounts until 1870, at which point all funds were merged into a joint "Miller & Lux" account. "Journal A," August 1869–December 1879, Miller & Lux Collection.

66. H. Miller, "Dictation," 16.

67. In the immediate vicinity of Las Ánimas, Miller & Lux came to own portions of ranchos Las Aromitas y Agua Caliente, Bolsa de San Felipe, Juristac, Tequesquite, Lomerias Muertas, Salsipuedes, San Justo, and Laguna Seca.

68. *Expediente,* dated 3 July 1802, Rancho Las Ánimas, in docket 496, Records of the General Land Office.

69. On the Castro family and their various landholdings, see Cowan, *Ranchos of California;* Augusta Fink, *Monterey County: The Dramatic Story of Its Past* (Santa Cruz: Western Tanager Press, 1972).

70. Talbot H. Green to Thomas Larkin, 12 July, 15 July, and 29 September 1842, in George Hammond, ed., *The Larkin Papers: Personal, Business, and Official Correspondence of Thomas Oliver Larkin, Merchant and United States Consul in California,* vol. 1 (Berkeley and Los Angeles: University of California Press, 1951–68), 246–47, 295; Clay, "Trade without Law," 38.

71. *Gilroy Advocate,* 11 January 1879.

72. *Henry Miller et al. v. Massey Thomas et al.* (1879), no. 5536, Santa Clara County District Court.

73. *Gilroy Advocate,* 1 November 1879; H. Miller, "Dictation," 16.

74. *Gilroy Advocate,* 1 July 1871; Horace S. Foote, *Pen Pictures from the Garden of the World, or, Santa Clara County, California* (Chicago: Lewis Publishing, 1886), 89–90.

75. Britton & Gray to Miller & Lux, 30 September 1869, Latta Collection. On Britton & Gray's involvement in land claims, see Gates, *Land and Law in California,* 49, 287.

76. S. O. Houghton to Miller & Lux, 2 April 1872, box 9, Latta Collection.

77. Foote, *Pen Pictures,* 202.

78. *Gilroy Advocate,* 3 October 1868.

79. For a good illustration of Miller & Lux's purchase of bottomlands, see their survey map of Township N.12 South, Range N.4 East in San Benito County, encompassing the lands adjacent to the Pajaro and San Benito Rivers. Map 36, Latta Collection.

80. *Gilroy Advocate,* 29 January 1870.

81. Ibid., 19 January 1869, and 3 June 1876.

82. Ibid., 14 June 1879.

83. Map 36, Latta Collection.

84. See the letter and county surveyor's report, 20 September 1869, box 7, Latta Collection.

85. Miller to Lux, 4 May 1873, Miller Papers; W. S. Smith to Henry Miller, 16 July 1873, box 13, and W. S. Smith to Miller & Lux, 2 December 1873, box 15, Latta Collection.

86. "Agreement between Henry Miller and S.P.R.R. Co., Rights of Way through Bloomfield Farm," 25 May 1872, Latta Collection.

87. A. C. Bassett to Miller & Lux, 9 September 1872, box 11, Latta Collection.

88. C[harles] Crocker to Henry Miller, 21 April 1871, box 9, Latta Collection. On the Southern Pacific's controversial practice of issuing free passes, see Deverell, *Railroad Crossing,* 128.

89. *Gilroy Advocate,* 28 September 1878.

90. Hiram Wentworth to Grover Cleveland, 28 December 1885, in docket 496, record group 49, Records of the General Land Office.

91. Phillips, *Indians and Intruders in Central California.*

92. Warren A. Beck and Ynez D. Haase, *Historical Atlas of California* (Norman: University of Oklahoma Press, 1974), 28–34.

93. Cowan, *Ranchos of California,* 83, 94, 99.

94. "Family Tree," folder 15, carton 732, Miller & Lux Collection. This document was mistakenly labeled as a family tree.

95. John Parrot to Abel Stearns, 17 June 1861, Stearns Collection. Paul Wallace Gates writes, "The most serious charges against Ogier were not his borrowing from persons bringing claims before him, his fondness for liquor and acceptance of gifts from attorneys, his absence while lobbying in Washington in behalf of claimants, but were his predilection in favor of claims, his inertia, his unwillingness to write out more than a few of his decisions, his approval of a two-league claim without even reading the decrees, and his contradictory decrees." Gates, *Land and Law in California,* 55–56.

96. H. Miller, "Dictation," 17.

97. Lux manuscript, prepared for Bancroft's *Chronicles of the Builders.*

98. Brenda Burnett Preston, *Thomas Hildreth: Early California Cattle Baron* (Aptos: Rio Del Mar Press, 1995).

99. H. Miller, "Dictation," 17.

100. Latta, "William J. Browning," 17–18, Latta Collection.

101. "Schedule A" of Orestimba Rancho, folder 29 C #1, carton 483, Miller & Lux Collection.

102. Numerous letters during this period make reference to Miller & Lux's interest in San Joaquin swampland. See William G. Collier to Henry Miller, 15 October 1869, box 7, Latta Collection; William M. Pierson to Charles Lux, 26 February 1869, Miller & Lux Collection; Britton & Gray to William Chapman, 21 February 1869, Miller & Lux Collection.

103. On Miller & Lux's relationship with Mariano Malarin, see M[ariano] Malarin to Charles Lux, 6 July 1875, box 20, Latta Collection; Miller to Lux, 17 April and 8 May 1869, Miller Papers. Malarin was born in California in 1827. Albert Shumate, *Mariano Malarin: A Life That Spanned Two Cultures,* vol. 26 (Cupertino: De Anza College Local History Studies, 1980).

104. Shumate, *Mariano Malarin,* 1–14.

105. H. Miller, "Dictation," 18.

106. Miller to Lux, 19 January 1869, Miller Papers.

107. Latta, "William J. Browning," 19.

108. Miller to Lux, 19 January and 25 April 1869, Miller Collection.

109. J. S. Deane to Miller & Lux, 14 July 1869, box 7, Latta Collection.

110. Miller to Lux, 28 May 1869, Miller Papers.

111. Miller to Lux, 11 June 1869, Miller Papers.

112. For examples of these views, see "Speech of Mr. [James] O'Sullivan," published in California Constitutional Convention, *Debates and Proceedings of the Constitutional Convention of the State of California Convened at the City of Sacramento, Saturday, September 28, 1878* (Sacramento: J. D. Young, 1881): 1136–37; George, *Our Land and Land Policy,* 14–17.

CHAPTER 3. PRIVATIZING THE SAN JOAQUIN LANDSCAPE

1. See Louie A. Gardella, "Just Passing Through," 171, Oral History Project, University of Nevada, Reno Library; *The Oregonian,* 6 February 1888; Torchiana, *California Gringos,* 4–5; Treadwell, *The Cattle King,* 301.

2. California State Board of Agriculture, *Biennial Report of the State Board of Agriculture for the Years 1870 and 1871,* 3:15–16.

3. George based his estimate on information from the State Board of Equalization, but he admits that "a comparison of the books of the various (county) Assessors would be the only means of forming even an approximate list." George, *Our Land and Land Policy,* 26. Due to the widespread use of "dummy" entrypersons by large landowners, even figures from the county assessment lists would have fallen short of the actual amount of land owned by various individuals.

4. "Land owned by Miller & Lux in San Joaquin Valley, May 15, 1874," Box ML (3) A, Latta Collection. Miller & Lux held 1,400.59 acres in Stanislaus County, 190,934.62 acres in Merced County, 170,825.26 acres in Fresno County, 880 acres in Tulare County, and 56,847.93 acres in Kern County.

5. The California State Board of Equalization released information on the size of landholdings that buttressed these beliefs. See the *Report of the State Board of Equalization of the State of California for the Years 1872 and 1873* (Sacramento, 1874). The figures from such reports were reprinted widely in newspapers throughout California. *San Francisco Chronicle* 28 and 30 October, and 1, 3, 7, and 13 November 1873.

6. Pisani, *From the Family Farm to Agribusiness,* 1–29. The California State Agricultural Society, founded in 1854, was an elite group of agriculturalists. By the early 1870s many of its leaders owned extensive tracts of land, and its annual publication was less critical of large, absentee landowners than the more radical California State Grange. For a comparison of the California State Agricultural Society and the Grange on land monopoly, see Gerald L. Prescott, "Farm Gentry vs. the Grangers: Conflict in Rural America," *California Historical Quarterly* 56 (winter 1977–78): 328–45.

7. On republicanism in nineteenth-century California, see Kelley, *Battling the Inland Sea;* Philip J. Ethington, *The Public City: The Political Construction of Urban Life in San Francisco, 1850–1900* (Cambridge: Cambridge University Press, 1994).

8. On the various motives of large landowners, see Nash, "Problems and Projects in the History of Nineteenth-Century California Land Policy," 327–40.

9. The origin of the term "skyfarming" is unclear, though Frank Latta cites it as a widely used label to describe San Joaquin farmers who "tried for sixty

years to grow grain from desert rainfall." Latta, "Rainmakers," 3, box 4 (2) 7, Skyfarming Collection, Huntington Library, San Marino, California.

10. Frank F. Latta, "Crop of 1868," box 4 (2) 5, Skyfarming Collection.

11. For the most comprehensive account of the San Joaquin's settler society, see Wallace Smith, *Garden of the Sun: A History of the San Joaquin Valley* (Los Angeles: Lymanhouse, 1939).

12. U.S. Census Office, *Compendium of the Ninth Census, 1870* (Washington, D.C.: Government Printing Office, 1872), 23; *Abstract of the Eleventh Census, 1890* (Washington, D.C.: Government Printing Office, 1896), 14. For a good table of state population figures, see W. Smith, *Garden of the Sun,* 234–38.

13. Sucheng Chan, *This Bittersweet Soil: The Chinese in California Agriculture, 1860–1920* (Berkeley and Los Angeles: University of California Press, 1986), 42–51.

14. California State Board of Equalization, *Report of the State Board of Equalization of the State of California for the Years 1872 and 1873,* 1–11, 22–23, 26–27.

15. David L. Phillips, *Letters from California* (Springfield: Illinois State Journal Company, 1877), 140, quoted in Pomeroy, *The Pacific Slope,* 124.

16. Pomeroy, *The Pacific Slope,* 102. On single-crop specialization, see Stoll, *The Fruits of Natural Advantage,* 16–31.

17. This was less true for the northernmost San Joaquin County, which had an evenly distributed population and less climatic variation.

18. For a general guide to the valley's natural features, see David Hornbeck, *California Patterns: A Geographical and Historical Atlas* (Mountain View, Calif.: Mayfield Publishing, 1983), 16–24. For a nineteenth-century scientific reading of the San Joaquin, see W. H. Hall, *Report of the State Engineer to the Legislature of the State of California.*

19. *Pacific Rural Press,* 31 March and 28 April 1877; *Stockton Daily Independent,* 24 and 28 April 1877.

20. Norris, *The Octopus,* 127–28.

21. W. Smith, *Garden of the Sun,* 248.

22. Alice L. Carothers, "The History of the Southern Pacific Railroad in the San Joaquin Valley" (M.A. thesis, Stanford University, 1934), 34–60; Carothers, "From Trail to Rail—the Story of the Beginning of Southern Pacific," *Southern Pacific Bulletin* (June 1928): 12–15; W. Smith, *Garden of the Sun,* 203–16.

23. *Fresno Expositor,* 8 December 1875. On farm colonies, see Virginia E. Thickens, "Pioneer Agricultural Colonies of Fresno County," *California Historical Quarterly* 25 (1946): 17–38, 169–77; Pisani, *From the Family Farm to Agribusiness,* 122–25.

24. This discussion draws upon the "Patent" books "C" through "H" stored in the Merced County Recorder's Office, Merced, California. For information on Miller & Lux's purchases from private landowners, see the "Index to Deeds," under the headings of "Grantor" and "Grantee," and the various "Deed" books.

25. On the various land acts and land grants that formed California's public domain, see Gates, *Land and Law in California,* 209–71; Liebman, *California Farmland,* 30–43; Robinson, *Land in California,* 147–98.

26. Patent book "D," Merced County Recorder's Office.

27. Beginning in the early 1870s Miller & Lux gave a Thanksgiving turkey to favored employees, helpful government officials, and other friends of the corporation.

28. George, *Our Land and Land Policy,* 17–23.

29. Patent books "C," "F," "G," and "H," Merced County Recorder's Office.

30. Miller to Lux, 23 April 1873, box 3, Latta Collection.

31. William G. Collier to Henry Miller, 15 October 1869, box 7, Latta Collection. See Map 12, n.d., Latta Collection.

32. William F. White, in California Constitutional Convention, *Debates and Proceedings,* 1150.

33. Collier's map shows that Miller & Lux purchased 11,520 contiguous acres of swampland roughly paralleling the San Joaquin River running south from Sanjon de Santa Rita. By claiming the land in this pattern, Miller & Lux enclosed over 45,000 acres of state swampland.

34. *Santa Cruz Sentinel,* 25 January 1868; *Fresno Expositor,* 2 February 1876. Chapman defended his land dealings in a long letter to the *San Francisco Bulletin,* claiming "that the speculation in these lands so loudly complained of, is leading to their actual cultivation, and is a benefit to the State rather than a curse." *San Francisco Bulletin,* 31 August 1868. For two views on Chapman and land speculation, see Gerald Nash, "Henry George Reexamined: William S. Chapman's Views on Land Speculation in Nineteenth-Century California," *Agricultural History* 33 (July 1959): 133–37; Pisani, "Land Monopoly in Nineteenth-Century California," *Agricultural History* 65 (fall 1991): 15–16.

35. William S. Chapman to Henry Miller, 27 September 1868, box ML 23 (1), Latta Collection.

36. Britton & Gray to Mr. Chapman, 21 February 1869, Miller Papers.

37. *Santa Cruz Sentinel,* 25 January 1868.

38. See Miller & Lux's account sheet for its payments to Chapman, box ML 23 (1) B, Latta Collection. On the varieties of land scrip, see Robinson, *Land in California,* 177–84.

39. Richard H. Stretch to John H. Bolton, 28 July 1876, box ML 7 (5), Latta Collection.

40. Miller to Lux, 20 May 1869, Miller Papers.

41. See "R. H. Stretch a/c for 1873," Journal A: August 1869–December 1879, 116, vol. 192, Miller & Lux Papers; *San Francisco City Directory for the year 1873* (San Francisco: Journal of Commerce Press, 1873), 34.

42. George W. Smith to Henry Miller, 6 January 1874, box 15, Latta Collection.

43. Ibid.

44. Charles Blair to Miller & Lux, 16 December 1876, box 25, Latta Collection. (Emphasis added.)

45. Both of Higley's successors fled office with tens of thousands of dollars left unaccounted for. Nash, "The California State Land Office," 347–56.

46. Bancroft, *History of California,* 6:690; *Sacramento Union,* 26 November 1873. Following his arrest, Higley was held prisoner at Johnson's Island. See Gates, *Land and Law in California,* 128.

47. On the Green Act, see Kelley, *Battling the Inland Sea,* 59–62; Hundley,

The Great Thirst, 78. Higley's lobbying for Miller & Lux is discussed in various correspondences: H. A. Higley to Miller & Lux, 28 May and 5 August 1869, Miller Papers; 15 October and 12 November 1873, box 14, Latta Collection.

48. Thomas Roulhac to Henry Miller, 24 March 1870, box 7, and Henry Miller to Charles Lux, 20 July 1870, box 1, Latta Collection.

49. William G. Collier to Henry Miller, 15 January 1871, box 8, and Thomas Roulhac to Henry Miller, 22 May 1870, box 7, Latta Collection.

50. California State Board of Equalization, *Report of the State Board of Equalization of the State of California for the Years 1870 and 1871* (Sacramento, 1872), 5–6, and *Report of the State Board of Equalization of the State of California for the Years 1872 and 1873,* 10–11; Nash, *State Government and Economic Development,* 208–9.

51. William Faymonville to Charles Lux, 20 August 1875, box 20, Latta Collection.

52. Fresno County Centennial Committee, *Fresno County Centennial Almanac* (Fresno: Fresno County Centennial Committee, 1956), 58, 66.

53. William Faymonville to Miller & Lux, 11 November 1869, box ML 7 (3) A, Latta Collection. As noted earlier, Miller & Lux purchased scrip in San Francisco at a fraction of its cash value, and presumably the treasurer then had to sell off Miller & Lux's scrip.

54. William Faymonville to Miller & Lux, 24 May 1870, box 7 (3) A, Latta Collection. For another example of lobbying on the firm's behalf, see Faymonville to Miller & Lux, 22 August 1871, box 9, Latta Collection.

55. T. F. Hassell to Miller & Lux, 13 February 1869, Miller Papers.

56. James C. Crocker to Henry Miller, 18 March 1869, Miller Papers.

57. D[avid] Shacklefford to Henry Miller, 24 March 1869, Miller Papers.

58. Henry Miller to Charles Lux, 3 February 1870, Miller Papers.

59. Henry Miller to Charles Lux, 27 April, 25 May, and 4 June 1871, box 2, Latta Collection.

60. J. C. Crocker to Miller & Lux, 4 March 1871, box 8, Latta Collection.

61. Henry Miller to Charles Lux, 28 December 1871, box 2, Latta Collection.

62. Pisani, *From the Family Farm to Agribusiness,* 95.

63. George H. Morrison, typescript biography of John Bensley, Bancroft Collection.

64. John Bensley to Henry Miller, 17 January 1870, box ML 7 (5), Latta Collection.

65. *Irrigation in California* (Sacramento: Record Steam Book and Job Printing House, 1873), 18.

66. Henry Miller to Charles Lux, 14 July 1871, box 1, Latta Collection.

67. Each share cost $100, and the company offered 100,000 shares for purchase. On Miller & Lux's accumulating interest in the company between 1871 and 1891, see "List of Stock Held by or for Miller & Lux Inc., in the San Joaquin and King's River Canal & Irrigation Company Incorporated," carton 483, Miller & Lux Collection.

68. *San Francisco Evening Post,* 18 May 1874; *Irrigation in California,* 13–14; San Joaquin and King's River Canal and Irrigation Company, *Report to the*

Stockholders (San Francisco: Woman's Publishing, 1874), 15; M. C. Miller, *Flooding the Courtrooms,* 42.

69. Latta, "The Fresno Scraper," 2, box 4 (2), Skyfarming Collection.

70. Robert M. Brereton, *Report on Messrs. Bensley & Co.'s Canal Project from Fresno Slough to Tide Water at Antioch* (San Francisco: A. L. Bancroft and Company, 1872), 13.

71. Robert M. Brereton, *Reminiscences of an Old English Civil Engineer* (Portland, Oreg.: Irwin-Hodson, 1908); Pisani, *From the Family Farm to Agribusiness,* 107–8.

72. Brereton, *Report,* 2.

73. Ibid., 15.

74. *San Joaquin Republican,* quoted in the *Sacramento Bee,* 23 May 1871. For a similar assessment, see the *Alta California,* 2 July 1871.

75. R. M. Brereton to Miller & Lux, 29 February 1872, box ML 7 (5), Latta Collection. The other trustees apparently did not know of Brereton's offer to Miller & Lux.

76. Henry Miller to Charles Lux, 1 March and 13 April 1872, box 3, Latta Collection. Brereton only corresponded with Lux subsequent to this meeting with Miller; Miller thereafter openly resented Brereton's role in the canal company and considered his technical advice on irrigation matters misdirected.

77. Pisani, *From the Family Farm to Agribusiness,* 111–12.

78. The canal company paid Miller & Lux $48,000 during 1873 for the leased property, which amounted to almost half of the company's expenditures for the year. During the same time period, the SJ&KRC&ICo collected less than $10,000 from water sales. One-quarter of this income came from Miller & Lux, who paid for water at the rate of $1.25 per acre. SJ&KRC&ICo, *Report to the Stockholders,* 14–15; and M. C. Miller, *Flooding the Courtrooms,* 42.

79. Henry Miller to Charles Lux, 28 May 1873, Miller Papers.

80. Henry Miller to Charles Lux, 16 June 1873, Miller Papers.

81. In 1873, the seven-member board of trustees included Isaac Friedlander, William Chapman, A. H. Rose, Nicholas Luning, John Bensley, J. Mora Moss, and Charles Webb Howard. The following year E. F. Northam, William Ralston, and Charles Lux replaced Friedlander, Rose, and Luning as trustees.

82. San Joaquin and King's River Canal and Irrigation Company, *Prospectus* (San Francisco: A. L. Bancroft and Company, 1873), 4.

83. Henry Miller, in particular, wanted to free up as much capital as possible in 1873. In August, he instructed Lux to "not take any more [SJ&KRC&ICo] stock than you have already promised to take," and he suggested that Lux order the abattoir to hasten its slaughtering rate. Miller was also fearful of their labor costs. The gangs of "Chinamen" that Miller & Lux employed to dig lateral irrigation ditches across its land would be "kept" for the month of August and then "let go." Henry Miller to Charles Lux, 26 July, 1 August, and 3 August 1873, Miller Papers.

84. Miller considered the vast project a "wild scheme" that could not have been completed even with public and private financial support. One source estimated the cost of the enterprise at $25 per acre, or $12,500,000 for 500,000

acres (which was only 10 percent of the land projected for irrigation). The overall water supply and the valley's topography also posed serious problems for constructing a canal system that could be used for transportation, despite Brereton's insistence that "an irrigation canal, should be, as a rule, laid out so as to serve for navigation" as well as for watering crops. Finally, as the next chapter will detail, the idea of using Tulare Lake as a reservoir for the canal was entirely unfeasible. H. Miller, "Dictation," 21–22; *San Francisco Chronicle*, 12 November 1875; R. M. Brereton, in "Pamphlets on California Irrigation," vol. 3, no. 29, 1, Bancroft Library, University of California at Berkeley.

85. On congressional support for the land-grant subsidy and the Alexander Commission, see Pisani, *From the Family Farm to Agribusiness*, 112–18.

86. Worster, *Rivers of Empire*, 102.

87. *Stockton Daily Independent*, 20 December 1873; *Weekly Colusa Sun*, 20 December 1873; *Pacific Rural Press*, 4 April 1874.

88. For example, one valley resident argued: "As an answer to the croakings of those that fear that irrigation may have the tendency of monopolizing lands, it has on the contrary the tendency to make small, well-cultivated farms and increase labor and population to an extraordinary extent." *Alta California*, 2 July 1871.

89. Gates, *Landlords and Tenants on the Prairie Frontier*, 266–302.

90. SJ&KRC&ICo., *Prospectus*, 8. (Emphasis added.)

91. *San Joaquin Republican*, reprinted in the *Sacramento Daily Bee*, 23 May 1871.

92. *Alta California*, 14 August 1871.

93. *Sacramento Daily Bee*, 23 May 1873.

94. Prescott, "Farm Gentry vs. the Grangers," 335. By 1875, there were 231 local Grange organizations in California, with a membership of almost fifteen thousand. Ezra Carr, *The Patrons of Husbandry of the Pacific Coast* (San Francisco: A. L. Bancroft and Company, 1875), 81–130; J. W. A. Wright, in *San Francisco Chronicle*, 2 November 1873.

95. *Sacramento Union*, 15 July 1873.

96. *San Francisco Chronicle*, 9 January 1873.

97. Miller & Lux had, however, established at least forty "renters" on the irrigated land that came to be known as Canal Farm. The renters grew mostly wheat and alfalfa on parcels of land ranging in size from 160 to 600 acres. The crops, by agreement, were then sold back to Miller & Lux, and the corporation retained the right to graze its cattle on the stubble. By 1875 some renters were deep in debt to Miller & Lux because of crop failures. J. C. Risk to Miller & Lux, 17 November 1875, box 22, Latta Collection. On the renters, see J. H. Ham to John Bolton, 7 and 21 July, 25 August, and 22 September 1875, box 21, Latta Collection; H. G. Tanner, "Account on M & L Farmers," 14 August 1877, box 28.

98. *Fresno Expositor*, 30 July 1873.

99. *San Francisco Evening Bulletin*, 18 May 1874. Apparently, the *Bulletin* was not invited to send a reporter to cover this event, likely because of its reputation for having an antimonopoly stance and an exposé style of reporting. Ethington, *The Public City*, 119.

100. *San Francisco Evening Post*, 18 May 1874. The branding mark was pre-

viously owned by the Hildreth brothers and was obtained along with Rancho Sanjon de Santa Rita in 1863.

101. *San Francisco Evening Post,* in "California Pamphlets," vol. 9, 398, Bancroft Library, University of California at Berkeley.

102. The first edition of Powell's *Report* was submitted to Secretary of the Interior Carl Schurz, April 1, 1878. Due to demand, a second edition was printed the following year. My citations refer to the 1962 edition, edited by Wallace Stegner. Powell, *Report on the Lands of the Arid Region.*

103. Henry Miller to Charles Lux, 28 May 1876, Miller Papers.

104. Henry Miller to Charles Lux, 22 and 29 March 1876, Miller Papers.

105. John Outcalt, *History of Merced County* (Los Angeles: Historic Record Company, 1925), 221.

106. Henry Miller to Charles Lux, 8 August 1877, Miller Papers.

107. "List of Stock Held by or for Miller & Lux in the San Joaquin and King's River Canal & Irrigation Company, Inc.," carton 483, Latta Collection.

108. Lavender, *Nothing Seemed Impossible,* 350–55.

109. Pisani, "Land Monopoly in Nineteenth-Century California," 25.

110. William Chapman to Miller & Lux, 28 September and 30 October 1876, Miller Papers; Brereton, *Reminiscences of an Old English Civil Engineer,* 25; Pisani, *From the Family Farm to Agribusiness,* 119.

111. Miller to Lux, 23 June 1873, Miller Papers. Miller & Lux slaughtered over a quarter of the beef cattle in the city, averaging approximately 1,000 a month (and 350 calves a month). Miller & Lux also supplied many of the smaller slaughterhouses with livestock. *San Francisco Commercial Herald and Market Review,* 13 January 1871.

112. B. P. Preston, *Thomas Hildreth,* 41–46.

113. In 1871, ten German and English banking companies purchased the Parrott & Company bank, which previously had supported Miller & Lux's land purchases. It was renamed the London & San Francisco Bank, Ltd., and the former U.S. senator and California governor Milton S. Latham became the bank's president. Parrott continued his involvement with the bank throughout the decade. Jostes, *John Parrott, Consul,* 190; Cross, *Financing an Empire,* 258–59, 399–400.

114. John Bolton to Henry Miller, 1 April 1876, box 24, Latta Collection; Henry Miller to Charles Lux, 27 May 1877, Miller Papers.

115. See Pisani, *From the Family Farm to Agribusiness,* 129; and Pisani, *To Reclaim a Divided West,* ch. 3; Hundley, *The Great Thirst,* 97–102.

116. J. R. McDonald to Miller & Lux, 8 November 1876, box 25, Latta Collection; *Prospectus of the West Side Irrigation District, San Joaquin Valley* (n.p., n.d.), Miller & Lux Collection.

117. Jeff Shannon to Miller & Lux, 17 March 1876, box 23, Latta Collection.

118. Miller & Lux's supplemental legislation was reported in the *Pacific Rural Press,* 1 April 1876. See Pisani, *From the Family Farm to Agribusiness,* 141–42.

119. Henry Miller to Charles Lux, 11 April 1877, Miller Papers.

120. On the injunction suit, see Treadwell, *The Cattle King,* 344–45; Pisani, *From the Family Farm to Agribusiness,* 147.

121. *San Francisco Evening Bulletin,* 18 May 1874.

122. The next two counties, in terms of acres irrigated, were Los Angeles

and Modoc, which had 56 and 196 individual irrigation ditches, respectively. California State Surveyor General, "Statistical Tables," in *Biennial Report of the Surveyor General of the State of California from August 1, 1877, to August 1, 1879* (Sacramento, 1880), 8–9.

123. Between 1864 and 1879, thirty-seven states drafted new constitutions. See Morton Keller, *Affairs of State: Public Life in Late Nineteenth-Century America* (Cambridge: Harvard University Press, 1977), 111.

124. A vast majority of the delegates, Harry Scheiber argues, "carried a reform banner in one hand and a 'Whites Only' placard in the other." Harry N. Scheiber, "Race, Radicalism, and Reform: Historical Perspective on the 1879 California Constitution," *Hastings Constitutional Law Quarterly* 17 (fall 1989): 51. On the Constitutional Convention and its delegates, see California Constitutional Convention, *Debates and Proceedings*; Carl Swisher, *Motivation and Political Technique in the California Constitutional Convention, 1878–79* (Claremont, Calif.: Pomona College, 1930); David Alan Johnson, *Founding the Far West: California, Oregon, and Nevada, 1840–1890* (Berkeley and Los Angeles: University of California Press, 1992), 254–58; and Ethington, *The Public City*, 279–82.

125. Ethington, *The Public City*, 242–86.

126. *Gilroy Advocate*, 16 February 1878. While the *Advocate* and many other newspapers around the state were outspoken critics of "Kearneyism," they simultaneously praised the "anticoolie" and "workingmen's" clubs in their own communities. See the *Gilroy Advocate*, 16 February and 20 April 1878.

127. Johnson, *Founding the Far West*, 255.

128. Deverell, *Railroad Crossing*, 46–56.

129. Patrick T. Dowling, in California Constitutional Convention, *Debates and Proceedings*, 1152.

130. James O'Sullivan, in ibid., 1137–38.

131. William P. Grace, in ibid., 1141.

132. For the text of the "minority report" of the Committee on Land and Homestead Exemptions, see California Constitutional Convention, *Debates and Proceedings*, 1136.

133. "Land and Homestead Exemptions," art. XVII, sec. II, *Constitution of the State of California*.

134. Thomas B. McFarland, in California Constitutional Convention, *Debates and Proceedings*, 1145.

135. Scheiber, "Race, Radicalism, and Reform," 41; and Richard Orsi, "*The Octopus* Reconsidered: The Southern Pacific and Agricultural Modernization in California, 1865–1915," *California Historical Quarterly* 54 (fall 1975): 197–220.

136. Patrick T. Dowling, in California Constitutional Convention, *Debates and Proceedings*, 1148.

137. *Constitution of the State of California*, art I, sec. I. (Emphasis added.)

138. Pisani, *From the Family Farm to Agribusiness*, 161; Scheiber, "Race, Radicalism, and Reform," 66–67.

139. See Scheiber, "Race, Radicalism, and Reform," 57–63.

140. Powell, *Report on the Lands of the Arid Region*, 8.

141. Ibid., 7.

CHAPTER 4. *LUX V. HAGGIN*

1. On California's early mining and timber industries, see Rodman Paul, *California Gold: The Beginning of Mining in the Far West* (Cambridge: Harvard University Press, 1947); Daniel A. Cornford, *Workers and Dissent in the Redwood Empire* (Philadelphia: Temple University Press, 1987); Richard Walker, "California's Debt to Nature: Natural Resources and the Golden Road to Capitalist Growth, 1848–1940," *Annals of the American Association of Geographers* (forthcoming).

2. Hyacinth [Powers], "Wayside Views of California," 229.

3. Norris, *The Octopus*, 130–31. For a close reading of this passage, see Merchant, "Reinventing Eden," 146.

4. *San Francisco Bulletin*, 29 October 1874. Muir's original and unedited version of this article is reprinted in *Los Tulares: Quarterly Bulletin of the Tulare County Historical Society* (December 1970).

5. On production and reproduction in a different historical context, see Merchant, *Ecological Revolutions*, 14–19. The California state engineer William Hammond Hall, a great booster for irrigation, wrote, "[Irrigation] means not only cultivation of crops, but also cultivation of irrigators. The question *How to secure a population of irrigators* may be regarded as presenting the fourth great problem of irrigation." W. H. Hall, *Report of the State Engineer to the Legislature of the State of California*, 121.

6. Merchant, *Ecological Revolutions*, 199; Donald Worster, *Nature's Economy: A History of Ecological Ideas* (Cambridge: Cambridge University Press, 1977), 1–55.

7. Urban, O'Neill, and Shugart, "Landscape Ecology," 119–27; Davis, "Los Angeles after the Storm," 221–41.

8. W. Preston, *Vanishing Landscapes*, 41–42.

9. Davis, "Los Angeles after the Storm," 226; David E. Bradbury, "The Physical Geography of the Mediterranean Lands," in *Mediterranean-Type Shrublands*, ed. Francesco di Castri et al. (New York: Elsevier Scientific Publishing, 1981), 53–62.

10. W. Preston, *Vanishing Landscapes*, 10–11. Preston identifies these different soils as lake deposits, weathered older alluvium, residual materials, and recent alluvium of alluvial fans and deltas. On the importance of soils to biotic diversity, see Michael G. Barbour and Valerie Whitworth, "California's Living Landscape," *Fremontia* 22 (summer 1994), 4–5.

11. A. A. Sargent, "Irrigation and Drainage," *Overland Monthly* 8 (July 1886): 19, 32.

12. Alexander, *Report*, 22–24.

13. Ibid., map 4, 39–40.

14. W. H. Hall, *Report of the State Engineer*, appendix b, 103, 7.

15. *San Francisco Bulletin*, 29 October 1874. In the unedited draft of this article, Muir mixed ideas of natural preservation with utilitarianism. He writes, "Californians have only to see to it that the forests on which the regular and manageable flow of the rivers depend are preserved, that storage reservoirs are made at the foot of the Range and all the bounty of the mountains put to use.

Then will theirs be the most foodful and beautiful of all the lowland valleys of like extent in the world."

16. George E. Freeman, "Among the Irrigators of Fresno County," *Overland Monthly* 9 (June 1887): 624. On Fresno's irrigation colonies, see Stoll, *The Fruits of Natural Advantage*, 33–43.

17. See the *Kern County Courier*, 23 November 1872, 19 April and 20 September 1873, and 3 and 4 October 1874; *Southern Californian*, 18 March 1875.

18. See John M. Day, "Public Ownership and Control of the Water, the Only Safety for the Irrigator," in *Report of the Special Committee of the United States Senate on the Irrigation and Reclamation of Arid Lands* (Washington, D.C.: Government Printing Office, 1890), 398; Zonlight, *Land, Water, and Settlement*, 257–60.

19. *Gilroy Advocate*, 21 September 1878. Other letters from "Pioneer" appeared 1 June, 24 August, 28 September, 5 October, and 30 November 1878.

20. J[ames]. C. Crocker to Henry Miller, 8 April 1870, box 8, Latta Collection.

21. "Riparian Suits Association," box ML 23 B, Latta Collection.

22. Mary Austin, *The Land of Little Rain* (Boston: Houghton Mifflin, 1903), 241; *Gilroy Advocate*, 30 November 1878.

23. George Derby drew his map for the Army Corps of Topographical Engineers following his exploration of the Tulare Basin. See Derby, *Report to the Secretary of War, Communications in Compliance with a Resolution of the Senate: A Report on the Tulare Valley*, 32nd Cong., 1st sess., 1852, Sen. Ex. Doc. 110. William Blake served as expedition geologist for the Transcontinental Railroad Survey, and he likely possessed a greater understanding of the region's landscape. William Blake, *Geological Report of Exploration and Surveys for a Railroad Route from the Mississippi River to the Pacific Ocean, under R. S. Williamson* (Washington, D.C.: Department of War, 1853).

24. W. H. Hall, *Report of the State Engineer*, appendix B, 66.

25. Horatio Livermore to Charles Lux, 3 July 1876, box ML 1 (2), Latta Collection.

26. Miller to Lux, 21 and 27 January 1877, Miller Papers.

27. Crocker to Lux, 28 February 1877, box 26, Latta Collection; Miller to Lux, 15 and 18 March 1877, Miller Papers.

28. *Gilroy Advocate*, 5 October 1878. On Gilroy's anti-Chinese groups, see the *Advocate*, 22 July and 16 September 1876, and 16 February and 20 April 1878.

29. *Gilroy Advocate*, 21 September 1878.

30. Miller to Lux, 23 March 1877, Miller Papers.

31. Miller to Lux, 21 January 1877, Miller Papers; Crocker to Lux, 30 March 1877, box 27, Latta Collection. Miller & Lux and Haggin had worked together prior to their confrontation over the Kern River, and as large landowners and ranchers they shared common interests. During the early 1870s, for instance, they formed the Southern California Stockraisers Association to oppose local "no fence" ordinances. See Zonlight, *Land, Water, and Settlement*, 7.

32. Documents related to the membership and proceedings of the Riparian Suits Association can be found in box ML (1) B, Latta Collection.

33. The "campaign expenses" document lists amounts paid to various individuals, including the editors of the *San Francisco Chronicle* and the *Evening Gazette* and Warren Olney, who would soon become an associate justice on the California Supreme Court. Immediately following the supreme court's ruling in favor of Miller & Lux, Olney penned an article for the *Overland Monthly* praising the verdict. See *Overland Monthly* 9 (January 1887): 40–50. During the first three months of 1885, Lux also issued numerous checks (made out to "Cash") in Sacramento ranging from $1,500 to $7,000 "connected with Legislative proceedings to Water rights."

34. Riparian Suits Association, "Statement of Principles," box ML 23 (1) B, Latta Collection. This statement included the following initial acreage for members: Cox & Clarke, 14,520 acres; Miller & Lux, 36,644 acres; John H. Redington, 13,283 acres; George Cornwell, 8,000 acres; L. H. Bonestell, 1,920 acres; Horatio Livermore, 22,541 acres; and Horatio Stebbins, 1,280 acres. On the bottom of this sheet Miller & Lux's acreage was combined with that of Redington, Bonestell, and Livermore, and part of Cox & Clarke's, for a total of 78,908 acres. Most likely, Miller & Lux paid their expenses and taxes until the suit was complete, at which time the land was legally transferred to Miller & Lux.

35. Alonzo Phelps, *Contemporary Biography of California's Representative Men* (San Francisco: Bancroft and Co., 1881), 325–26; Pisani, *From the Family Farm to Agribusiness*, 193–203. Haggin's San Francisco ventures included the California Steam Navigation Company, the State Telegraph Company (Western Union), the Pacific Ice Company, Potrero Gas Light Company, the California Street Road, Risdon Iron Works, and the Sutro Tunnel. See Zonlight, *Land, Water, and Settlement*, 62–63.

36. Malone, *The Battle for Butte*, 26–31.

37. *Stockton Daily Independent*, 4 December 1873; *Kern County Weekly Courier*, 17 January and 9 May 1874; the *San Francisco Chronicle*, 17 January 1874.

38. *Kern County Courier*, 3 October 1874.

39. The Desert Land Act allowed settlers to purchase up to 640 acres of land for $1.25 an acre, with the stipulation that the land was required to be irrigated within three years' time.

40. *Kern County Courier-Californian*, 20 May 1880. Since Haggin rarely appeared in Kern County, local newspapers often relied on his statement and collection of desert land affidavits, published in James Ben Ali Haggin, *The Desert Lands of Kern County, California—Affidavits of Various Residents of Said County* (San Francisco: C. H. Street, 1877). For criticism of Haggin's actions, see the *Visalia Delta*, 8 December 1877, and 25 January 1878; *San Francisco Chronicle*, 5, 6, 7, and 11 January 1878.

41. *Kern County Courier-Californian*, 31 October 1878.

42. *Kern County Courier*, 24 April 1875.

43. *San Francisco Chronicle*, 29 January 1878.

44. *Bakersfield Californian*, 3 May 1877, and 10 September 1871; Pisani, *From the Family Farm to Agribusiness*, 200–201.

45. "Homeseekers and Development Number," *Bakersfield Californian*, 1 January 1910, p. 18.

46. *Visalia Delta,* 8 November 1878.

47. Horwitz, *The Transformation of American Law,* 31–62; Steinberg, *Nature Incorporated,* 16.

48. The best source on the various conflicts surrounding *Lux* v. *Haggin* is Pisani, *From the Family Farm to Agribusiness,* 191–249. On riparian and appropriative water law, see Gordon R. Miller, "Shaping California Water Law, 1781–1928," *Southern California Quarterly* (spring 1973): 9–37; Eric T. Freyfogle, "*Lux* v. *Haggin* and the Common Law Burden of Modern Water Rights," *University of Colorado Law Review* 57 (spring 1986): 485–525.

49. One local editor wrote, "All the parties in the suit seem to consider the riparian questions settled, so the question . . . is whether the Buena Vista Slough is or is not a natural channel of the Kern River." *Kern County Weekly Courier,* 26 May 1881, cited in Pisani, *From the Family Farm to Agribusiness,* 209–10.

50. *Lux* v. *Haggin* (1881), "Argument of Hall McAllister," 2. The phrase "time immemorial" was previously used to assert prescriptive (and not riparian) water rights. In common law, it meant that those rights were ancient and beyond memory. McAllister flipped this usage to assert that the river itself "had run from time immemorial," thereby justifying Miller & Lux's riparian claims. See Steinberg, *Nature Incorporated,* 143–44.

51. *Lux* v. *Haggin* (1881), "Argument of Hall McAllister," 70.

52. Joseph Kinnicut Angell, *A Treatise on the Law of Watercourses,* 5th ed. (Boston: Brown and Co., 1854).

53. *Lux* v. *Haggin* (1881), "Argument of Hall McAllister," 73.

54. These two examples were cited by McAllister and John Garber during the case. *McComber* v. *Godfrey,* 108 Mass., 219–22; *Swett* v. *Cutts,* 50 New Hampshire, 429.

55. *McComber* v. *Godfrey,* 108 Mass., 219–22. (Emphasis added.)

56. Horwitz, *The Transformation of American Law,* 31; Steinberg, *Nature Incorporated,* 16.

57. Scheiber and McCurdy, "Eminent-Domain Law and Western Agriculture," 115–16.

58. In California's leading water rights case of the gold era, *Irwin* v. *Phillips* (1855), the court recognized the need of mining enterprises to appropriate water "without which the most important interests of the mineral regions would remain without development." *Irwin* v. *Phillips* established an important precedent for water appropriators as well as the primacy of economic enterprise in water allocation, which the district court ruling in *Lux* v. *Haggin* duly noted and reaffirmed. *Irwin* v. *Phillips,* 5 Cal. 140 (1855), 146.

59. *Lux* v. *Haggin* (1881), "Argument of Hall McAllister," 18.

60. Ibid., 74.

61. Ibid., 18–19. (Emphasis added.)

62. Ibid., 70, 145.

63. Ibid., "Argument of John Garber," 3, and Garber, "Statement of Facts," i.

64. Ibid., "Argument of George Flournoy," 39.

65. Ibid., "Decision of Hon. Benjamin Brundage," 27.

66. Ibid., 7, 24.

67. Ibid., "Argument of Hall McAllister," 159.

68. A variety of sources document the changing course of Kern River. See ibid., "Testimony of George H. Mendell," vol. 3, 246–53; McAllister, "Oral Argument," 94–99; Sargent, "Irrigation and Drainage," 29–30; and Rafael Cuen oral history, box 4 (1), Latta Collection.

69. W. Preston, *Vanishing Landscapes,* 22–25; and Hilgard et al., *Report,* 50–52.

70. W. H. Hall, *Report of the State Engineer,* appendix B, 66.

71. "Testimony of J. F. Clyne," in "Estate of Henry Miller," 1381, carton 593, Miller & Lux Collection.

72. *Lux v. Haggin,* 4 P. 919 (1884), "Brief for Appellants in Reply," 9, 19, cited in Pisani, *From the Family Farm to Agribusiness,* 213.

73. A concise summary of McKinstry's ruling can be found in Pisani, *From the Family Farm to Agribusiness,* 228–29.

74. McKinstry, in Supreme Court of California, *Report of Cases Determined in the Supreme Court of the State of California,* vol. 69 (San Francisco: Bancroft-Whitney, 1906), 343.

75. Ibid., 418.

76. Ibid., 390–91. (Emphasis in original.)

77. *Lux v. Haggin* (1881), "Argument of George Flournoy," 39, and "Argument of Hall McAllister," 18, 145.

78. "Homeseekers and Development Number," 19.

79. "Contract and Agreement between Henry Miller and others of the first part and James B. Haggin and others of the second part, July 28, 1888," carton 594, Miller & Lux Collection.

80. Sargent, "Irrigation and Drainage," 30.

81. Hyacinth [Powers], "Wayside Views of California," 229.

82. Hilgard et al., *Report,* 50–54; W. Preston, *Vanishing Landscapes,* 139. On Eugene Hilgard, see Stoll, *The Fruits of Natural Advantage,* 48–50.

83. Hilgard et al., *Report,* 51.

84. Ibid., 52.

85. Ibid., 44, 50. Alkalinity is caused by the natural evaporation of water on the surface of the land. Reclamation and irrigation increased the amount of salts brought to the surface. As Hilgard noted, "The more water [that] evaporates from the surface of the soil within a season the more alkali salts will be drawn to the surface." (34)

86. William Hammond Hall, "Irrigation in California," *National Geographic Magazine* 1 (1889): 286. See also Elwood Mead, *Report of the Irrigation Investigations in California* (Washington, D.C.: Government Printing Office, 1901), 222; Warren Olney, "The Present Status of the Irrigation Problem," *Overland Monthly* 9 (January 1887): 48.

87. Mead, *Report,* 263–66.

88. Andrew N. Cohen, "The Hidden Costs of California's Water," in *Life on the Edge: A Guide to California's Endangered Natural Resources* (Santa Cruz, Calif.: BioSystems Books, 1994), 289.

89. Katibah, "A Brief History of Riparian Forests in the Central Valley of

California" (paper presented at the California Riparian Systems Conference, University of California at Davis, 17–19 September 1981), 26–27.

90. Anne Sands, "The Value of Riparian Habitat," *Fremontia* 10 (April 1982): 3–4; Thompson, "Riparian Forests of the Sacramento Valley, California," 294–315; Mount, *California Rivers and Streams*, 52–82.

91. For an excellent discussion of both the treatment of insects in the fields and the insecticide industry, see Stoll, *The Fruits of Natural Advantage*, 94–123.

92. T. S. Palmer, *The Jack Rabbits of the United States* (Washington, D.C.: Government Printing Office, 1896).

93. Frank Latta, "William J. Browning," 23–26, Latta Collection.

94. T. S. Palmer, *The Jack Rabbits of the United States*, 47–64.

95. McCullough, *The Tule Elk*. On population estimates, see 25–26.

96. Ibid., 26.

97. H. Miller, "Dictation," 13.

98. C. Hart Merriam, "The Elk's Last Stand," *Scientific Monthly* 13 (1921): 465–75.

99. *Gilroy Advocate*, 21 September 1878.

100. *Gilroy Advocate*, 28 September 1878.

101. *Lux v. Haggin* (1881), "Testimony of S. W. Wible," 482.

102. "Homeseekers and Development Number," 20.

103. *Visalia Delta*, 8 November 1878, cited in Worster, *Rivers of Empire*, 104.

104. M. C. Miller, *Flooding the Courtrooms*, 20.

105. *Kern County Gazette*, 22 May 1880.

106. Ibid.

107. O. Brown, "Statement of O. Brown," in *Report of the Special Committee of the United States Senate on the Irrigation and Reclamation of Arid Lands* (Washington, D.C.: Government Printing Office, 1890), 288.

108. Day, "Public Ownership and Control of the Water," 398.

109. The population of Fresno County rose by 89 percent and that of Tulare County rose by 66 percent. Zonlight, *Land, Water, and Settlement*, 316.

110. Day, "Public Ownership and Control of the Water," 397–98.

111. *Kern County Record*, 13 April 1883; *Kern County Gazette*, 11 December 1886.

112. *Kern County Gazette*, 11 December 1886.

113. Columbia Division, "Dues for Labor, January 1890," Box 715, Miller & Lux Collection.

114. W. H. Hall, *Report of the State Engineer*, 121.

115. Immediately following the *Lux v. Haggin* decision, irrigators throughout the state organized a "State Irrigation Convention" that sought legislative action for statewide irrigation districts. They portrayed riparian water rights as the main instrument of water monopoly but failed to see how the law of appropriation also produced monopolistic tendencies. The resulting Wright Act of 1887 (which promoted irrigation districts) failed to produce a rapid increase in irrigated acreage. During the 1890s, the amount of irrigated land increased by only 44 percent, compared to 500 percent during the previous decade. See Pisani, *From the Family Farm to Agribusiness*, 230–82.

CHAPTER 5. LABORING ON THE LAND

1. Joseph Warren Matthews, "Diary 1869–1900," Joseph Warren Matthews Papers, Bancroft Library, University of California at Berkeley. On the "wage-workers' frontier," see Schwantes, *Hard Traveling*.

2. On western migrant labor in different industries, see Schwantes, *Hard Traveling*; McWilliams, *Factories in the Field*; Chan, *This Bittersweet Soil*; Emmons, *The Butte Irish*; Robbins, *Hard Times in Paradise*; Cornford, *Workers and Dissent in the Redwood Empire*; Gregory R. Woirol, *In the Floating Army: F. C. Mills on Itinerant Life in California, 1914* (Urbana: University of Illinois Press, 1992); Don Mitchell, *The Lie of the Land: Migrant Workers and the California Landscape* (Minneapolis: University of Minnesota Press, 1996).

3. On segmentation practices, see David M. Gordon, Richard Edwards, and Michael Reich, *Segmented Work, Divided Workers: The Historical Transformation of Labor in the United States* (Cambridge: Cambridge University Press, 1982); Walter Licht, *Working for the Railroad: The Organization of Work in the Nineteenth Century* (Princeton: Princeton University Press, 1983), 221–25; Rich Halpern, *Down on the Killing Floor: Black and White Workers in Chicago's Packinghouses, 1904–54* (Urbana: University of Illinois Press, 1997), 23–32. On the racialization of social groups in the West and the nation, see David R. Roediger, *The Wages of Whiteness: Race and the Making of the American Working Class* (New York: Verso Press, 1991), 95–166; Alexander Saxton, *The Indispensable Enemy: Labor and the Anti-Chinese Movement in California* (Berkeley and Los Angeles: University of California Press, 1971), 3–45; Tomas Almaguer, *Racial Fault Lines: The Historical Origins of White Supremacy in California* (Berkeley and Los Angeles: University of California Press, 1994).

4. Cletus Daniel, *Bitter Harvest: A History of California Farmworkers, 1870–1941* (Ithaca: Cornell University Press, 1981), 71. The pioneering works on California migrant labor include Levi Varden Fuller, "The Supply of Agricultural Labor as a Factor in the Evolution of Farm Organization in California" (Ph.D. diss., University of California at Berkeley, 1939); Paul S. Taylor, "Foundations of California Rural Society," *California Historical Society Quarterly* 24 (1945): 193–228; McWilliams, *Factories in the Field*. For a pointed critique of McWilliams's "factory" thesis, see David Vaught, "An Orchardist's Point of View: Harvest Labor Relations on a California Almond Ranch, 1892–1921," *Agricultural History* 69 (fall 1995): 563–91.

5. R. White, *The Organic Machine*, 1–15.

6. While a few of the vaqueros were Californios by birth, the majority were born either in Mexico or in California after statehood. California's dominant white population increasingly referred to them as "Mexicans" regardless of their place of origin, especially in their role as agricultural laborers.

7. For example, see the oral histories of José Messa and Rafael Cuen, box 4 (1), Latta Collection. On the cultural contributions of Mexican vaqueros to California ranching, see Terry G. Jordan, *North American Cattle-Ranching Frontiers: Origins, Diffusion, and Differentiation* (Albuquerque: University of New Mexico Press, 1993), 241–65; Arnold R. Rojas, *The Vaquero* (Santa Barbara: McNally and Loftin, 1964).

8. Miller & Lux's decentralized system of accounting in the late 1860s makes it difficult to estimate the total number of vaqueros employed (or the total number of employees). Henry Miller kept separate account books for his Las Animas–Bloomfield Farm employees. The *Gilroy Advocate* estimated that Bloomfield Farm regularly employed 35–150 "farm hands, ordinary laborers, mechanics and vaqueros." Miller & Lux likely kept accounts for its other employees in separate books. *Gilroy Advocate*, 3 June 1876.

9. Miller to Lux, 9 January 1874, box 4, Latta Collection. Castro had purchased property near Monterey in 1872, and he likely invested his wages in improvements. See Fink, *Monterey County*, 208.

10. Miller to Lux, 1 January 1875, box 5, Latta Collection.

11. David Montejano, *Anglos and Mexicans in the Making of Texas, 1836–1986* (Austin: University of Texas Press, 1987), 82–89; Alonzo, *Tejano Legacy*, 97–101; David G. Gutierrez, *Walls and Mirrors: Mexican Americans, Mexican Immigrants, and the Politics of Ethnicity* (Berkeley and Los Angeles: University of California Press, 1995), 39–60.

12. "S.H. [Slaughterhouse] Employees Pay Roll," June 1880, box 7 (3) B, Latta Collection. The other two employees who earned $30 a month were named Brodrick and Zimmerman.

13. "Miller & Lux [Firebaugh] Ledger," April 1885-February 1895, box ML 7 (3) B, Latta Collection.

14. "Payroll at Santa Rita Ranch for July 1900," box 3 (1) B, Latta Collection.

15. The Southern Division was constituted by the properties in Tulare and Kern Counties, roughly the region surrounding Buena Vista Slough. Its different payrolls included the Buttonwillow Ranch, the Cattle Department, Guyana Ranch, Maples Ranch, Panama Ranch, Wible Ranch, and various "hay" and "thresher camps."

16. "Southern Ranches," June 1905–December 1908, vol. 145, Latta Collection.

17. Another example of this practice occurred when Miller sent José Antonio Eigilo to work as a vaquero in Nevada. Eigilo's wife (along with another young woman) served as ranch cook, and the combined wages for the three of them amounted to $40 a month. Miller to Holloway, 13 December 1887, box 5, Latta Collection.

18. Rafael Cuen, oral history, box 4 (1), Latta Collection; Rojas, *The Vaquero*, 120–21.

19. "Southern Ranches," Latta Collection.

20. According to Horace Torchiana, who served as a Miller & Lux superintendent between 1895 and 1901, employees could speak any language among themselves, "but any man who [came] in contact with the management must speak English." Torchiana, *California Gringos*, 211.

21. Of the sixty-five employees listed on the payroll for the Cattle Department in February 1908, ten surnames are repeated twice and a couple are repeated three or four times.

22. U.S. Congress, *Report of the United States Immigration Commission*

(Washington, D.C.: Government Printing Office, 1911), cited in California State Relief Administration, *Migratory Labor in California* (San Francisco, 1936), 26.

23. Stoll, *The Fruits of Natural Advantage,* 150–52.

24. J. Leroy Nickel to the commissioner general of immigration, 8 March 1918, carton 494, Miller & Lux Collection.

25. J. F. Clyne to Nickel, 8 November 1918, carton 494, Miller & Lux Collection.

26. Chan, *This Bittersweet Soil;* 361. Chan's study remains the only one to address Chinese cooks in detail. For general studies of Chinese labor in agriculture, see Ronald Takaki, *Strangers from a Different Shore: A History of Asian Americans* (New York: Penguin Books, 1989), 21–178; Saxton, *The Indispensable Enemy;* Ping Chiu, *Chinese Labor in California, 1850–1880* (Madison: State Historical Society of Wisconsin, 1963); Sylvia Sun Minnick, *SAMFOW: The San Joaquin Chinese Legacy* (Fresno, Calif.: Panorama West Publishers, 1988).

27. Torchiana, *California Gringos,* 24. For similar testimony, see Paul P. Parker, "Along the Dirty Plate Route," *California Folklore Quarterly* 3 (January 1944): 16–20; Orville Foster, "The Men of Miller-Lux," *Old West* (summer 1973): 32–34, 58–60.

28. *Gilroy Advocate,* 16 February 1878. On the "southern movement" of Chinese from the mining regions and the Bay Area, see Chan, *This Bittersweet Soil,* 45–51. Ping Chiu estimates that reclamation projects employed between 5,000 and 6,000 Chinese workers during the peak years of 1874 and 1875. Chiu, *Chinese Labor in California,* 72. Also see John Thompson, *Discovering and Rediscovering the Fragility of Levees and Land in the Sacramento–San Joaquin Delta, 1870–1879 and Today* (Sacramento: California Department of Water Resources, 1982).

29. "Chinamen—Big Jim Gangs #1 & #2, for March 1873," box 8 (3), Latta Collection. The debts often entailed transportation cost from China, subsistence, and a fee from the contractor.

30. The "payroll" section of the "Statement of Expenses from 8/19/73–9/17/73" includes this data: "Payroll: White Labor 3,684.07, Chinese Labor 9,641.50." See box ML 1 (5) B. Totals for Chinese labor during the month of August are contained in box ML 8 (2).

31. *Southern Californian,* 4 March 1875; Chan, *This Bittersweet Soil,* 332–33; Saxton, *The Indispensable Enemy,* 215–18.

32. Miller to Lux, 1 August 1873, Miller Papers.

33. Miller to Lux, 12 May 1876, Miller Papers. Miller did not specify the race or ethnicity of the suspected strikers. Miller's opposition to M. L. Stangroom is discussed in Miller to Lux, 14 November 1877, Miller Papers.

34. Only a few canal company payrolls exist for the 1870s. These are contained in boxes ML 1 (5) C, 1 (5) E, 8 (2), and 8 (3), Latta Collection; and carton 738, Miller & Lux Collection. Miller occasionally made reference to Chinese labor; see his letters dated 26 July and 1 August 1873, and 14 November 1877, Miller Papers.

35. For instance, see "Miller & Lux ledger, April 1885-February 1895," vol. 54, ML box 7 (3) B, Latta Collection.

36. H. Miller, "Dictation," 25.

37. "Ranch Instructions," 2, Lux Family Papers.

38. H. Miller, "Dictation," 25.

39. In 1874, Miller asked the San Francisco office to engage a "girl" for "housework" at the Canal Farm. Upon her arrival in July, Miller wrote that "she want[ed] to go right back. . . . I don't think you [took] great pains to tell her what kind of a place she has to go to." San Francisco office manager John Bolton responded, "This is the same story all over the country; these girls engage, get passage paid and have the trip and then refuse to stay." Miller to Lux, 14 July 1874, box 4, Latta Collection.

40. "Time Book and Pay-Roll for the Month of July, 1908," carton 737, Miller & Lux Collection.

41. "Miller & Lux [Firebaugh] Ledger," April 1885-February 1895.

42. "Southern Ranches [Payroll], June 1905-December 1908." See the labor account books for the Dos Palos Division that cover the years 1901 through 1912, carton 737, Miller & Lux Collection.

43. Chan, *This Bittersweet Soil,* 368.

44. P. Parker, "Along the Dirty Plate Route," 16. Also see the oral history of John Dugain, box ML 4–5 (1), Latta Collection.

45. The only non-Chinese Asian I have discovered who worked for Miller & Lux was "S. Yashimoto." He served as a cook at the Chester Ranch in Kern County in 1908. It is very likely, however, that other Japanese immigrants worked for the firm in the early twentieth century.

46. Hans Christian Palmer, "Italian Immigration and the Development of California Agriculture" (Ph.D. diss., University of California at Berkeley, 1965), appendix, tables XXIX and XXX, 360–64. On Portuguese and Italian immigrants, see August Mark Vaz, *The Portuguese in California* (Oakland: I.D.E.S. Supreme Council, 1965); Micaela Di Leonardo, *The Varieties of Ethnic Experience: Kinship, Class, and Gender among California Italian Americans* (Ithaca: Cornell University Press, 1984).

47. *Pacific Rural Press,* cited in Sally Miller, "Changing Faces of the Central Valley: The Ethnic Presence," *California History* 74 (summer 1995): 186–88; H. C. Palmer, "Italian Immigration and the Development of California Agriculture," 152.

48. See Theodore Saloutos, "The Immigrant in Pacific Coast Agriculture, 1880-1940," *Agricultural History* 49 (spring 1975): 193–94.

49. J[ohn]. W. Schmitz to Charles Lux, 14 December 1875, box 22, Latta Collection; Miller to Lux, 12 May 1876, Miller Papers.

50. Joseph Warren Matthews to Rebecca Matthews, 2 April 1899, box 1, Matthews Papers.

51. Matthews to Rebecca Matthews, 19 March 1899, Matthews Papers; Thompson, "The Fragility of Levees and Land," 11–17.

52. Joseph Warren Matthews "Diary," 18 April 1899, and Matthews to Rebecca Matthews, 15 April 1899, box 1, Matthews Papers.

53. James A. Young and B. Abbott Sparks, *Cattle in the Cold Desert* (Logan: Utah State University Press, 1985), 128–30.

54. See the yearly inventories of the firm's assets contained in volumes 1

(1885–89), 2 (1897–1900), 4 (1900–02), 11 (1902–04), and 17 (1904–06). The largest stockpiles of feed were located at Bloomfield Farm and Poso Farm.

55. "Miller & Lux [Firebaugh] Ledger," April 1885-February 1895, box ML 7 (3) B, Latta Collection.

56. Foster, "The Men of Miller-Lux," 59.

57. "Miller & Lux [Firebaugh] Ledger," April 1885-February 1895, box ML 7 (3) B, Latta Collection.

58. H. C. Palmer, "Italian Immigration and the Development of California Agriculture," appendix, table XLI, 380–83.

59. "Estimated Inventory," Miller & Lux Ledger, vol. 17, 28 February 1905, Latta Collection.

60. These places employed over two-thirds of the total labor force. The work site names were misleading: "Parson" had lost his "place" to Miller & Lux, no Dutchman labored at Dutch Boys, and hogs were allowed onto the Hog Camp fields only after the hay had been cut and stacked.

61. H. C. Palmer, "Italian Immigration," 80–96.

62. Employees could keep accounts at Miller & Lux's stores in Firebaugh or Los Banos, and any purchases were deducted from their wages and recorded in the payrolls. For Koenig's account, see "Miller & Lux [Firebaugh] Ledger," April 1885-February 1895, vol. 54, box 7 (3) B, Latta Collection.

63. *Fresno Evening Expositor,* 28 April 1890.

64. Ibid.

65. Ibid.

66. Richard Maxwell Brown, *No Duty to Retreat: Violence and Values in American History and Society* (Norman: University of Oklahoma Press, 1994), 87–127.

67. The *Expositor*'s sketch (three-quarters profile) depicted Koenig with a full beard, carefully cropped hair, a formidable forehead, and deep-set eyes. He very much resembled a younger Henry Miller.

68. *Fresno Evening Expositor,* 28 April 1890.

69. Carleton Parker, *The Casual Laborer and Other Essays* (New York: Harcourt, Brace, and Howe, 1920); Eric H. Monkkonen, ed., *Walking to Work: Tramps in America, 1790–1935* (Lincoln: University of Nebraska Press, 1984); Woirol, *In the Floating Army.*

70. P. Parker, "Along the Dirty Plate Route," 16.

71. See Matthews's "Diary" and letters, March-April 1899, Matthews Papers.

72. *San Francisco Bulletin,* 14 April 1877.

73. Richard Steven Street, "Tattered Shirts and Ragged Pants: Accommodation, Protest, and the Coarse Culture of California Wheat Harvesters and Threshers, 1866–1900," *Pacific Historical Review* 67 (November 1998): 573–608.

74. P. Parker, "Along the Dirty Plate Route," 17.

75. Matthews to Rebecca Matthews, 26 March 1899, Matthews Papers.

76. P. Parker, "Along the Dirty Plate Route," 16.

77. On Central Valley labor shortages, see Vaught, "An Orchardist's Point of View": 563–91. For one example of Miller & Lux's experiencing an undersupply of laborers, see Henry Miller to Joseph Walter Schmitz, 7 June 1900, J. Walter Schmitz Papers, J. W. Schmitz III Papers.

78. Torchiana, *California Gringos,* 158.
79. *San Francisco Call,* 14 March 1895.
80. On San Francisco's meatpacking industry, see Roger R. Olmsted and Nancy L. Olmsted, *Rincon de las Salinas y Potrero Viejo—the Vanished Corner* (San Francisco: San Francisco Clean Water Management Program, November 1981); Joseph A. Blum, "South San Francisco: The Making of an Industrial City," *California History* 63 (spring 1984): 114–34.
81. "Slaughterhouse Employees. Payroll," June 1880, box 7 (3) b, Latta Collection.
82. Issel and Cherny, *San Francisco, 1865–1932,* 72; Halpern, *Down on the Killing Floor,* 23–30.
83. "Butchertown Pay Roll," 20 June 1914, vol. 155, Miller & Lux Collection; Charles Lux, "Autobiographical Statement," Bancroft Collection; Charles Steward to J. Leroy Nickel, 7 November 1913, carton 105, Miller & Lux Collection.
84. Halpern, *Down on the Killing Floors,* 21–30.
85. Michael Kazin, *Barons of Labor: The San Francisco Building Trades and Union Power in the Progressive Era* (Urbana: University of Illinois Press, 1987), 13–35.
86. Thomas Walker Page, "The San Francisco Labor Movement in 1901," *Political Science Quarterly* 17 (1902): 673–75; Robert Knight, *Industrial Relations in the San Francisco Bay Area, 1900–1918* (Berkeley and Los Angeles: University of California Press, 1960), 70–71; *San Francisco Call,* 16 March 1911.
87. On this point, see Cronon, *Nature's Metropolis,* 340.
88. Ted White, cited in Olmsted and Olmsted, *Rincon de Las Salinas y Potrero Viejo,* 125.
89. "Estimated Inventory, February 28, 1905," vol. 17, and "Meat Department, December 30, 1899," vol. 2, Miller & Lux Collection.
90. The majority listed were foreign-born, single men between the ages of twenty-one and forty, each of whom had spent over six years as a "casual laborer." The respondents most often cited "common labor," "ranch work," and "teamster" as their "first job" and as their "last regular job." Commission of Immigration and Housing, *Report on Unemployment* (Sacramento: State Printing Office, 1914), appendix C-10, 47–53.
91. Labor charges were broken down as follows: "ranch labor," $451,954.91; "slaughterhouse labor," $72,766.65; "sheep labor," 61,022.44; top-management salaries, $80,762.15; "subsistence" for laborers, $113,957.02; and "legal expenses," $17,261.94. Other significant figures included "freight" expenses, $184,613.88; ranch, sheep, and slaughterhouse expenses, $300,488.95; and taxes, $110,823.95. Operating expenses for the year totaled $1,691,614.62. "Estimated Inventory, 28 February 1905," vol. 17, Latta Collection.

CHAPTER 6. CONFRONTING NEW ENVIRONMENTS

1. *San Francisco Call,* 16, 18, and 20 March 1887; *Kern County Californian,* 19 March 1887.
2. Lux's will bequeathed funds (ranging from $2,500 to $15,000) to the

Ladies' Protection and Relief Society; Sarah B. Cooper's Golden Gate Kindergarten Association; the Boys' and Girls' Aid Society; orphan asylums run by Protestant, Catholic, and Hebrew foundations; and six other San Francisco charities. *San Francisco Call,* 22 March 1887. Miranda Wilmarth Lux died on 20 September 1894. For information on the Lux School of Industrial Training, see the Lux Family Papers; box ML 7 (1), Latta Collection; and Beth Jersey Crowder, "The Lux School: A Little Gem of Education for Women," *California History* 65 (September 1986): 209–12.

3. *San Francisco Call,* 15 September 1894. The agreement is contained in "Charles Lux Legal Papers," carton 739, Miller & Lux Collection. A similar agreement, signed on 24 June 1875, is in the Lux Family Papers.

4. Litigation between the two parties dragged on for the next twenty years, but they reached a preliminary agreement in 1897. After paying an undisclosed amount to Lux's heirs, Miller reincorporated the firm as Miller & Lux, Inc., and his private landowning company (the Las Animas & San Joaquin Land Company) controlled the vast majority of stock in this new firm. Litigation between the two parties would continue until 1910, when Miller made a final $5 million payment to Lux's heirs. Files #13 and #27, carton 671, Miller & Lux Collection; *San Francisco Call,* 25 October 1901.

5. For an evaluation of the literature dealing with corporate managerialism, see John, "Elaborations, Revisions, and Dissents," 151–200.

6. On water litigation in particular, see M. C. Miller, *Flooding the Courtrooms.*

7. During the 1880s, according to one study, "very large" firms included those with net assets exceeding $10 million. After 1900 at least a hundred corporations had assets exceeding $15 million (including Miller & Lux), and a handful of firms had assets exceeding $100 million. Thomas Navin and Marion Sears, "The Rise of a Market for Securities," *Business History Review* 29 (June 1955): 105–138; Gordon, Edwards, and Reich, *Segmented Work, Divided Workers,* 108.

8. Recent studies of California agribusiness include David Vaught, *Cultivating California: Growers, Specialty Crops, and Labor, 1875–1920* (Baltimore: Johns Hopkins University Press, 1999); Stoll, *The Fruits of Natural Advantage;* Gilbert Gonzalez, *Labor and Community: Mexican Citrus Worker Villages in a Southern California County* (Urbana: University of Illinois Press, 1994); Mitchell, *The Lie of the Land.* Also see Lawrence J. Jelinek, *Harvest Empire: A History of California Agriculture* (San Francisco: Boyd and Fraser Publishing, 1979); Daniel, *Bitter Harvest;* and Liebman, *California Farmland.*

9. Jacob Adler, *Claus Spreckels: The Sugar King in Hawaii* (Honolulu: University of Hawaii Press, 1966); Peterson, *The Bonanza Kings,* 108–37; Malone, *The Battle for Butte,* 34–56; Cox, *Mills and Markets;* Robbins, *Colony and Empire,* 83–120.

10. Peter Hall, ed., *Von Thunen's Isolated State* (New York: Pergamon Press, 1966). On central place theory, see Cronon, *Nature's Metropolis,* 48–54.

11. A. S. Mercer, "The Cattle Industry of California," in *Report of the Bureau of Animal Industry,* by U.S. Bureau of Animal Industry (Washington, D.C.: General Printing Office, 1886), 239–53. Miller served as one of Mercer's main sources of information, and he was one of a few ranchers who allowed Mercer to use his name in connection with the deadly cattle disease.

12. Mercer, "Cattle Industry of California," 245; Miller to Lux, 1 July 1877, Miller Papers.

13. Splenic fever causes the spleen (or melt) to become twice its normal size. Regions with infected cattle, which sometimes comprised a single ranch, became known as areas of "big melt." Outbreaks tended to occur in regions with hot climates that did not have cold winters.

14. For a good discussion of purchasing Oregon and Nevada cattle, see Miller to Lux, 29 August 1876. On this purchase, Miller considered $.03 per pound (in Nevada) a fair price. But he concluded, "You better buy them by the head, not pay[ing] him over $26 per head. . . . We to pay the freight but all other expenses and loses [sic] he to bear." On problems with transportation, see Henry Miller to Southern Pacific Railroad, 18 March 1874, box 4, Latta Collection.

15. Margaret Justine Lo Piccolo, "Some Aspects of the Range Cattle Industry of Harney County, Oregon, 1870–1900" (M.A. thesis, University of Oregon, 1962); Peter K. Simpson, *The Community of Cattlemen: A Social History of the Cattle Industry in Southeastern Oregon, 1869–1912* (Moscow, Idaho: University of Idaho Press, 1987); J. Orin Oliphant, "The Eastward Movement of Cattle from the Oregon Country," *Agricultural History* 20 (January 1946): 19–43; Oliphant, "The Cattle Herds and Ranches of the Oregon Country, 1860–1890," *Agricultural History* 21 (October 1947): 217–38; Oliphant, *On the Cattle Ranges of the Oregon Country* (Seattle: University of Washington Press, 1968); Jordan, *North American Cattle-Ranching Frontiers,* 241–66.

16. *Walla Walla (Wash.) Union,* 9 September 1882; Oliphant, "Cattle Herds and Ranches of the Oregon Country," 223. N. A. H. Mason was a partner in Overfelt & Company during the 1870s, and he served as Miller & Lux's main supplier of cattle. F. A. Hyde was a land scrip dealer in Oregon. On his land purchases for Miller & Lux and his 1908 conviction, see the "Letterbook" for the years 1887–88, carton 710, Miller & Lux Collection; *San Francisco Call,* 23 June 1908. Some of John Wheeler's letters are contained in this book as well, but also see J. S. Wheeler to Miller & Lux, 4 February, 26 April, 2 July, 4 August, and 10 September 1887, box ML 3 (2) B, Latta Collection. For records of dummy entrypersons used in northern Nevada, see file 1, carton 671, Miller & Lux Collection.

17. John Wheeler to Miller & Lux, 2 and 11 July 1887. The "Articles of Incorporation" for the Pacific Live Stock Company are contained in file 1, carton 671, Miller & Lux Collection. Miller & Lux ordered large amounts of barbed wire from Boston for the Pacific Live Stock Company; see "Letterbook," 151, carton 710, Miller & Lux Collection.

18. *Silver State,* 24 May, 17 June, 8 August, and 23 and 28 December 1889; *East Oregon Herald,* 1 August 1889, and 9 January 1890; Lo Piccolo, "The Range Cattle Industry," 108–9. Todhunter & Devine owned over 150,000 acres in eastern Oregon; it had been valued at $2,230,000 in 1887. Simpson, *Community of Cattlemen,* 33.

19. In the first published history of eastern Oregon, the Pacific Live Stock Company was portrayed as "opposing . . . anything having a tendency to promote settlement." See *An Illustrated History of Baker, Grant, Malheur, and Har-*

ney Counties (Chicago: Western Historical Publishers, 1902), cited in Simpson, *Community of Cattlemen,* 37.

20. Miller & Lux received this swampland along the Silvies River from Todhunter & Devine in 1887, but settlers took possession of various tracts following an 1888 decision by the General Land Office, which ruled the original claims invalid. Miller & Lux petitioned the secretary of the interior, receiving a favorable ruling in 1891. See Lo Piccolo, "The Range Cattle Industry," 63–64.

21. *East Oregon Herald,* 16 September 1889; Simpson, *Community of Cattlemen,* 36–37.

22. The Pacific Live Stock Company stockpiled "county" land scrip for just this purpose. In this letter, Gilcrest suggested using "Forest Reserve Scrip." John Gilcrest to Henry Miller, 12 April 1899, carton 715, Miller & Lux Collection. For the company's collection of land scrip, see the Pacific Livestock Ledger, 1887–95, vol. 174, Latta Collection.

23. Henry Miller to F. M. Payne, 30 July 1913, carton 95, Miller & Lux Collection.

24. One local story recounts this latter practice. The Oregon historian Peter Simpson writes, "Henry Miller, dressed in his rough clothes and out riding alone, chanced upon a homesteader cutting open one of the Company's beeves. Miller dismounted and, expert butcher that he was, helped the man 'gut out' the carcass. As Miller did so, he asked the homesteader what the steer's owners would say if they caught him. 'Aw hell!' the homesteader is supposed to have replied, 'they stole so many theirselves they wouldn't miss this one.' 'Well, I'm Henry Miller,' the butcher replied, 'and if you won't tell on me, I won't tell on you.'" Simpson, *Community of Cattlemen,* 121.

25. For yearly totals, see "Labor Account," Pacific Live Stock Company Ledger, 1887–95, vol. 174, Latta Collection.

26. Henry Miller to W. R. Hayes, 9 October 1893, Harney County Library, Burns, Oregon.

27. Henry Miller to H. N. Fulgham, 20 December 1894, Lux Papers.

28. Henry Miller to J. G. Holloway, 13 December 1887, Miller Papers.

29. Simpson, *Community of Cattlemen,* 118.

30. C. J. Columbet to Henry Miller, 3 September 1910, carton 400, Miller & Lux Collection.

31. *East Oregon Herald,* 30 October 1895; *Harney Times,* 19 July 1893. During the 1890s, various newspapers reported that Miller & Lux "owned" or "controlled" over 14 million acres. This figure most likely referred to the corporation's water rights, which allowed it to control ten times the amount of land it actually owned. For similar figures, see the *Kern Standard,* 1 January 1898; *Seattle Post-Intelligencer,* 8 September 1918.

32. Lo Piccolo, "The Range Cattle Industry," 122; M. C. Miller, *Flooding the Courtrooms,* 122–24. Henry Miller to H. N. Fulgham, 24 December 1891, 30 January 1892, 28 May 1894, and Anonymous to Miller, 24 May 1894, Lux Family Papers.

33. *An Illustrated History of Baker, Grant, Malheur, and Harney Counties,* 738.

34. "Minutes of Meeting, 27 November 1899," file 13, carton 715, Miller & Lux Collection.

35. Chandler, *The Visible Hand*, 6–11; Lamoreaux and Raff, eds., *Coordination and Information*, 3–5; Gordon, *Segmented Work, Divided Workers*, 108–11.

36. Chandler, *The Visible Hand*, 4.

37. Miller & Lux ledger, vol. 1: 31 March 1889; vol. 2: 1 January 1900, Miller & Lux Collection.

38. Miller & Lux ledger, vol. 1, Miller & Lux Collection; "The Story of the First J. Walter Schmitz and Family," *Madera County Historian* 6 (October 1966): 1–5; J. Walter Schmitz Papers, J. W. Schmitz III Papers.

39. Miller & Lux ledger, June 1897-February 1900, vol. 2, Miller & Lux Collection.

40. Miller to Schmitz, 29 December 1897, J. Walter Schmitz Papers, J. W. Schmitz III Papers.

41. See W. M. Wiley oral history, box ML 4 (1), Latta Collection. A good source of information on many managers is J. M. Guinn, *History of the State of California and Biographical Record of the San Joaquin Valley, California* (Chicago: Chapman Publishers, 1905).

42. Torchiana, *California Gringos*, 248–50.

43. Ibid., 221–27.

44. Ibid., 89, 5.

45. Ibid., 12.

46. C. J. Columbet to Thomas Rutledge, 29 October 1909, box ML 35 (4), Latta Collection.

47. See the statement by Miller & Lux's secretary, David Brown, contained in "Estate of Henry Miller, Deceased, Hearing before Inheritance Tax Appraisers," 266, carton 593, Miller & Lux Collection.

48. Miller's own son, Henry Miller Jr., never took part in the company's affairs, and he died in 1907. On Nickel's role in the firm, see his testimony in "Estate of Henry Miller," 76, Miller & Lux Collection; Joseph Patzen oral history, box ML 7(4), Latta Collection.

49. R[ichard]. L. Adams, "Estimate of Working Capital for California Ranches," in J. Leroy Nickel to F. H. Raffo, 17 November 1913, file 479, carton 100, Miller & Lux Collection.

50. In a thinly veiled attack on Nickel's management, one manager wrote, "The whole trouble in my opinion is . . . that of trying to run a business at long range, and not obtaining the knowledge of detail which comes from intimate association with the business. Also from the failure to consider what effect certain policies will have on expenses of operation and quality of product. To have our organization capable of producing results, the operating and selling departments [and] also the executive must work for the same end." Charles A. Stewart to J. Leroy Nickel, 7 November 1913, box ML 35 (4), Latta Collection.

51. Bolton to Miller, 29 October 1874, box 19, Latta Collection.

52. The rented portion of Canal Farm was split between the "upper" and "lower" farm, each one comprising approximately 3,500 acres. Renters worked plots ranging from 150 to 450 acres. They paid Miller & Lux an unknown sum

per year as rent, and until 1877 they paid the canal company $1.50 an acre for water. After 1877, Miller & Lux rented and sharecropped out a great deal more land, usually with water included. Until the 1890s, all of the renters listed had northern European surnames. See "Account on Miller & Lux Farmers," 14 August 1877, box 28, Latta Collection.

53. Ham to Bolton, 7 and 15 July 1875, box 20, and 25 August 1875, box 21, Latta Collection.

54. Ham to Bolton, 22 September 1875, box 21, Latta Collection.

55. Ham to Bolton, 13 December 1875, box 22, Latta Collection.

56. Miller to Leonard, 2 August 1904, carton 738, Miller & Lux Collection.

57. See Charles Rodemer oral history, box ML 4; and "Los Banos Office ledger, 1887–89," vol. 84, Latta Collection.

58. Henry Miller demanded that meals taken by his employees at neighboring ranches or at boardinghouses be paid for, and conversely, that visitors (and tramps) to his ranches always receive a free meal. The "meal tokens" apparently standardized this practice. Miller & Lux would reimburse the proprietors who honored the tokens. See the notes of Frank Latta, box ML 4(1), Latta Collection.

59. Mary Watson, for example, worked at Dos Palos Farm as the "washerwoman" between 1901 and 1909. She earned $5 a month and likely came to the ranch one day a week from the town of Dos Palos. Other ranches also hired women to do the washing; in some cases, the ranch cook assumed this job. Female workers began to appear on the slaughterhouse payrolls with some regularity after 1905. But nine years later, they still accounted for only a small percentage of the $4,000 weekly payroll, and their salaries averaged only half that of their male coworkers. By 1914, women were segmented into two of the slaughterhouses' twenty-one different departments—five clerked in the "Administrative" department, and two labored in the "Lard" department. They earned $7–$12 a week compared to $13–$23 paid to men in those two departments. Dos Palos ledger, 1901–10, carton 737, and Butchertown payroll, 20 June 1914, vol. 155, Miller & Lux Collection.

60. Malone, *The Battle for Butte,* 131–58.

61. The name *Baden* derived from Charles Lux's place of birth. It encompassed his country house and surrounding acreage, as well as a railroad station called Baden.

62. Jimmy M. Skaggs, *Prime Cut: Livestock Raising and Meatpacking in the United States, 1607–1983* (College Station: Texas A and M University Press, 1986), 59; Blum, "South San Francisco, 114–34.

63. Sklar, *The Corporate Reconstruction of American Capitalism;* Andrew Sayer and Richard Walker, *The New Social Economy: Reworking the Division of Labor* (Cambridge, Mass.: Basil Blackwell, 1992).

64. The Armour Company reported that, because the company operated at full potential, each two-year steer earned them an estimated $.59 profit. With their economy of scale, realizing a profit as low as this allowed Armour and other Chicago meatpackers to underprice local packers. Cronon, *Nature's Metropolis,* 251. While no similar information exists on Miller & Lux's costs and profits for a single steer, data does confirm that the cost of buying a 1,260-pound steer

in Chicago was equivalent to the cost of raising a 968-pound steer in California. Will C. Barnes and James Jardine, "Live Stock Production in the Eleven Far Western Range States," *Meat Situation in the United States,* pt. 2 (Washington, D.C.: Government Printing Office, 1916), 27, 31.

65. Skaggs, *Prime Cut,* 103.

66. The Butchers' Board of Trade, *Programme of the Second Annual Festivities* (San Francisco: n.p., 1901), Bancroft Library, University of California at Berkeley. For a good example of the propaganda drive, see the *San Francisco Voice of Labor,* 26 January 1895.

67. Butchers' Board of Trade, "Butchers' Day Bulletin," 22 May 1901, Bancroft Library, University of California at Berkeley.

68. Blum, "South San Francisco," 123.

69. This strategy had worked to Miller's advantage before in his dealings with the San Francisco organizers of the San Joaquin and King's River Canal & Irrigation Company. See chapter 3.

70. "Minutes of the Board of Directors Meeting of the Western Meat Company," 24 May 1894, carton 474, Miller & Lux Collection.

71. Miller was also wary of the BBT as a labor-capital organization, and in 1901 he fractured the alliance by refusing to sell meat to the city's butcher shops that posted union cards in their windows. Page, "The San Francisco Labor Movement in 1901," 673–74.

72. "Members of the Butchers' Board of Trade," in *Souvenir Album and Program,* 1903, Bancroft Library, University of California at Berkeley; and Blum, "South San Francisco," 125.

73. *San Francisco Chronicle,* 25 January 1899; *San Francisco Enterprise,* 18 June 1898.

74. Treadwell, *The Cattle King,* 350–53.

75. Upton Sinclair, *The Jungle* (1906; reprint, New York: Penguin Books, 1990), 342.

76. See Skaggs, *Prime Cut,* 119–28.

77. In various sectors of the economy, Martin Sklar concludes, "large corporate sentiment . . . favored federal regulation not only to preempt state or local authority but, more positively, to facilitate, legitimize, police, and complement corporate regulation of the market." Sklar, *The Corporate Reconstruction of American Capitalism,* 434.

78. J. Ogden Armour, *The Packers, the Private Car Lines, and the People* (Philadelphia: Henry Altemus, 1906), 368, 379.

79. Charles Stewart to J. Leroy Nickel, 15 November 1913, carton 147, Miller & Lux Collection.

80. See Skaggs, *Prime Cut,* 128.

81. Miller & Lux to [the New York Produce exchange dealer] H. W. Calef, 17 November 1913, carton 105, Miller & Lux Collection.

82. On the loss of markets in Vancouver, see Miller & Lux to Mr. Bellstedt, 21 July 1912, carton 95, Miller & Lux Collection. On Baden's regional expansion, see Blum, "South San Francisco," 131.

83. Antitrust litigation forced the dissolution of the National Packing Company in 1912, and the Consent Decree of 1920 supposedly dissolved the Cattle

Trust for good. But despite these measures, market domination by the "Big Five" continued. Skaggs, *Prime Cut,* 100–108.

84. In addition to meatpacking plants, South San Francisco soon included other industries: W. P. Fuller Lead and Color Works, Pacific Jupiter Steel, Selby Smelting & Lead, Doak Steel, and Bethlehem Steel. See Blum, "South San Francisco," 126–27; Walker, "Industry Builds the City," 8. On competition to secure cattle, see W. D. Duke to Henry Miller, 19, 20, and 25 August 1910, carton 400, Miller & Lux Collection.

85. Charles A. Stewart to J. Leroy Nickel, 7 November 1913, box ML 35 (4), Latta Collection. On total sales for 1913, see R. L. Adams, "Estimate of Working Capital for California Ranches," file 464, carton 100, Miller & Lux Collection.

86. Stewart to Nickel, 15 November 1913, folder 50, carton 105, Miller & Lux Collection.

87. Skaggs, *Prime Cut,* 77.

88. Vaught, *Cultivating California,* ch. 1; David Vaught, "Factories in the Field Revisited," *Pacific Historical Review* 66 (May 1997): 149–84; Stoll, *The Fruits of Natural Advantage,* 94–123.

89. Stoll, *The Fruits of Natural Advantage,* 63–93.

90. The value of the state's fruits and nuts increased from $28 million in 1900 to $51 million in 1910. California was the nation's leading producer of table grapes, lemons, winter vegetables, plums, prunes, raisins, and apricots. The value of California farmland jumped from $630 million in 1900 to $2.8 billion in 1925, despite a small decrease in farm acreage. Vaught, *Cultivating California,* ch. 3; Robert Glass Cleland and Osgood Hardy, *March of Industry* (Los Angeles: Powell Publishing, 1929), 97, cited in Stoll, *The Fruits of Natural Advantage,* 121.

91. W. M. Wiley oral history, box ML 4 (1), Latta Collection; Lawrence, "Henry Miller and the San Joaquin Valley," 138.

92. Leon K. David to J. Leroy Nickel, 4 December 1913, file 448, carton 100, Miller & Lux Collection; M. C. Miller, *Flooding the Courtrooms,* 120.

93. Between 1900 and 1910, average land values increased one-and-a-half-fold in Fresno and Kern Counties, threefold in Merced County, and fourfold in Tulare County. Land values escalated by nearly the same rates in the following decade. The firm's taxes increased by 38 percent between 1909 and 1913. M. C. Miller, *Flooding the Courtrooms,* 120. The following table shows the rise of land values in the valley and California as a whole. See Thomas J. Pressly and William H. Scofield, eds., *Farm Real Estate Values in the United States by Counties, 1850–1959* (Seattle: University of Washington Press, 1965), 68. The figures express average value per acre.

	1900	1910	1920
Fresno	29	74	212
Kern	7	18	44
Merced	12	36	78
Madera	10	21	65
Tulare	16	66	167
Statewide	25	52	105

94. "Estimated Inventory," 28 February 1905, vol. 17, file 28, carton 671, Miller & Lux Collection.

95. Walker, "Industry Builds the City."

96. "Notice for Posting," carton 350, Miller & Lux Collection; John Dugain oral history, box ML 4–5 (1), Latta Collection.

97. Daniel T. Rodgers, "In Search of Progressivism," *Reviews in American History* 10 (December 1982): 113–32; Wiebe, *The Search for Order,* 164–95; and Sklar, *The Corporate Reconstruction of American Capitalism,* 31–34. On progressivism in California, see William Deverell and Tom Sitton, eds., *California Progressivism Revisited* (Berkeley and Los Angeles: University of California Press, 1994); and George Mowry, *The California Progressives* (Berkeley and Los Angeles: University of California Press, 1951).

98. Miller & Lux were accused of accepting rebates for interstate commerce— specifically, the shipment of lumber, wool, and cattle from Oregon. The firm's shipping manager, John Dillon, argued that the rebate was only on that part of the shipment within state borders, making it a state and not a federal crime. *San Francisco Call,* 11, 17, 19, and 23 June 1908.

99. *San Francisco Call,* 23 June 1908. On Hyde's land acquisition for Miller & Lux, see "Letterbook" for 1887–88, carton 710, Miller & Lux Collection.

100. See Lo Piccolo, "The Range Cattle Industry," 67.

101. John Gilcrest to J. Leroy Nickel, 31 August 1913, file 42, carton 95, Miller & Lux Collection.

102. Christopher McGrory Klyza, *Who Controls Public Lands? Mining, Forestry, and Grazing Policies, 1870–1990* (Chapel Hill: University of North Carolina Press, 1996), 110; Langston, *Forest Dreams, Forest Nightmares,* 75–78; and Samuel P. Hayes, *Conservation and the Gospel of Efficiency: The Progressive Conservation Movement, 1890–1920* (Cambridge: Harvard University Press, 1959), 49–65.

103. Charles H. Shinn to Henry Miller, 21 January, 11 and 25 April 1908, and 12 January 1909, carton 400, Miller & Lux Collection; Charles H. Shinn, "A Wizard of the Garden," *The Land of Sunshine* 14 (February 1901): 39.

104. M. C. Miller, *Flooding the Courtrooms,* 26.

105. *Fresno Morning Republican,* 20 September 1914. For a water conservation study directed by Elwood Mead, see U.S. Department of Agriculture, *Report of Irrigation Investigations in California* (Washington, D.C.: Government Printing Office, 1901), 257–58.

106. *Report of the Conservation Commission of the State of California* (Sacramento: Government Printing Office, 1912): 28, cited in M. C. Miller, *Flooding the Courtrooms,* 103.

107. For a discussion of the water commission and the legislation, see M. C. Miller, *Flooding the Courtrooms,* 102–113. "Wasteful" irrigation was defined as the application of more than 2.5 acre-feet of water per year to uncultivated lands.

108. William G. Kerckhoff to Henry E. Huntington, 2 May 1903, box 102, Henry E. Huntington Collection, Huntington Library, San Marino, California; *San Francisco Chronicle,* 23 June 1903. Miller & Lux and the Kern County Land

Company opposed the construction of a canal proposed by the Pacific Light & Power Company, and for this reason Kerckhoff believed "it would be a serious matter for [Miller & Lux's] Attorney to be appointed to this Judgeship."

109. The two most prominent examples of organized action and violence were the Oxnard sugar beet strike of 1903 and the Wheatland riot of 1913. On the Oxnard strike and the formation of the Japanese-Mexican Labor Association, see Tomas Almaguer, "Racial Domination and Class Conflict in Capitalist Agriculture: The Oxnard Sugar Beet Workers' Strike of 1903," in *Working People of California*, ed. Daniel Cornford (Berkeley and Los Angeles: University of California Press, 1995), 183–207. On the Wheatland riot and hop pickers' strike, see Mitchell, *The Lie of the Land*, 36–57; Vaught, "Factories in the Field Revisited," 149–84.

110. On range deterioration in the Far West, see Simpson, *Community of Cattlemen*, 139; Lo Piccolo, "The Range Cattle Industry," 107–10; United States Department of Agriculture, "Live Stock Production in the Eleven Far Western Range States," *Meat Situation in the United States* (Washington, D.C.: Government Printing Office, 1916), 57, 83.

111. J. Leroy Nickel to F. W. Holbert, 23 November 1913, file 463, carton 100, Miller & Lux Collection.

112. W. L. Preston, *Vanishing Landscapes: Land and Life in the Tulare Lake Basin* (Berkeley and Los Angeles: University of California Press, 1981), 141–42.

113. Haslam, Dawson, and Johnson, *The Great Central Valley*, 184; W. Preston, *Vanishing Landscapes*, 208; Stoll, *The Fruits of Natural Advantage*, 161–62.

114. Miller & Lux, "Farming Instructions," 158, box 6, Latta Collection; Mead, *Irrigation Investigations in California*, 253.

115. J. F. Clyne to J. Leroy Nickel, 23 December 1922, carton 386, Miller & Lux Collection. Clyne believed that opening up drainage channels would lower the water table to "normal" levels. Miller & Lux engineer W. C. Hammatt disagreed with Clyne's assessment of the situation and called for immediate data collection in order to study the problem. W. C. Hammatt to J. Leroy Nickel, 26 December 1922, carton 386, Miller & Lux Collection.

116. See Clyne and Ogden's testimonies in "Estate of Henry Miller," 1249–1365. While they certainly underestimated the properties' value for tax inheritance purposes, the soil problems they discuss were unquestionably accurate.

117. Harry M. Ohlendorf, "Aquatic Birds and Selenium in the San Joaquin Valley," and Arthur W. Kilness and Jerry L. Simmons, "Toxic Effects of Selenium on Wildlife Species and Other Organisms," in *Selenium and Agricultural Drainage: Implications for the San Francisco Bay and the California Environment* (Berkeley: Proceedings of the Second Selenium Symposium, 1985): 14–24, 52–59; Haslam, Dawson, and Johnson, *The Great Central Valley*, 220–22; Worster, *Rivers of Empire*, 323–24.

118. José Messa oral history, 5 October 1939, box ML 4 (1), Latta Collection.

119. Henry Miller to D. O. Leonard, 28 December 1905, carton 738, Miller & Lux Collection.

CONCLUSION

1. For information on Miller's final years, see the testimonies by Nellie Miller Nickel, J. Leroy Nickel, and E. Frank Campbell in "Estate of Henry Miller," vol. 1, carton 593, Miller & Lux Collection.

2. Gray Brechin, "Sailing by Byzantium: The Architecture of the Panama Pacific International Exhibition," *California History* 62 (summer 1983): 106–21; Robert W. Rydell, *All the World's a Fair: Visions of Empire at American International Expositions, 1876–1916* (Chicago: University of Chicago Press, 1984), 208–33.

3. "Testimony of E. Frank Campbell," in "Estate of Henry Miller," vol. 1, carton 148. Campbell was Miller's private assistant and nurse.

4. The federal government alone demanded $4 million in inheritance taxes, and nonpayment increased that amount to $6 million. Deed of Trust, 1 July 1910, Miller & Lux Incorporated to Mercantile Trust Company of San Francisco; Deed of Trust, 15 June 1920, Miller & Lux Incorporated to Bank of California, carton 594, Miller & Lux Collection. For the legal aspects of this debt, see M. C. Miller, *Flooding the Courtrooms*, 149–52.

5. Miller & Lux to Holders of First Mortgage Bonds of Miller & Lux Incorporated, 5 February 1918, and Treadwell to Britton & Gray, 23 October 1918, carton 166, Miller & Lux Collection; M. C. Miller, *Flooding the Courtrooms*, 149.

6. *San Francisco Chronicle*, 19 February and 15 March 1930. The actual "HH" branding iron today hangs in the Bakersfield office of George Nickel Jr.

7. See the oral history of Turner Hudson McBaine, 114–20, Bancroft Library, University of California at Berkeley. McBaine represented one side of the Nickel family in court proceedings.

8. In 1939, the Bureau of Reclamation paid Miller & Lux $2.45 million for "excess water flooding its 'uncontrolled' grasslands" as part of the Central Valley Project. State and federal government purchases of the firm's remaining water rights far exceeded this amount. M. C. Miller, *Flooding the Courtrooms*, 173.

9. I am grateful to Henry Bowles and George Nickel Jr. for information on their respective family businesses.

10. For a discussion of this point, see Igler, "The Industrial Far West."

11. M. C. Miller, *Flooding the Courtrooms*, 6, 179.

Bibliography

ARCHIVAL AND MANUSCRIPT COLLECTIONS

Bancroft, Hubert Howe. Hubert Howe Bancroft Collection, Bancroft Library, University of California at Berkeley.

Barlow, Samuel. Samuel Barlow Collection, Huntington Library, San Marino, California.

California Private Land Claims. Bancroft Library, University of California at Berkeley (microfilm).

Haight, Henry. Henry Haight Papers, Huntington Library, San Marino, California.

Hayes, Benjamin. Benjamin Hayes Collection. Bancroft Library, University of California at Berkeley.

Houghton, Sherman O. Sherman O. Houghton Papers, Huntington Library, San Marino, California.

Huntington, Henry E. Henry E. Huntington Collection, Huntington Library, San Marino, California.

Larkin, Thomas O. Thomas O. Larkin Papers. Bancroft Library, University of California at Berkeley.

Latham, Milton Slocum. Milton Slocum Latham Papers, Huntington Library, San Marino, California.

Latta, Frank. Frank Latta Collection. Huntington Library, San Marino, California.

Lux, Charles. "Dictation of Charles Lux, Esq." Bancroft Library, University of California at Berkeley.

———. Lux Family Papers. California Historical Society, San Francisco.

Matthews, Joseph Warren. Joseph Warren Matthews Papers. Bancroft Library, University of California at Berkeley.

Miller, Henry. "Dictation of Henry Miller, Esq." Bancroft Library, University of California at Berkeley.

———. Henry Miller Papers. Bancroft Library, University of California at Berkeley.

Miller & Lux Collection. Bancroft Library, University of California at Berkeley.

Records of the General Land Office. Bancroft Library, University of California at Berkeley (microfilm).

Skyfarming Collection. Huntington Library, San Marino, California.

Stearns, Abel. Abel Stearns Collection. Huntington Library, San Marino, California.

Vallejo, Mariano G. "Historical and Personal Memoirs Relating to Alta California." Typescript translation by Earl R. Hewitt, Manuscript Collection, Bancroft Library, University of California at Berkeley.

NEWSPAPERS AND PERIODICALS

Alta California
Bakersfield Californian
California Farmer
California Fish and Game
Commercial Herald and Market Review
Daily Journal of Commerce
Fresno Expositor
Gilroy Advocate
Kern County Courier
Kern County Record
Los Angeles Southern News
Los Tulares
Overland Monthly
Pacific Rural Press
Sacramento Bee
Sacramento Daily Union
Sacramento Union
San Francisco Bulletin
San Francisco Call
San Francisco Chronicle
San Francisco Evening Bulletin
San Francisco Evening Post
San Francisco Voice of Labor
San Joaquin Republican
San Jose Mercury
San Mateo Times
Santa Cruz Sentinel
Southern Californian
Stockton Independent
Sunset
Visalia Delta

PRIMARY BOOKS, REPORTS, AND ARTICLES

Alexander, B. S. *Report of the Board of Commissioners on the Irrigation of the San Joaquin, Tulare, and Sacramento Valleys of the State of California.* Washington, D.C.: Government Printing Office, 1874.

Armour, J. Ogden. *The Packers, the Private Car Lines, and the People.* Philadelphia: Henry Altemus, 1906.

Austin, Mary. *Earth Horizon.* New York: Literary Guild, 1932.

———. *The Land of Little Rain.* Boston: Houghton Mifflin, 1903.

Bancroft, H. H. *Chronicles of the Builders of the Commonwealth.* San Francisco: History Company, 1891–92.

Blake, William. *Geological Report of Exploration and Surveys for a Railroad Route from the Mississippi River to the Pacific Ocean, under R. S. Williamson.* Washington, D.C.: Government Printing Office, 1853.

Bosqui, Edward. *Memoirs.* San Francisco: n.p., 1904.

Brereton, Robert M. *Reminiscences of an Old English Civil Engineer.* Portland, Oreg.: Irwin-Hodson, 1908.

———. *Report on Messrs. Bensley and Co.'s Canal Project from Fresno Slough to Tide Water at Antioch.* San Francisco: Bancroft and Company, 1872.

Brewer, William H. *Up and Down California in 1860–64: The Journal of William H. Brewer.* Berkeley and Los Angeles: University of California Press, 1966.

Brown, O. "Statement of O. Brown." In *Report of the Special Committee of the United States Senate on the Irrigation and Reclamation of Arid Lands.* Washington, D.C.: Government Printing Office, 1890.

Bryant, Edwin. *What I Saw in California.* Santa Ana: Fine Arts Press, 1936.

Burton, Maria Amparo Ruiz. *The Squatter and the Don.* San Francisco: S. Carson and Company, 1885.

Butchers' Board of Trade. *Programme of the Second Annual Festivities.* San Francisco: n.p., 1901. Bancroft Library, University of California at Berkeley.

California Constitutional Convention. *Debates and Proceedings of the Constitutional Convention of the State of California Convened at the City of Sacramento, Saturday, September 28, 1878.* Sacramento: J. D. Young, 1880.

California State Board of Agriculture. *Biennial Report of the State Board of Agriculture for the Years 1870 and 1871.* Sacramento, 1872.

California State Board of Equalization. *Report of the State Board of Equalization of the State of California for the Years 1872 and 1873.* Sacramento, 1874.

———. *Report of the State Board of Equalization of the State of California for the Years 1870 and 1871.* Sacramento, 1872.

California State Relief Administration. *Migratory Labor in California.* San Francisco, 1936.

California State Surveyor General. *Biennial Report of the Surveyor General of the State of California from August 1, 1877, to August 1, 1879.* Sacramento, 1880.

Camp, C. L. *James Clyman, American Frontiersman, 1792–1881.* San Francisco: California Historical Society, 1928.

Carr, Ezra. *The Patrons of Husbandry of the Pacific Coast.* San Francisco: A. L. Bancroft and Company, 1875.

Cronise, Titus Fey. *The Natural Wealth of California*. San Francisco: H. H. Bancroft and Company, 1868.

Day, John M. "Public Ownership and Control of the Water, the Only Safety for the Irrigator." *Report of the Special Committee of the United States Senate on the Irrigation and Reclamation of Arid Lands*. Washington, D.C.: Government Printing Office, 1890.

Evermann, Barton Warren. "An Attempt to Save California Elk." *California Fish and Game* 1 (1915): 85–97.

Freeman, George E. "Among the Irrigators of Fresno." *Overland Monthly* 9 (June 1887): 621–27.

George, Henry. *Our Land and Land Policy*. San Francisco: White and Bauer, 1871.

Guinn, J. M. "Exceptional Years." *History Society of Southern California* (1890): 33–39.

Haggin, James Ben Ali. *The Desert Lands of Kern County, California — Affidavits of Various Residents of Said County*. San Francisco: C. H. Street, 1877.

Hall, William Hammond. "Irrigation in California." *National Geographic Magazine* 1 (1889): 277–91.

——. *Report of the State Engineer to the Legislature of the State of California — Session of 1880*. Sacramento: State Office of Printing, 1880.

Hilgard, E. W., et al. *Report on the Climatic and Agricultural Features and Agricultural Practices and Needs of the Arid Regions of the Pacific Coast*. Washington, D.C.: Government Printing Office, 1882.

Hyacinth, Socrates [Stephen Powers]. "Wayside Views of California." *Overland Monthly* 2 (1869): 227–32.

Jackson, Helen Hunt. *Ramona*. New York: Roberts Brothers, 1884.

Maloney, Alice B. *Fur Brigade to the Bonaventura: John Work's California Expedition, 1832–33*. San Francisco: California Historical Society, 1945.

Mead, Elwood. *Report of the Irrigation Investigations in California*. Washington, D.C.: Government Printing Office, 1901.

Memorial and Biographical History of the Counties of Fresno, Tulare, and Kern, California. Chicago: Lewis Publishing, 1890.

Mercer, A. S. "The Cattle Industry of California." In *Report of the Bureau of Animal Industry*, by U.S. Bureau of Animal Industry, 239–53. Washington, D.C.: General Printing Office, 1886.

Muir, John. *The Mountains of California*. New York: Century, 1894.

Norris, Frank. *The Octopus*. New York: Doubleday, Page, and Company, 1901.

Olney, Warren. "The Present Status of the Irrigation Problem." *Overland Monthly* 9 (January 1887): 40–50.

Palmer, T. S. *The Jack Rabbits of the United States*. Washington, D.C.: Government Printing Office, 1896.

Perkins, James E. "Sheep Husbandry in California." *Transactions of the California State Agricultural Society* (1863): 134–45.

Phelps, Alonzo. *Contemporary Biography of California's Representative Men*. San Francisco: Bancroft and Company, 1881.

Powell, John Wesley. *Report on the Lands of the Arid Region of the United States*. 1878. Reprint, Cambridge: Harvard University Press, 1963.

Prospectus of the West Side Irrigation District, San Joaquin Valley. N.p., n.d. Miller & Lux Collection, Bancroft Library, University of California at Berkeley.

Rojas, Arnold R. *The Vaquero.* Santa Barbara: McNally and Loftin, 1964.

Royce, Josiah. *California: From the Conquest in 1846 to the Second Vigilance Committee in San Francisco.* New York: Alfred A. Knopf, 1948.

San Joaquin and King's River Canal and Irrigation Company. *Report to the Stockholders.* San Francisco: Woman's Publishing, 1874.

———. *Prospectus.* San Francisco: A. L. Bancroft and Company, 1873.

Sargent, A. A. "Irrigation and Drainage." *Overland Monthly* 8 (July 1886): 19–32.

Sinclair, Upton. *The Jungle.* New York: Doubleday, Page, and Company, 1906.

Stuart, Charles D. *Casa Grande, a California Pastoral.* New York: Henry Holt and Company, 1906.

Supreme Court of California. *Report of Cases Determined in the Supreme Court of the State of California.* Vol. 69. San Francisco: Bancroft-Whitney, 1906.

Thompson, R. A. *Historical and Descriptive Sketch of Sonoma County, California.* Philadelphia: L. H. Everts and Company, 1877.

Torchiana, H. A. Van Coenen. *California Gringos.* San Francisco: Paul Elder and Company, 1930.

U.S. Department of Agriculture. *Report of Irrigation Investigations in California.* Washington, D.C.: Government Printing Office, 1901.

U.S. Department of State. *Cattle and Dairy Farming: Reports from the Consuls of the United States on Cattle and Dairy Farming and the Markets for Cattle, Beef, and Dairy Products in the Several Districts.* Washington, D.C.: Government Printing Office, 1887.

SECONDARY SOURCES

Abbott, Carl. "Regional City and Network City: Portland and Seattle in the Twentieth Century." *Western Historical Quarterly* 23 (August 1992): 293–322.

Adler, Jacob. *Claus Spreckels: The Sugar King in Hawaii.* Honolulu: University of Hawaii Press, 1966.

Almaguer, Tomas. *Racial Fault Lines: The Historical Origins of White Supremacy in California.* Berkeley and Los Angeles: University of California Press, 1994.

Alonzo, Armando C. *Tejano Legacy: Rancheros and Settlers in South Texas, 1734–1900.* Albuquerque: University of New Mexico Press, 1998.

Anderson, M. Kat, Michael G. Barbour, and Valerie Whitworth. "A World of Balance and Plenty: Land, Plants, Animals, and Humans in a Pre-European California." *California History* 76 (summer-fall 1997): 12–47.

Anderson, Terry L., and Peter J. Hill. *The Political Economy of the American West.* Lanham: Rowman and Littlefield, 1994.

Aron, Stephen. *How the West Was Lost: The Transformation of Kentucky from Daniel Boone to Henry Clay.* Baltimore: Johns Hopkins University Press, 1996.

Bakken, Gordon Morris. *Practicing Law in Frontier California.* Lincoln: University of Nebraska Press, 1991.

Barbour, Michael G., and Valerie Whitworth. "California's Living Landscape." *Fremontia* 22 (summer 1994): 1–8.

Barron, Hal S. *Mixed Harvest: The Second Great Transformation in the Rural North, 1870–1930.* Chapel Hill: University of North Carolina Press, 1997.

Barth, Gunther. *Instant Cities: Urbanization and the Rise of San Francisco and Denver.* New York: Oxford University Press, 1982.

———. "Metropolism and Urban Elites in the Far West." In *The Age of Industrialism in America: Essays in Social Structure and Cultural Values,* ed. Frederic Cople Jaher, 158–87. New York: Free Press, 1968.

Bartolome, James. "*Stipa Pulchra,* a Survivor from the Pristine Prairie." *Fremontia* 9 (April 1981): 3–6.

Beck, Warren A., and Ynez D. Haase. *Historical Atlas of California.* Norman: University of Oklahoma Press, 1974.

Beers, Henry Putney. *Spanish and Mexican Records of the American Southwest.* Tucson: University of Arizona Press, 1979.

Bishofberger, Thomas E. "Early Flood Control in the California Central Valley." *Journal of the West* 14 (July 1975): 80–92.

Blackford, Mansel G. *The Politics of Business in California, 1890–1920.* Columbus: Ohio State University Press, 1977.

Blum, Joseph A. "South San Francisco: The Making of an Industrial City." *California History* 63 (spring 1984): 114–34.

Blumler, Mark. "Invasion and Transformation of California's Valley Grassland, a Mediterranean Analogue Ecosystem." In *Ecological Relations in Historical Times: Human Impact and Adaptation,* ed. Robin A. Butlin and Neil Roberts. Oxford: Blackwell Press, 1995.

———. "Some Myths about California Grasslands and Grazers." *Fremontia* 20 (April 1992): 22–27.

Botkin, Daniel B. *Discordant Harmonies: A New Ecology for the Twenty-first Century.* New York: Oxford University Press, 1990.

Bradbury, David E. "The Physical Geography of the Mediterranean Lands." In *Mediterranean-Type Shrublands,* ed. Francesco di Castri et al., 53–62. New York: Elsevier Scientific Publishing, 1981.

Brechin, Gray. *Imperial San Francisco: Urban Power, Earthly Ruin.* Berkeley and Los Angeles: University of California Press, 1999.

———. "Sailing by Byzantium: The Architecture of the Panama Pacific International Exhibition." *California History* 62 (summer 1983): 106–21.

Brown, Richard Maxwell. *No Duty to Retreat: Violence and Values in American History and Society.* Norman: University of Oklahoma Press, 1994.

Buell, Lawrence. *The Environmental Imagination: Thoreau, Nature Writing, and the Formation of American Culture.* Cambridge: Harvard University Press, 1995.

Bunting, Robert. *The Pacific Raincoast: Environment and Culture in an American Eden, 1778–1900.* Lawrence: University Press of Kansas, 1997.

Burcham, L. T. *California Range Land.* Publication no. 7. Davis: University of California at Davis, Center for Archaeological Research, 1981.

Camarillo, Albert. *Chicanos in a Changing Society: From Mexican Pueblos to American Barrios in Santa Barbara and Southern California, 1848–1930.* Cambridge: Harvard University Press, 1979.

Carothers, Alice L. "The History of the Southern Pacific Railroad in the San Joaquin Valley." M.A. thesis, Stanford University, 1934.

———. "From Trail to Rail—the Story of the Beginning of Southern Pacific." *Southern Pacific Bulletin* (June 1928): 12–15.

Chan, Sucheng. *This Bittersweet Soil: The Chinese in California Agriculture, 1869–1910.* Berkeley and Los Angeles: University of California Press, 1986.

Chandler, Alfred D. *The Visible Hand: The Managerial Revolution in American Business.* Cambridge: Harvard University Press, 1977.

Chiu, Ping. *Chinese Labor in California, 1850–1880.* Madison: State Historical Society of Wisconsin, 1963.

Clark, Christopher. *The Roots of Rural Capitalism: Western Massachusetts, 1780–1860.* Ithaca: Cornell University Press, 1990.

Clawson, James W. *Landscape Ecology: Study of Mediterranean Grazed Ecosystems.* Nice: Proceedings of the Man and the Biosphere Symposium, 1989.

Clay, Karen Bradley. "Trade without Law: Private-Order Institutions in Mexican California." *Journal of Law, Economics, and Organization* 13 (April 1997): 202–32.

———. "Economic Institutions in Theory and History." Ph.D. diss., Stanford University, 1994.

Cleland, Robert Glass. *The Cattle on a Thousand Hills: Southern California, 1850–80.* San Marino: Huntington Library, 1941.

Cobb, James C. *Industrialization and Southern Society, 1877–1984.* Lexington: University of Kentucky Press, 1984.

Cochran, Thomas. *Frontiers of Change: Early Industrialism in America.* New York: Oxford University Press, 1981.

Conzen, Kathleen Neils. "Germans." In *Encyclopedia of American Ethnic Groups.* Cambridge: Harvard University Press, 1980.

———. *Immigrant Milwaukee, 1836–1860: Accommodation and Community in a Frontier City.* Cambridge: Harvard University Press, 1976.

Conzen, Michael P. "The Maturing Urban System in the United States." *Annals of the Association of American Geographers* 67 (March 1977): 88–108.

Cornford, Daniel. *Workers and Dissent in the Redwood Empire.* Philadelphia: Temple University Press, 1987.

———, ed. *Working People of California.* Berkeley and Los Angeles: University of California Press, 1995.

Cowan, Robert G. *Ranchos of California.* Fresno: Academy Library Guild, 1956.

Cox, Thomas R. *Mills and Markets: A History of the Pacific Coast Lumber Industry to 1900.* Seattle: University of Washington Press, 1974.

Cronon, William. *Nature's Metropolis: Chicago and the Great West.* New York: W. W. Norton and Company, 1991.

———. "Modes of Prophecy and Production: Placing Nature in History." *Journal of American History* 76 (March 1990): 1122–31.

———. *Changes in the Land: Indians, Colonists, and the Ecology of New England.* New York: Hill and Wang, 1983.

———, ed. *Uncommon Ground: Toward Reinventing Nature.* New York: W. W. Norton and Company, 1995.

Crosby, Alfred W. *Ecological Imperialism: The Biological Expansion of Europe, 900–1900.* Cambridge: Cambridge University Press, 1986.

Cross, Ira. *Financing an Empire: History of Banking in California.* San Francisco: S. J. Clarke Publishing, 1927.

Crowder, Beth Jersey. "The Lux School: A Little Gem of Education for Women." *California History* 65 (September 1986): 209–12.

Daniel, Cletus. *Bitter Harvest: A History of California Farmworkers, 1870–1941.* Ithaca: Cornell University Press, 1981.

Dary, David. *Cowboy Culture: A Saga of Five Centuries.* Lawrence: University of Kansas Press, 1981.

Dasmann, Raymond. *California's Changing Environment.* San Francisco: Boyd and Fraser Publishing, 1981.

———. *The Destruction of California.* New York: Collier Books, 1966.

Davis, Mike. *Ecology of Fear: Los Angeles and the Imagination of Disaster.* New York: Metropolitan Books, 1998.

———. "The Case for Letting Malibu Burn." *Environmental History Review* 19 (summer 1995): 1–36.

———. "Los Angeles after the Storm: The Dialectic of Ordinary Disaster." *Antipode* 27 (July 1995): 221–41.

Decker, Peter R. *Fortunes and Failures: White Collar Mobility in Nineteenth-Century San Francisco.* Cambridge: Harvard University Press, 1978.

Deverell, William. *Railroad Crossing: Californians and the Railroad, 1850–1910.* Berkeley and Los Angeles: University of California Press, 1994.

Deverell, William, and Tom Sitton, eds. *California Progressivism Revisited.* Berkeley and Los Angeles: University of California Press, 1994.

DeVoto, Bernard. "The West: A Plundered Province." *Harper's* (August 1934): 355–64.

Diaz, Henry F., and Vera Markgraf, eds. *El Niño: Historical and Paleoclimatic Aspects of the Southern Oscillation.* New York: Cambridge University Press, 1992.

Di Leonardo, Micaela. *The Varieties of Ethnic Experience: Kinship, Class, and Gender among California Italian Americans.* Ithaca: Cornell University Press, 1984.

Ebright, Malcolm. *Land Grants and Lawsuits in Northern New Mexico.* Albuquerque: University of New Mexico Press, 1994.

Egli, Ida Rae. *No Rooms of Their Own: Women Writers of Early California.* Berkeley: Heyday Books, 1992.

Emmons, David M. *The Butte Irish: Class and Ethnicity in an American Mining Town, 1875–1925.* Urbana: University of Illinois Press, 1989.

Erlandson, Jon M., and Kevin Bartoy. "Protohistoric California: Paradise or Pandemic?" *Proceedings of the Society for California Archeology* 9 (1996): 304–9.

Ethington, Philip J. *The Public City: The Political Construction of Urban Life in San Francisco, 1850–1900.* Cambridge: Cambridge University Press, 1994.

Evernden, Neil. *The Social Creation of Nature*. Baltimore: Johns Hopkins University Press, 1992.

Fink, Augusta. *Monterey County: The Dramatic Story of Its Past*. Santa Cruz: Western Tanager Press, 1972.

Flamming, Douglas. *Creating the Modern South: Millhands and Managers in Dalton, Georgia, 1884–1984*. Chapel Hill: University of North Carolina Press, 1992.

Foner, Eric. *Reconstruction: America's Unfinished Revolution, 1863–1877*. New York: Harper and Row, 1988.

Foote, Horace S. *Pen Pictures from the Garden of the World, or, Santa Clara County, California*. Chicago: Lewis Publishing, 1886.

Foster, Orville. "The Men of Miller-Lux." *Old West* (summer 1973): 32–34, 58–60.

Freyfogle, Eric T. "*Lux v. Haggin* and the Common Law Burden of Modern Water Rights." *University of Colorado Law Review* 57 (spring 1986): 485–525.

Frink, Maurice, W. Turrentine Jackson, and Agnes Wright. *When Grass Was King*. Boulder: University of Colorado Press, 1956.

Fuller, Levi Varden. "The Supply of Agricultural Labor as a Factor in the Evolution of Farm Organization in California." Ph.D. diss., University of California at Berkeley, 1939.

Garrison, Myrtle. *Romance and History of California Ranchos*. San Francisco: Harr Wagner Publishing, 1935.

Gates, Paul Wallace. *Land and Law in California: Essays on Land Policies*. Ames: Iowa State University Press, 1991.

———. *Landlords and Tenants on the Prairie Frontier: Studies in American Land Policy*. Ithaca: Cornell University Press, 1973.

Gayton, A. H., and Stanley Newman. "Yokut and Western Mono Myths." *Anthropological Records* 5 (October 1940): 2–48.

Gjerde, Jon. " 'Roots of Maladjustment' in the Land: Paul Wallace Gates." *Reviews in American History* 19 (March 1991): 142–53.

Gogan, J. P., and Reginald H. Barrett. "Comparative Dynamics of Introduced Tule Elk Populations." *Journal of Wildlife Management* 51 (1987): 20–27.

Gonzalez, Gilbert. *Labor and Community: Mexican Citrus Worker Villages in a Southern California County*. Urbana: University of Illinois Press, 1994.

Gordon, David M., Richard Edwards, and Michael Reich. *Segmented Work, Divided Workers: The Historical Transformation of Labor in the United States*. Cambridge: Cambridge University Press, 1982.

Graham, Richard. "The Investment Boom in British-Texas Cattle Companies, 1880–1885." *Business History Review* 34 (1960): 421–45.

Gregory, James N. *American Exodus: The Dust Bowl Migration and Okie Culture in California*. New York: Oxford University Press, 1989.

Gressley, Gene. *Bankers and Cattlemen*. Lincoln: University of Nebraska Press, 1966.

Griswold del Castillo, Richard. *The Los Angeles Barrio, 1850–1890: A Social History*. Berkeley and Los Angeles: University of California Press, 1979.

Guinn, J. M. *History of the State of California and Biographical Record of the San Joaquin Valley, California.* Chicago: Chapman Publishers, 1905.

Gutierrez, David G. *Walls and Mirrors: Mexican Americans, Mexican Immigrants, and the Politics of Ethnicity.* Berkeley and Los Angeles: University of California Press, 1995.

Hall, Peter, ed. *Von Thunen's Isolated State.* New York: Pergamon Press, 1966.

Halpern, Rich. *Down on the Killing Floor: Black and White Workers in Chicago's Packinghouses, 1904–54.* Urbana: University of Illinois Press, 1997.

Hammond, George. *The Larkin Papers: Personal, Business, and Official Correspondence of Thomas Oliver Larkin, Merchant and United States Consul in California.* Berkeley and Los Angeles: University of California Press, 1951–68.

Haslam, Gerald, Robert Dawson, and Stephen Johnson. *The Great Central Valley: California's Heartland.* Berkeley and Los Angeles: University of California Press, 1994.

Hass, Lisbeth. *Conquests and Historical Identities in California, 1769–1936.* Berkeley and Los Angeles: University of California Press, 1995.

Hays, Samuel P. *Conservation and the Gospel of Efficiency: The Progressive Conservation Movement, 1890–1920.* Cambridge: Harvard University Press, 1959.

———. *The Response to Industrialism, 1885–1914.* Chicago: University of Chicago Press, 1957.

Heady, H. F., J. W. Bartolome, M. D. Pitt, G. D. Savelle, and M. C. Stroud. "California Prairie." In *Natural Grasslands: Introduction and Western Hemisphere,* ed. Robert T. Coupland. New York: Elsevier, 1991.

Heizer, Robert F., and Albert B. Elsasser. *The Natural World of California Indians.* Berkeley and Los Angeles: University of California Press, 1980.

Heizer, Robert F., and M. A. Whipple. *The California Indians.* Berkeley and Los Angeles: University of California Press, 1975.

Hendry, George W., and Margaret P. Kelley. "The Plant Content of Adobe Bricks." *California Historical Society Quarterly* 4 (1925): 361–73.

Hittell, John. *History of California.* San Francisco: n.p., 1897.

Holland, Marjorie, et al., eds. *Ecotones: The Role of Landscape Boundaries in the Management and Restoration of Changing Environments.* New York: Chapman and Hall, 1991.

Hornbeck, David. *California Patterns: A Geographical and Historical Atlas.* Mountain View, Calif.: Mayfield Publishing, 1983.

———. "The Patenting of California's Private Land Claims, 1851–1885." *Geographical Review* 69 (October 1979): 434–48.

———. "Land Tenure and Rancho Expansion in Alta California, 1784–1846." *Journal of Historical Geography* 4 (fall 1978): 371–90.

Horwitz, Morton. *The Transformation of American Law, 1770–1860.* Cambridge: Harvard University Press, 1977.

House, Albert V. "The Samuel Latham Mitchell Barlow Papers in the Huntington Library." *Huntington Library Quarterly* 28 (August 1965): 341–52.

Hundley, Norris. *The Great Thirst: Californians and Water, 1770s–1990s.* Berkeley and Los Angeles: University of California Press, 1992.

Hurley, Andrew. *Environmental Inequalities: Class, Race, and Industrial Pollu-*

tion in Gary, Indiana, 1945–1980. Chapel Hill: University of North Carolina Press, 1995.

Igler, David. "The Industrial Far West: Region and Nation in the Late Nineteenth Century." *Pacific Historical Review* 69 (May 2000): 159–92.

———. "When Is a River Not a River?: Reclaiming Nature's Disorder in *Lux v. Haggin.*" *Environmental History* 1 (April 1996): 52–69.

———. "Industrial Cowboys: Corporate Ranching in Late Nineteenth-Century California." *Agricultural History* 69 (spring 1995): 201–15.

Irrigation in California. Sacramento: Record Steam Book and Job Printing House, 1873.

Issel, William, and Robert W. Cherny. *San Francisco, 1865–1932: Politics, Power, and Urban Development.* Berkeley and Los Angeles: University of California Press, 1982.

Jelinek, Lawrence J. *Harvest Empire: A History of California Agriculture.* San Francisco: Boyd and Fraser Publishing, 1979.

John, Richard R. "Elaborations, Revisions, Dissents: Alfred D. Chandler, Jr.'s, *The Visible Hand* after Twenty Years." *Business History Review* 71 (summer 1997): 151–200.

Johnson, David Alan. *Founding the Far West: California, Oregon, and Nevada, 1840–1890.* Berkeley and Los Angeles: University of California Press, 1992.

Jordan, Terry G. *North American Cattle-Ranching Frontiers: Origins, Diffusion, and Differentiation.* Albuquerque: University of New Mexico Press, 1993.

Jostes, Barbara Donohoe. *John Parrott, Consul, 1811–1884: Selected Papers of a Western Pioneer.* San Francisco: Lawton and Alfred Kennedy, 1972.

Kahn, Judd. *Imperial San Francisco: Politics and Planning in an American City, 1897–1906.* Lincoln: University of Nebraska Press, 1979.

Kammen, Michael G. *Mystic Chords of Memory: The Transformation of Tradition in American Culture.* New York: Random House, 1993.

Katibah, Edwin F. "A Brief History of Riparian Forests in the Central Valley of California." Paper presented at the California Riparian Systems Conference, University of California at Davis, 17–19 September 1981.

Kazin, Michael. *Barons of Labor: The San Francisco Building Trades and Union Power in the Progressive Era.* Urbana: University of Illinois Press, 1987.

Keller, Morton. *Affairs of State: Public Life in Late Nineteenth-Century America.* Cambridge: Harvard University Press, 1977.

Kelley, Robert. *Battling the Inland Sea: American Political Culture, Public Policy, and the Sacramento Valley, 1850–1986.* Berkeley and Los Angeles: University of California Press, 1989.

King, Joseph E. *A Mine to Make a Mine: Financing the Colorado Mining Industry, 1859–1902.* College Station: Texas A and M University Press, 1977.

Klyza, Christopher McGrory. *Who Controls Public Lands? Mining, Forestry, and Grazing Policies, 1870–1990.* Chapel Hill: University of North Carolina Press, 1996.

Kollman, Wolfgang, and Peter Marschalck. "German Emigration to the United States." *Perspectives in American History* 7 (1973): 499–554.

Kolodny, Annette. *The Land before Her: Fantasy and Experience of the Ameri-*

can Frontier, 1630–1860. Chapel Hill: University of North Carolina Press, 1984.

Kulikoff, Allan. "The Transition to Capitalism in Rural America." *William and Mary Quarterly* 46 (January 1989): 120–44.

Lamoreaux, Naomi R. *The Great Merger Movement in American Business, 1895–1904*. Cambridge: Cambridge University Press, 1985.

Lamoreaux, Naomi R., and Daniel M. G. Raff, eds. *Coordination and Information: Historical Perspectives on the Organization of Enterprise*. Chicago: University of Chicago Press, 1994.

Langston, Nancy. *Forest Dreams, Forest Nightmares: The Paradox of Old Growth in the Inland West*. Seattle: University of Washington Press, 1995.

Lavender, David. *Nothing Seemed Impossible: William C. Ralston and Early San Francisco*. Palo Alto: American West Publishing, 1975.

Lawrence, William D. "Henry Miller and the San Joaquin Valley." M.A. thesis, University of California at Berkeley, 1933.

Leibhardt, Barbara. "Interpretation and Causal Analysis: Theories in Environmental History." *Environmental Review* 12 (spring 1988): 23–36.

Leopold, Starker. *Wild California: Vanishing Lands, Vanishing Wildlife*. Berkeley and Los Angeles: University of California Press, 1985.

Lewis, Henry T. *Patterns of Indian Burning in California: Ecology and Ethnohistory*. Anthropological Papers no. 1. Ramona: Ballena Press, 1973.

Licht, Walter. *Industrializing America: The Nineteenth Century*. Baltimore: Johns Hopkins University Press, 1995.

———. *Working for the Railroad: The Organization of Work in the Nineteenth Century*. Princeton: Princeton University Press, 1983.

Liebman, Ellen. *California Farmland: A History of Large Agricultural Landholdings*. Totowa: Rowman and Allanheld, 1983.

Limerick, Patricia Nelson. *Legacy of Conquest: The Unbroken Past of the American West*. New York: W. W. Norton and Company, 1987.

Lo Piccolo, Margaret Justine. "Some Aspects of the Range Cattle Industry of Harney County, Oregon, 1870–1900." M.A. thesis, University of Oregon, 1962.

Lotchin, Roger W. *San Francisco, 1846–1856: From Hamlet to City*. New York: Oxford University Press, 1974.

Lyman, George D. *Ralston's Ring: California Plunders the Comstock Lode*. New York: Scribner's, 1937.

Malone, Michael P. *The Battle for Butte: Mining and Politics on the Northern Frontier, 1864–1906*. Helena: Montana Historical Society Press, 1981.

Mann, Susan Archer. *Agrarian Capitalism in Theory and Practice*. Chapel Hill: University of North Carolina Press, 1990.

Marien, Mary Warner. "Imaging the Corporate Sublime." In *Carleton Watkins: Selected Text and Bibliography*, ed. Mary Rule. Boston: G. K. Hall and Company, 1993.

Marx, Leo. *The Machine in the Garden: Technology and the Pastoral Ideal in America*. New York: Oxford University Press, 1964.

McCullough, Dale R. *The Tule Elk: Its History, Behavior, and Ecology*. Berkeley and Los Angeles: University of California Press, 1971.

McEvoy, Arthur F. *The Fisherman's Problem: Ecology and Law in the California Fisheries, 1850–1980*. New York: Cambridge University Press, 1986.

McPhee, John. *Assembling California*. New York: Farrar, Straus, and Giroux, 1994.

———. *The Control of Nature*. New York: Farrar, Straus, Giroux, 1989.

McWilliams, Carey. *Factories in the Field: The Story of Migratory Farm Labor in California*. Boston: Little, Brown, and Company, 1939.

Merchant, Carolyn. "William Cronon's *Nature's Metropolis*." *Antipode* 26 (April 1994): 135–40.

———. *Ecological Revolutions: Nature, Gender, and Science in New England*. Chapel Hill: University of North Carolina Press, 1989.

———. *The Death of Nature: Women, Ecology, and the Scientific Revolution*. San Francisco: Harper and Row, 1980.

Merriam, C. Hart. "The Elk's Last Stand." *Scientific Monthly* 13 (1921): 465–75.

Miller, M. Catherine, *Flooding the Courtrooms: Law and Water in the Far West*. Lincoln: University of Nebraska Press, 1993.

Miller, Sally. "Changing Faces of the Central Valley: The Ethnic Presence." *California History* 74 (summer 1995): 175–89.

Minnick, Sylvia Sun. *SAMFOW: The San Joaquin Chinese Legacy*. Fresno: Panorama West Publishers, 1988.

Mitchell, Don. *The Lie of the Land: Migrant Workers and the California Landscape*. Minneapolis: University of Minnesota Press, 1996.

Moehring, Eugene. "The Comstock Urban Network." *Pacific Historical Review* 66 (August 1997): 337–62.

Monkkonen, Eric H. *Walking to Work: Tramps in America, 1790–1935*. Lincoln: University of Nebraska Press, 1984.

Monroy, Douglas. *Thrown among Strangers: The Making of Mexican Culture in Frontier California*. Berkeley and Los Angeles: University of California Press, 1990.

Montejano, David. *Anglos and Mexicans in the Making of Texas, 1836–1986*. Austin: University of Texas Press, 1987.

Mount, Jeffrey F. *California Rivers and Streams: The Conflict between Fluvial Process and Land Use*. Berkeley and Los Angeles: University of California Press, 1995.

Mowry, George. *The California Progressives*. Berkeley and Los Angeles: University of California Press, 1951.

Nash, Gerald D. "The California State Land Office, 1858–1898." *Huntington Library Quarterly* 27 (August 1964): 347–56.

———. *State Government and Economic Development: A History of Administrative Policies in California, 1849–1933*. Berkeley: Institute of Government Studies, 1964.

———. "Problems and Projects in the History of Nineteenth-Century Land Policy." *Arizona and the West* 2 (winter 1960): 327–40.

———. "Henry George Reexamined: William S. Chapman's Views on Land Speculation in Nineteenth-Century California." *Agricultural History* 33 (July 1959): 133–37.

Navin, Thomas R. "The 500 Largest American Industrials in 1917." *Business History Review* 44 (autumn 1970): 360–86.

Norris, Robert M., and Robert W. Webb. *Geology of California.* New York: John Wiley and Sons, 1990.

Oliphant, J. Orin. *On the Cattle Ranges of the Oregon Country.* Seattle: University of Washington Press, 1968.

———. "The Cattle Herds and Ranches of the Oregon Country, 1860–1890." *Agricultural History* 21 (October 1947): 217–38.

———. "The Eastward Movement of Cattle from the Oregon Country." *Agricultural History* 20 (January 1946): 19–43.

Olmsted, Roger R., and Nancy L. Olmsted. *Rincon de las Salinas y Potrero Viejo—the Vanished Corner.* San Francisco: San Francisco Clean Water Management Program, November 1981.

Opie, John. *The Law of the Land: Two Hundred Years of American Farmland Policy.* Lincoln: University of Nebraska Press, 1987.

Orsi, Richard. "*The Octopus* Reconsidered: The Southern Pacific and Agricultural Modernization in California, 1865–1915." *California Historical Quarterly* 54 (fall 1975): 197–220.

Osborn, John. *Railroads and Clearcuts.* Spokane: Inland Empire Public Lands Council, 1995.

Outcalt, John. *History of Merced County.* Los Angeles: Historic Record Company, 1925.

Padilla, Genaro. "The Recovery of Chicano Nineteenth-Century Autobiography." *American Quarterly* 40 (September 1988): 286–306.

Page, Brian, and Richard Walker. "*Nature's Metropolis:* The Ghost Dance of Christaller and Von Thunen." *Antipode* 26 (April 1994): 152–62.

———. "From Settlement to Fordism: The Agro-Industrial Revolution in the American Midwest." *Economic Geography* 67 (October 1991): 281–315.

Page, Thomas Walker. "The San Francisco Labor Movement in 1901." *Political Science Quarterly* 17 (1902): 672–75.

Palmer, Hans Christian. "Italian Immigration and the Development of California Agriculture." Ph.D. diss., University of California at Berkeley, 1969.

Palmquist, Peter E. *Carleton E. Watkins: Photographer of the American West.* Albuquerque: University of New Mexico Press, 1983.

Panayi, Panikos. *German Immigrants in Britain during the Nineteenth Century, 1815–1914.* Oxford: Berg Publishers, 1995.

Parker, Carleton. *The Casual Laborer and Other Essays.* New York: Harcourt, Brace, and Howe, 1920.

Parker, Paul P. "Along the Dirty Plate Route." *California Folklore Quarterly* 3 (January 1944): 16–20.

Pascoe, Peggy. "Miscegenation Law, Court Cases, and Ideologies of 'Race' in Twentieth-Century America." *Journal of American History* 83 (June 1996): 44–69.

Paul, Rodman. *The Far West and the Great Plains in Transition, 1859–1900.* New York: Harper and Row, 1988.

———. *California Gold: The Beginning of Mining in the Far West.* Cambridge: Harvard University Press, 1947.

Peterson, Richard. *The Bonanza Kings: The Social Origins and Business Behavior of Western Mining Entrepreneurs, 1870–1900.* Lincoln: University of Nebraska Press, 1977.

Phillips, George H. *Indians and Intruders in Central California, 1769–1849.* Norman: University of Oklahoma Press, 1993.

Pina, Joaquin. "Diario de la espedicion al Valle de San Jose al mando del Alferez de caballeria C. Mariano Guadalupe Vallejo." In "Expeditions to the Interior of California, Central Valley, 1820–1840," ed. S. F. Cook *Anthropological Records* 20 (February 1962): 177.

Pisani, Donald J. *To Reclaim a Divided West: Water, Law, and Public Policy, 1848–1902.* Albuquerque: University of New Mexico Press, 1992.

——. "Land Monopoly in Nineteenth-Century California." *Agricultural History* 65 (fall 1991): 15–35.

——. *From the Family Farm to Agribusiness: The Irrigation Crusade in California and the West, 1850–1931.* Berkeley and Los Angeles: University of California Press, 1984.

Pitt, Leonard. *The Decline of the Californios: A Social History of the Spanish-Speaking Californians, 1846–1890.* Berkeley and Los Angeles: University of California Press, 1966.

Pomeroy, Earl. *The Pacific Slope: A History of California, Oregon, Washington, Idaho, Utah, and Nevada.* New York: Alfred A. Knopf, 1966.

Post, Charles. "The American Road to Capitalism." *New Left Review* 133 (1982): 30–51.

Pred, Allan. *Urban Growth and City-Systems in the United States, 1840–1860.* Cambridge: Harvard University Press, 1980.

——. *City-Systems in Advanced Economies.* New York: John Wiley, 1977.

Prescott, Gerald L. "Farm Gentry vs. the Grangers: Conflict in Rural America." *California Historical Quarterly* 56 (winter 1977–78): 328–45.

Preston, Brenda Burnett. *Thomas Hildreth: Early California Cattle Baron.* Aptos: Rio Del Mar Press, 1995.

Preston, William. "Serpent in the Garden: Environmental Change in Colonial California." *California History* 76 (summer-fall 1997): 260–98.

——. "Serpent in Eden: Dispersal of Foreign Diseases into Pre-Mission California." *Journal of California and Great Basin Anthropology* 18 (1996): 2–37.

——. *Vanishing Landscapes: Land and Life in the Tulare Lake Basin.* Berkeley and Los Angeles: University of California Press, 1981.

Pulling, Hazel Adele. "California's Fence Laws and the Range Cattle Industry." *Historian* 8 (April 1946): 140–55.

Robbins, William G. *Colony and Empire: The Capitalist Transformation of the American West.* Lawrence: University of Kansas Press, 1994.

——. *Hard Times in Paradise: Coos Bay, Oregon, 1850–1986.* Seattle: University of Washington Press, 1988.

——. "The 'Plundered Province' Thesis and the Recent Historiography of the American West." *Pacific Historical Review* 55 (November 1986): 577–97.

Robinson, W. W. *Land in California: The Story of Mission Lands, Ranchos, Squatters, Mining Claims, Railroad Grants, Land Script, Homesteads.* Berkeley and Los Angeles: University of California Press, 1948.

Rodgers, Daniel T. "In Search of Progressivism." *Reviews in American History* 10 (December 1982): 113–32.

Roediger, David R. *The Wages of Whiteness: Race and the Making of the American Working Class.* New York: Verso Press, 1991.

Rolle, Andrew. "Turbulent Waters: Navigation and California's Southern Central Valley." *California History* 75 (summer 1996): 128–37.

Rose, Carol M. *Property and Persuasion: Essays on the History, Theory, and Rhetoric of Ownership.* Boulder: Westview Press, 1994.

Rydell, Robert W. *All the World's a Fair: Visions of Empire at American International Expositions, 1876–1916.* Chicago: University of Chicago Press, 1984.

Saloutos, Theodore. "The Immigrant in Pacific Coast Agriculture, 1880–1940." *Agricultural History* 49 (spring 1975): 182–201.

Sands, Anne. "The Value of Riparian Habitat." *Fremontia* 10 (April 1982): 3–4.

———. *Riparian Forests in California.* Special Publication no. 15. Davis, Calif.: Davis Institute of Ecology, 1977.

Saxton, Alexander. *The Indispensable Enemy: Labor and the Anti-Chinese Movement in California.* Berkeley and Los Angeles: University of California Press, 1971.

Schama, Simon. *Landscape and Memory.* New York: Random House, 1996.

Scheiber, Harry N. "Race, Radicalism, and Reform: Historical Perspective on the 1879 California Constitution." *Hastings Constitutional Law Quarterly* 17 (fall 1989): 35–80.

Scheiber, Harry N., and Charles W. McCurdy. "Eminent-Domain Law and Western Agriculture, 1849–1900." *Agricultural History* 49 (January 1975): 112–30.

Schmitt, Martin F. *The Cattle Drives of David Shirk.* Portland: Champoeg Press, 1956.

Schoenherr, Allan. *A Natural History of California.* Berkeley and Los Angeles: University of California Press, 1992.

Schwantes, Carlos Arnaldo. *Hard Traveling: A Portrait of Work Life in the New Northwest.* Lincoln: University of Nebraska Press, 1994.

Scranton, Philip. *Endless Novelty: Specialty Production and American Industrialization, 1865–1925.* Princeton: Princeton University Press, 1997.

———. *Figured Tapestry: Production, Markets, and Power in Philadelphia Textiles, 1885–1897.* Cambridge: Cambridge University Press, 1989.

Shuck, Oscar T. *History of the Bench and Bar of California.* Los Angeles: Commercial Printing House, 1901.

Shumate, Albert. *Mariano Malarin: A Life That Spanned Two Cultures.* Vol. 26. Cupertino: De Anza College Local History Studies, 1980.

Simpson, Peter K. *The Community of Cattlemen: A Social History of the Cattle Industry in Southeastern Oregon, 1869–1912.* Moscow: University of Idaho Press, 1987.

Skaggs, Jimmy M. *Prime Cut: Livestock Raising and Meatpacking in the United States, 1607–1983.* College Station: Texas A and M University Press, 1986.

Sklar, Martin J. *The Corporate Reconstruction of American Capitalism, 1890–1916.* Cambridge: Cambridge University Press, 1988.

Smith, Duane A. *Mining America: The Industry and the Environment, 1800–1915.* Lawrence: University of Kansas Press, 1987.

Smith, Henry Nash. *Virgin Land: The American West as Symbol and Myth.* Cambridge: Harvard University Press, 1950.

Smith, Wallace. *Garden of the Sun: A History of the San Joaquin Valley.* Los Angeles: Lymanhouse, 1939.

Spence, Mary Lee. *The Expeditions of John Charles Fremont.* Chicago: University of Illinois Press, 1970.

Stanger, Frank. "A California Rancho under Three Flags." *California Historical Society Quarterly* 17 (September 1938): 245–59.

Steinberg, Theodore. *Slide Mountain: Or the Folly of Owning Nature.* Berkeley and Los Angeles: University of California Press, 1995.

———. *Nature Incorporated: Industrialization and the Waters of New England.* Cambridge: Cambridge University Press, 1990.

Stoll, Steven. *The Fruits of Natural Advantage: Making the Industrial Countryside in California.* Berkeley and Los Angeles: University of California Press, 1998.

Storper, Michael, and Richard Walker. *The Capitalist Imperative: Territory, Technology, and Industrial Growth.* Cambridge: Blackwell Publishers, 1989.

Street, Richard Steven. "Tattered Shirts and Ragged Pants: Accommodation, Protest, and the Coarse Culture of California Wheat Harvesters and Threshers, 1866–1900." *Pacific Historical Review* 67 (November 1998): 573–608.

———. "A Kern County Diary: The Forgotten Photographs of Carleton E. Watkins, 1881–1888." *California History* 61 (winter 1983): 242–63.

Swisher, Carl. *Motivation and Political Technique in the California Constitutional Convention, 1878–79.* Claremont, Calif.: Pomona College, 1930.

Takaki, Ronald. *Stranger from a Different Shore: A History of Asian Americans.* New York: Penguin Books, 1989.

Taylor, Paul S. "Foundations of California Rural Society." *California Historical Society Quarterly* 24 (1945): 193–228.

Thickens, Virginia E. "Pioneer Agricultural Colonies of Fresno County." *California Historical Quarterly* 25 (1946): 17–38, 169–77.

Thompson, John. *Discovering and Rediscovering the Fragility of Levees and Land in the Sacramento–San Joaquin Delta, 1870–1879 and Today.* Sacramento: California Department of Water Resources, 1982.

Thompson, Kenneth. "Riparian Forests of the Sacramento Valley, California." *Annals of the Association of American Geographers* 51 (September 1961): 294–314.

Trachtenberg, Alan. *The Incorporation of America: Culture and Society in the Gilded Age.* New York: Hill and Wang, 1982.

Treadwell, Edward F. *The Cattle King: A Dramatized Biography.* New York: Macmillan, 1931.

Urban, Dean, Robert V. O'Neill, and Herman H. Shugart Jr. "Landscape Ecology." *Bioscience* 37 (February 1987): 119–27.

Vaught, David. *Cultivating California: Growers, Specialty Crops, and Labor, 1875–1920.* Baltimore: Johns Hopkins University Press, 1999.

———. "Factories in the Field Revisited." *Pacific Historical Review* 66 (May 1997): 149–84.

———. "An Orchardist's Point of View: Harvest Labor Relations on a California Almond Ranch, 1892–1921." *Agricultural History* 69 (fall 1995): 563–91.

Vaz, August Mark. *The Portuguese in California*. Oakland: I.D.E.S. Supreme Council, 1965.

Waldrop, M. Mitchell. *Complexity: The Emerging Science at the Edge of Order and Chaos*. New York: Simon and Schuster, 1992.

Walker, Richard. "California's Debt to Nature: Natural Resources and the Golden Road to Capitalist Growth, 1848–1940." *Annals of the American Association of Geographers* (forthcoming).

———. "Industry Builds the City: The Suburbanization of Manufacturing in the San Francisco Bay Area, 1850–1945." *Journal of Historical Geography* (forthcoming).

———. "Another Round of Globalization in San Francisco." *Urban Geography* 17 (January 1996): 60–94.

———. "Landscape and City Life: Four Ecologies of Residence in the San Francisco Bay Area." *Ecumene* 2 (1995).

Walton, John. *Western Times and Water Wars: State, Culture, and Rebellion in California*. Berkeley and Los Angeles: University of California Press, 1992.

Webb, Walter Prescott. "The American West, Perpetual Mirage." *Harper's Magazine* 214 (May 1957): 25–31.

Weber, Charles M. *An Approach to a California Public Works Plan*. Stockton: Weber Foundation, 1960.

Weber, Devra. *Dark Sweat, White Gold: California Farm Workers, Cotton, and the New Deal*. Berkeley and Los Angeles: University of California Press, 1994.

White, Richard. "The Nationalization of Nature." *Journal of American History* 88 (December 1999): 976–986.

———. *Remembering Ahanagran: Storytelling in a Family's Past*. New York: Hill and Wang, 1998.

———. *The Organic Machine: The Remaking of the Columbia River*. New York: Hill and Wang, 1995.

———. *It's Your Misfortune and None of My Own: A History of the American West*. Norman: University of Oklahoma Press, 1991.

———. "American Environmental History: The Development of a New Historical Field." *Pacific Historical Review* 54 (1985): 297–335.

———. *Land Use, Environment, and Social Change: The Shaping of Island County, Washington*. Seattle: University of Washington Press, 1980.

Whitten, David O. *The Emergence of Giant Enterprise, 1860–1914*. Westport: Greenwood Press, 1983.

Wiebe, Robert H. *The Search for Order, 1877–1920*. New York: Hill and Wang, 1967.

Woirol, Gregory R. *In the Floating Army: F. C. Mills on Itinerant Life in California, 1914*. Urbana: University of Illinois Press, 1992.

Worster, Donald. "Ecologies of Order and Chaos." *Environmental History Review* 14 (spring-summer 1990): 1–18.

———. *Rivers of Empire: Water, Aridity, and the Growth of the American West*. New York: Pantheon Books, 1985.

————. *Nature's Economy: A History of Ecological Ideas.* Cambridge: Cambridge University Press, 1977.

Wright, Doris Marion. "The Making of Cosmopolitan California: An Analysis of Immigration, 1848–1870." *California Historical Quarterly* 20 (March 1941): 334–45.

Young, James A., and B. Abbott Sparks. *Cattle in the Cold Desert.* Logan: Utah State University Press, 1985.

Zonlight, Margaret Aseman Cooper. *Land, Water, and Settlement in Kern County California, 1850–1890.* New York: Arno Press, 1979.

Index

Page numbers in **boldface** refer to illustrations.

Compositor:	Integrated Composition Systems, Inc.
Text:	10/13 Sabon
Display:	Sabon
Printer and binder:	Edwards Brothers, Inc.
Indexer:	Jeanne Moody, Beaver Wood Assoc.
Cartographer:	Bill Nelson

Lightning Source UK Ltd.
Milton Keynes UK

9 780520 245341